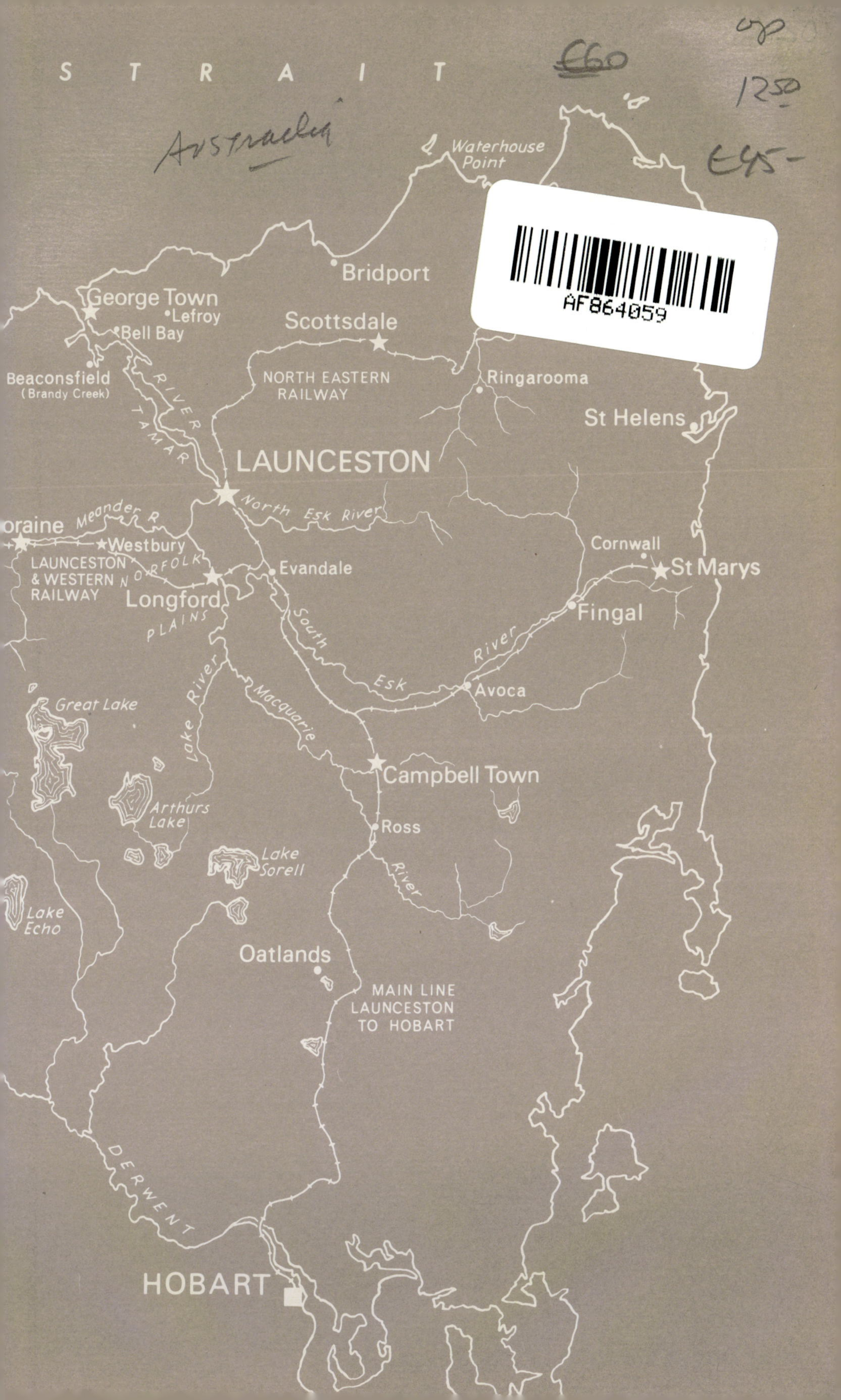
S T R A I T
Australia
£60
1250
£45-
Waterhouse Point
Bridport
George Town
Lefroy
Bell Bay
Scottsdale
Beaconsfield
(Brandy Creek)
NORTH EASTERN RAILWAY
RIVER TAMAR
Ringarooma
St Helens
LAUNCESTON
North Esk River
oraine
Meander R
Westbury
LAUNCESTON & WESTERN RAILWAY
NORFOLK PLAINS
Longford
Evandale
Cornwall
St Marys
Fingal
South Esk River
Avoca
Great Lake
Lake River
Macquarie
Campbell Town
Arthurs Lake
Ross
Lake Sorell
River
Lake Echo
Oatlands
MAIN LINE LAUNCESTON TO HOBART
DERWENT
HOBART
AF864059

Australia

o p

12.50

LAUNCESTON BANK FOR SAVINGS

1835–1970

12.50

In this edition two hundred
presentation copies have been
numbered and signed by the author

Henry Dowling

Launceston Bank for Savings

1835–1970

A HISTORY OF AUSTRALIA'S OLDEST SAVINGS BANK

E. A. BEEVER

MELBOURNE UNIVERSITY PRESS

First published 1972
Printed in Australia by
Halstead Press Division, John Sands Pty Ltd, Sydney for
Melbourne University Press, Carlton, Victoria 3053
Registered in Australia for transmission by post as a book

ISBN 0 522 84021 3
Dewey Decimal Classification Number 332.209946

Foreword

I was very pleased to be invited to write a brief foreword for this book, because the history of the Launceston Bank for Savings is more than a story of a successful banking enterprise—it reflects something of the history of Australia itself.

The Launceston Bank for Savings, while contributing to commercial and community development in Tasmania, has had a part in Australia's growth to nationhood.

It is, I believe, the oldest savings bank in the British Commonwealth outside of Great Britain, being founded only twenty-five years after the first savings bank was formed in Scotland.

The Launceston Bank for Savings opened its doors in 1835, the year which saw the establishment—from Launceston—of a settlement that was to become the city of Melbourne.

It is a trustee savings bank with a proud record of initiative and community responsibility. I have no doubt that this book is merely a consolidation of the past, and that the future will see the Launceston Bank for Savings maintaining and furthering its part in the life of Tasmania and of the nation.

R. G. MENZIES

Preface

The Launceston Bank for Savings is an unusual, and in some respects unique institution. It is the oldest surviving savings bank and one of two private but non-dividend-paying savings banks remaining in Australia; with the Hobart Savings Bank, it proudly continues as it was first established, in the British 'trustee' tradition. It has also been a remarkably successful institution. Without government guarantees, operating in an environment much less favourable than most Australian banks and always vulnerable because of its small size, survival alone would have been a major achievement. But it has done much more than survive. In the past half-century particularly, the Launceston Bank for Savings has been a vigorous and expanding institution, more than holding its place in an increasingly competitive sphere of financial activity.

For these reasons the Bank's history in itself is of considerable interest. However, the present study is intended to be rather more than just an institutional history, in two important respects. Firstly, I hope that it may contribute to a greater understanding of the history of Australian savings banking, a much neglected area of historical investigation. For this purpose the Launceston Bank for Savings has great advantages. Its records are excellent. The ledgers record every transaction made by depositors from the day the Bank opened its doors, and the new-account books record personal details of every depositor since 1849; from this and other material it is possible to reconstruct in some detail who were the depositors, what were their occupations and where they lived, the manner in which they saved, and how they were influenced by such events as depressions, mining booms, or financial scares. Furthermore, the very smallness of the Bank, which may seem in one respect to detract from its significance, has made it practicable to consider many aspects with a thoroughness that would be impossible for larger mainland institutions. Examples include the role of individuals in making and executing decisions, the pattern of the Bank's investments in the nineteenth century, and in the twentieth century the operation of branch banking.

Secondly, the history of the Launceston Bank for Savings is necessarily the history of a region as well as a bank, for the two are intertwined. In the nineteenth century those who directed the fortunes of the Bank were among those who directed the fortunes of Launceston, and this characteristic has continued to the present. Because it has had a strong and continuous preference for employing funds locally, the Bank's investments have for most of the time reflected the capital needs of northern Tasmania. Above all, the pattern of deposits has been directly determined in many ways by the area's changing economic fortunes. In turn, one must also add, the Bank's fortunes have helped to shape those of the region. If at first only modestly, the funds accumulated in the Bank have increasingly assisted in the growth of northern Tasmania. Today, perhaps more than ever, the Launceston Bank for Savings provides a major portion of the funds for local development, particularly for housing and municipal authorities.

E. A. BEEVER

September 1971

Acknowledgments

This history has been formally commissioned by the Launceston Bank for Savings. At all times, however, I have had unrestricted access to all the Bank's records and, more importantly, complete freedom in expressing judgements, favourable or unfavourable. The Bank has provided liberally for research assistance, travel to Hobart and Sydney in search of material, and many visits to Launceston; at Head Office the hospitality, provision of working space and assistance in assembling records have been all that one could have wished, provided frequently at considerable inconvenience to bank officers. It has been possible to visit many of the Bank's branches, again frequently at considerable inconvenience to the branch managers and staff. With the Bank's assistance I have also been able to acquire much information and understanding from past officers, and others unconnected with the Bank; although it is invidious to single out individuals, special mention must be made of the past general manager, Mr Ronald S. Tyson, whose remarkable memory and willingness to spend hours in conversation proved particularly helpful. Members of the Executive Committee, the present general manager, Mr B. Leslie Hooper, and many of his staff have provided much additional information of great value.

I am particularly indebted to my wife Margot, not merely for her constant patience and encouragement, but also for her major professional contribution to the history. She handled much of the initial research, offered innumerable constructive suggestions, and undertook a large part of the laborious and painstaking final preparation of the manuscript.

I am also indebted to Mr Frank Ellis, Director of the Queen Victoria Museum and Art Gallery, Launceston, for the part he played in initiating the present history and much subsequent assistance; to Mrs Jean Eckert-Smith, for her efficient and perceptive work as research assistant for some months; and to Professor Geoffrey Blainey, for many invaluable and detailed comments on the manuscript.

I am most grateful to the staff of several libraries and institutions for their assistance and co-operation: in Launceston, the Northern Regional

Library and the Queen Victoria Museum and Art Gallery; in Hobart, the State Archives, State Library of Tasmania; in Sydney, the Mitchell Library, the Library of New South Wales; and in Melbourne, the La Trobe Library, the Newspaper and Reference divisions of the State Library of Victoria, and the Baillieu and Giblin Libraries at the University of Melbourne.

Contents

Illustrations

PLATES

Illustrations

MAPS

Introduction

The instinct to save is a widespread and powerful force in human nature. Lacking this instinct, man would have remained primitive, always at the mercy of those conditions which nature imposed upon him. But, through this instinct to save, man's ability to hoard food and build shelter for his kith and kin became part of the long but successful struggle towards economic freedom. That goal has now been achieved and whether we think of a wealthy citizen, a prosperous business, or a thriving community, we know that past savings have made possible the accumulation of capital represented in these examples. For, wherever we look today the capital required for economic growth had its origin somewhere, sometime, in the surplus of production over consumption—in individual saving, in business saving, in community saving.

As our history will show, the founders of savings banking were philanthropists whose primary aim was to encourage thrift in the less-affluent members of the community as a protection against poverty and sickness. The necessity 'to save for a rainy day' was the philosophy on which savings banking was based, and the fact that regular saving demanded considerable self-discipline and so played its part in character building was a moral factor highly favoured by social reformers.

The founding of the Launceston Bank for Savings was inspired by philanthropy, in like manner to the course of events in Britain a generation earlier. Deposits were sought almost exclusively from the poorer sections of the population, and it is therefore not surprising that individual amounts were quite small and total deposits too insignificant to have any impact on the overall economy of the country. As time went on, deposits tended to come from the more enterprising and more affluent members of the community, and this trend, frowned on to some extent by those who felt it to be a departure from the original purpose of savings banking, has continued with ever-increasing force to the present time.

How different is the situation today from that of our very early years!

Increasing prosperity has made possible for the thrifty citizen oppor-

B

tunities undreamed of a century ago. Individual thrift now quite commonly leads to home ownership, provision of business capital, security in retirement, or the delights of travel. Furthermore, this development of personal saving has led to a vast increase in the total funds of savings banks themselves, enabling them to play a significant part in the general development of our country.

One need only study the investments of our own Bank to see this financial progress. At 31 August 1971 home ownership loans to depositors totalled $19,000,000, loans to local authorities in northern Tasmania $19,000,000, and investments in Commonwealth Loans $10,500,000. These figures demonstrate that the instinct to save is strong and active in our community. Not only is there a healthy accumulation of capital for the individual saver, but the community as a whole is benefiting from the substantial local investment which flows from our depositors' collective balances. These are interesting and impressive figures when considered in relation to the comparatively small population served by the Launceston Bank for Savings.

Our Bank came into being in 1835 as the result of the efforts of a number of high-minded citizens, and until the first Act of Parliament provided a legal basis for savings banks, the administration and, in fact, the destiny of the Bank rested entirely on the integrity of these self-appointed trustees. It is a tremendous credit to them during the period when bankruptcies were only too frequent (from 1839 to 1843, insolvencies in Launceston amounted to £676,865, one person in four becoming bankrupt), the savings of the people deposited with our Bank were secure. One might quote the case of the bank, Archers, Gilles and Company, which had the custody of our Bank's funds from 1840 to 1843. When their own bank was about to fail, it was arranged that the funds of our Bank were repaid without loss.

Two other major crises serve to demonstrate the high calibre of those in charge of the Bank. The vicious and quite unwarranted attack made in 1862 by the original chairman, the Reverend W. H. Browne, might well have caused the Bank to founder were it not for the resolute conduct and obvious integrity of the ruling board of Managers. Much later, the disasters of the nineties heralded by the collapse of the Van Diemen's Land Bank scarcely affected the steady growth of our Bank. For this immunity we must credit the skill and knowledge of the Managers over many years for their wise selection of investments for depositors' funds.

Our Bank weathered these storms and came through unscathed. Today all savings banks must comply with the experienced and highly developed legislation of the Commonwealth Banking Act so that the dangers of the past can never be repeated.

The Launceston Bank for Savings is unique in Australia. We are the older of the two surviving trustee savings banks in our country. With our friends, the Hobart Savings Bank, we are preserving the tradition set by Henry Duncan in 1810. Inherent in this tradition is the practice of trustee savings banks to operate locally, under local direction. That this practice is not outmoded is demonstrated by the fact that deposits in our Bank exceed by far those of any other savings bank in the areas in which we operate. This is a happy recognition of the importance of the personal relationship in savings banking and of what a progressive community can achieve through local initiative, loyalty and service.

What of the future?

We live in a dynamic and exciting era. Standards of living are rising rapidly in consonance with greater productivity. The speedier growth of affluence may well call for changes in the type of service required by our depositors, changes which at present cannot be foreseen. Whatever these may be, the Launceston Bank for Savings, as a community-owned institution administered by dedicated people, will surely be able to meet them and so preserve that personal relationship in service which has been a precious and characteristic feature of our Bank throughout its long and varied history.

SINCLAIR J. THYNE,
President

CHAPTER ONE

The Origins of 'An Excellent Institution'

Tasmania and Launceston in 1835

Over the years the early history of Tasmania, known until 1855 as Van Diemen's Land, has come to be identified with the worst excesses of a brutal and ugly system of convict transportation. Yet to many at the time such an image could not have been further from the truth. Visitors to Van Diemen's Land in the 1820s and 1830s were captivated and inspired by the island's landscape, its lushness and its ruggedness, and by its friendly climate. 'This is indeed a lovely country', wrote an anonymous correspondent to *The Times* of London in 1829. 'Take the climate of Italy, the mountain scenery of Wales, the fertility of England,—combine these, and you have Van Diemen's Land.' With its accessible fertile soils and soft climate this land of beauty also seemed a land of plenty. The same correspondent continued, with a degree of good-humoured exaggeration, 'positively, cattle, sheep, kangaroos, hogs, dogs, children, and other animals, increase so fast as to become a nuisance.'

To many British migrants of the 1820s and 1830s Van Diemen's Land was the land of promise. Nature had been generous to the island. Its government was also generous. To men of means it gave away, or sold at nominal cost, large parcels of the best land in the colony; for good measure it supplied cheap convict labour to work the land. For a time such attractions more than compensated for the colony's remoteness and the smallness of its community. During the 1820s and early 1830s as many free settlers came to Van Diemen's Land as to the more spacious and longer-established mainland settlement of New South Wales. By 1835 the free and convict population of the island together numbered nearly 40,000, an impressive increase over the 5,000 Europeans who had occupied it fifteen years earlier.

In 1835 rather more than a third of Van Diemen's Land's inhabitants lived in or around Hobart, the colony's capital and main port, in the south-east of the island. Nearly another third also lived in the south-east, along the narrow but fertile valleys of the Derwent and Coal Rivers and their tributaries. Most of the rest lived in one area to the north, the rolling, lightly wooded country drained by the complex of rivers which became the Tamar Estuary, and in the town of Launceston where those rivers finally converged. Overall, the Van Diemen's Land settlement consisted of a fairly narrow, though uneven belt of country stretching north-south across the island. East of this belt was uninhabited, except for a ribbon of settlement along the narrow valley of the South Esk, extending almost to the east coast. Westwards, more than half the island, was unoccupied, and indeed largely unexplored, except for the remote and insubstantial outposts of the Van Diemen's Land Company at Emu Bay and Circular Head, and the government penal establishment at Macquarie Harbour.

In 1835, as at all times, the island relied on the outside world not merely for its prosperity but for its survival. A large part of its needs and wants was imported and was paid for in a variety of ways. Earlier, when it was simply a penal establishment, the settlement was succoured by the British Treasury. Payments for provisions to the Commissariat (or government store), outlays on public works, and the incomes of the many civil and military government personnel had been for long the life-blood of the island's economy. In 1835 sustenance from this official source was still important, but now more important were the island's real and rapidly multiplying exports. First and foremost was the wool from the wealthier farmers' expanding flocks. Sheep-raising was located mainly in the 'Midlands', the central district of the island, and wool was shipped out through both Hobart and Launceston. Second to wool were the 'fisheries' products, the much-prized oil and bone from whales, and the oil and skins from seals; whales and seals once abounded off Van Diemen's Land, though seals were scarce now. Third still, but potentially very important, was the export of wheat. The cultivation of wheat, initially concentrated in the south of the island, was now developing rapidly in the north, particularly on the fertile river plains in the vicinity of Launceston.

Already by 1835 the northern port had become a proud rival to the colony's capital. Launceston had a population of only about 5,000 compared to Hobart's 13,000, but in the north Launceston was as important as Hobart was in the south. This small metropolis nestled in the arena of what an earlier explorer had called a vast amphitheatre of hill and forest—perhaps not so spectacularly situated as Hobart on its magnificent harbour beneath the towering Mount Wellington, but impressive nonetheless. Here two fresh-water rivers, the North Esk, meandering sluggishly around the east of the town, and the South Esk, emerging from the rugged Cataract Gorge, converged to enter the tidal waters of the Tamar Estuary. The port facilities were bad: much of the waterfront was low-lying and swampy, and the 'tortuous, narrow and incommodious' Tamar Estuary was a captain's nightmare; by contrast, Hobart boasted 'a harbour fitted to contain the navies of the world'. Nevertheless Launceston was the natural centre of the north, at the head of navigation, if vexatious navigation, of the dominant river system, and with a strongly expanding farm hinterland. Immediately to the south and west was highly productive and open plains country, soon to become the granary of the island. Further south were the rich grazing lands of the Midlands, geographically orientated more to the north than the south. Location and hinterland were more important than port facilities; in 1835 the value of Launceston's exports exceeded that of Hobart's.

Launceston's earlier growth had been erratic. The town had an exceptionally prolonged and somewhat painful birth as the governing authorities of Britain, the mother-colony of New South Wales, and Van Diemen's Land itself vacillated for twenty years about the site of the official northern base. In 1824 the final shift was made from the mouth of the Tamar to the head of navigation at Launceston. The boost to growth which this provided was reinforced in the following year when Van Diemen's Land achieved full colonial status, independent from New South Wales. Under Lieutenant-Governor George Arthur, reputed to be more kindly disposed to the north than most governors, Launceston became a government boom town; it had a large convict establishment with all the penal paraphernalia of gaols, barracks, Commissariat stores, a sizeable military detachment, and several civil administrative departments, each with headquarters and residences.

Before long, however, the town's productive and trading possibilities enveloped its penal foundations. By 1835 it had become a thriving and diversified capitalist community. On the northern edge of the town, the bank of the North Esk, was a small cluster of wharves backed by the warehouses of numerous merchants. Around the town, but especially on the low-lying land to the west, were several manufacturing establishments, including breweries, tanneries, flour mills and a distillery. The main residential area, to the south, was even then extending up the slopes of the surrounding hills. Houses were mainly timber, but there was a scattering of brick residences, including some 'really elegant looking mansions'. Launceston already had many of the trappings of civilization: churches, though as yet more congregations than places of worship, a number of private schools or 'seminaries', two newspapers, a circulating library, a turf club, and even a theatre of sorts. Most of the live entertainment, however, was to be found in the public houses, a facility with which Launceston was generously endowed.

For all these marks of advance Launceston was still young and raw and somewhat rural. Animals wandered at large through the streets, and market gardening was conducted along the main commercial thoroughfare. The still-unmade streets were a source of universal complaint, as was the lack of a public water-supply, which left the northern town uncomfortably vulnerable to southern wit. 'The good simple folk of Launceston', a Hobart newspaper had commented, 'cannot get up a temperance society for want of wholesome water.'

Launceston society in 1835 resembled that of other Australian settlements of the time. About three out of five Launcestonians had come to Van Diemen's Land as convicts. Most of these were convicts still under sentence, ranging from prisoners in public gangs to ticket-of-leave men, but there were already a considerable number of expirees. Together they appear to have been little different from their unfortunate counterparts elsewhere—a class described by *The Times*' anonymous correspondent as 'well fed, well clothed, very indolent, and very miserable—trading, cheating, canting, lying, praying, swearing, drinking, dissipating. . .'. Convicts and ex-convicts were poor material for the creation of a new community. But being numerous and preponderantly male, they provided the basis of a workforce which might otherwise have been critically scarce.

The remainder of Launceston's population was about equally divided between the native-born and the free immigrant. The native-born were almost all children and as yet too young to have a creative role in the community's life. In complete contrast were the free immigrants. Although among these were some of slender means, including assisted immigrants, the majority were monied and of social standing, 'the middling class', as the contemporary almanac described them, 'allowed by all moralists to be the happiest, and by all political economists the most useful in a state.' In Launceston they were certainly the most active and powerful class, dominating the affairs of town and region as government officials, lawyers, doctors and priests, merchants, manufacturers and landowners. Frequently they spread their energies widely over a range of 'respectable' activities. Many urban gentlemen held rural properties, perhaps a characteristic of the pioneer community, but also a reflection of geography; so much rich land was only a coach ride from town. By 1835 Launceston's 'middling class' was sufficiently large and cohesive to have begun a three-pronged assault on the unoccupied mainland across Bass Strait.

A meeting of philanthropists

A few months before the historic expeditions of Batman and Fawkner, eight of Launceston's 'middling class' met with a more modest and philanthropic purpose. During January 1835 four Launceston businessmen, two government officials, a clergyman and a neighbouring landowner held a meeting, in their own words, 'to take into consideration the propriety of establishing a Savings Bank in Launceston'.*

Apart from their social status, these eight men shared certain characteristics which fitted them well for the job in hand. Almost all were prominent in the town's affairs, especially its major political issues and its charitable organizations. Almost all were evangelical Anglicans or staunch Nonconformists and demonstrated in good works the sincerity of their religious faith. And with one exception they were very young men, a clear reflection of the town's youthfulness. Seven of the eight men were under forty, and two were not yet thirty years old.

The one relatively old man of the group was Philip Oakden, aged fifty. Although the evidence is scant it points to Oakden as the main instigator of the movement which established the Launceston Bank for Savings, and it may well have been at Oakden's house in High Street that the eight men met. Later Oakden seems to have taken on the mantle of senior adviser to the Bank. Generous, honest, dignified, and fervently Wesleyan, Oakden promoted many worthy causes, ranging from the Bank for Savings, the Mechanics Institute and St John's Hospital, to his own church and its Sunday-school. A merchant by profession, he was prone to serious misfortune. As a young businessman in London he had become bankrupt; subsequently he made good, first in Germany then in Van Diemen's Land, to which he migrated in 1833, but he was to lose a large portion of his gains in Port Phillip business ventures around 1840. Later he promoted the Launceston Shipping Company, but its first vessel, named *Philip Oakden* in his honour, was shipwrecked, bringing disaster to the company. Perhaps Oakden's most lasting business achievement was the role he played in establishing the Union Bank. In 1837 he was in England on behalf of the local Tamar Bank to negotiate an amalgamation with the proposed new bank. There he found the Union Bank scheme lagging, but through persistence and influential contacts was largely instrumental in breathing new life into it.

The man who, next to Oakden, was perhaps most influential in initiating the plan for a savings bank was the Reverend Doctor William Henry Browne, thirty-four years of age and Anglican priest to the parish of Launceston, a position he had held since his arrival in the colony in 1828. Browne, who could boast a Doctorate of Laws from Trinity College, Dublin, was a formidable combination of Irishman and evangelical: eloquent, fearless, energetic and contentious. On one occasion, confronted by four bushrangers about to burgle his house, he calmly talked them into a *quiet*

* The exact date of the meeting is uncertain. The Minutes record 7 January, the diary of the Rev. Dr W. H. Browne (the clergyman present) 22 January. Since it is likely that the Minute-book entry was written up at some later time, Browne's date of 22 January is probably the correct one. The meeting was not reported in the press.

robbery, in consideration for his wife, then in confinement. On the other hand, in his confrontations with his church superiors he was not always so successful. This turbulent figure immersed himself in worthy causes, like most of the group who had met to form the savings bank. Three months previously Browne had chaired a meeting to establish a benevolent society in Launceston. A few days later his name headed the list of those sponsoring a meeting to acknowledge George Augustus Robinson's work with the Aborigines of Van Diemen's Land. Later Browne was to be conspicuous in the Bible Society, the Church Grammar School, and perhaps above all, the Bank for Savings. Until 1850 he generally chaired meetings of its Trustees and Managing Committee. After that he became a bitter opponent of the Bank, and made many enemies in the process, but according to his biographer, being Irish, enjoyed the controversy.

Youngest member of the group was the twenty-four-year-old Henry Dowling junior, son of a well-known Baptist minister of the same name. Dowling resembled closely in temperament the much older Oakden, but had perhaps more business ability, particularly a talent for organization. Henry Dowling was to have a distinguished and exceptionally long career in northern Tasmanian affairs, long partly because he lived to seventy-five, but mainly through precocity. He had come to Van Diemen's Land at the age of twenty to pave the way for the rest of his family. Within a year, after working briefly for the *Hobart Town Courier*, he became editor and publisher of John Fawkner's *Launceston Advertiser*. In 1834 Dowling opened a large 'stationery warehouse', which he then promoted vigorously in the advertising columns of the newspaper. In more senses than one, Dowling had achieved a remarkable business maturity before his twenty-fifth birthday. Yet he still found time to participate actively in local public affairs, for which, like Oakden and Browne, he had an insatiable appetite. Later the Launceston Bank for Savings was to become the chief of these interests; indeed for many years Dowling virtually *was* the Bank.

Two other members of the group were to be prominent in the Bank's early years. Isaac Sherwin was a thirty-year-old merchant-landowner, another devout Wesleyan who was to have a distinguished record in charitable affairs. Sherwin had interests in southern Van Diemen's Land and was absent from Launceston for some time after the first meeting. However, he returned in 1838 to open a Launceston branch of the Commercial Bank of Tasmania, riding overland, according to legend, flaunting account-books and cash with contemptuous disregard for bushrangers. Sherwin later became the first paid manager of the Launceston Bank for Savings.

The other man who was to have a dominant place in the Bank's affairs was Lewis Gilles, thirty-seven years old, in the colony since 1822, ex-naval officer and now professional banker as managing director and accountant of the newly formed Tamar Bank. His brother, Osmond Gilles, had been in business in England with Oakden and was later to play an important part in establishing the colony of South Australia. Through his position in the Tamar Bank, then the Union Bank, and finally his own bank, Archers, Gilles and Company, Lewis Gilles held and recorded the funds of the Launceston Bank for Savings in its early years. Gilles may have been the 'professional' of the gathering, but he also was active in public life. His name appears in connection with both the Benevolent Society and Robinson testimonial late in 1834, and in March 1835 he chaired a public meeting to discuss certain government proposals for the north; at this meeting he was appointed to a deputation to visit the Lieutenant-Governor about Launceston's water-supply.

The three remaining members of the group had less influence on the Bank after it was launched than Oakden, Browne, Dowling, Sherwin and Gilles. George Palmer Ball was a wealthy landowner near Longford. Then twenty-eight years old, he has been described as 'a gentleman of religious and retired habits'. Ball was a close friend of Browne, and was also closely linked with Oakden and Gilles as a director of the Tamar Bank. Perhaps because he was preoccupied with running a large rural enterprise, however, he had no formal connection with the Launceston Bank for Savings after the initial meeting. George Whitcomb, aged thirty-one, also held land and was prominent in public affairs, but was primarily a government official, with a senior post in the Customs Department in Launceston. Later in 1835, however, he left the colony for many years. Theodore Bryant Bartley was also aged thirty-one and also a government official, Whitcomb's superior in the Customs Department, though in addition he held the important post of under-sheriff of the district. In this capacity he had played an important part in the capture of the bushranger Matthew Brady, and been rewarded with land. Bartley apparently continued to be active against bushrangers; on 20 March 1834 landowners inserted a special advertisement in the *Advertiser* expressing their appreciation of the 'promptitude, energy and decision' with which he personally had arrested a band of 'evil-disposed persons . . . who had justly acquired a most disreputable notoriety'. The tough Bartley was also an evangelical Anglican, 'a pious man' according to the Quaker, James Backhouse.

The origins and philosophy of savings banking

The seven younger men at the meeting were about the same age as savings banking itself, and had grown up in Britain during its formative years. Savings banks, in the form they eventually assumed, had evolved over about fifteen years, from the late 1790s to the early 1810s. Early 'charity' banks, which were heavily subsidized by philanthropists and bound depositors to strict rules of conduct, during this time gave way to genuinely self-supporting institutions which did not include moral reform in their formal constitutions and so could operate by greatly simplified rules and regulations. The Reverend Henry Duncan's parish bank, established at Ruthwell in Scotland in 1810, is often said to have been the first of these prototype savings banks, but the Edinburgh Savings Bank, founded three years later, which did not allow depositors to share in its management, did not enquire into their moral conduct and did not penalize irregular savers, as the Ruthwell Bank did, resembles more closely the modern savings bank. Its establishment was followed by a rapid multiplication of savings banks in England and Scotland, particularly after the introduction of sympathetic legislation in 1817 that, among other things, provided for the investment of accumulated funds in government stock on favourable terms. Meanwhile savings banks were also multiplying rapidly on the east coast of the United States, after a pioneer bank was established at Philadelphia in 1816. The late 1810s and early 1820s were the buoyant and confident formative years of savings banking in the English-speaking world, years in which the new institutions were much discussed and publicized and people probably took more interest in their fortunes than at any other time in their history.

By the mid-1830s the savings bank, though still young, was an entrenched institution with well-rounded philosophy and arguments. From the start it was designed for the less-affluent members of society, referred to variously, according to social outlook, from the vague and inoffensive 'great mass of the population', or euphemistic 'industrious classes', to the class-conscious 'lower orders', 'humbler classes' and 'the governed'. In fact, the great mass of the population was as diverse as the names it received, ranging from the destitute to the highly trained and self-consciously respectable artisans. The savings banks were intended to serve all less-affluent groups, but primarily the main intermediate groups of unskilled labourers, domestic servants, and the semi-skilled factory and building 'mechanics'.

The savings banks had two complementary objectives. One was to curb 'unnecessary' personal expenditure among workers who, it was widely believed, were prone to self-indulgence, to spend lavishly on food, on frivolous dress, and above all on alcohol; drunkenness was looked upon as the besetting sin of the workers. To eliminate such social vices was regarded as good in itself, but savings banking meant also accumulating money for future use; this was its second basic objective. Thrifty workers would eventually receive many benefits from their savings. In the main these were of the 'rainy day' type. The accumulation of wealth would guard against the ever-present threat of destitution resulting from sickness or unemployment, from old age or death of the earning member of the family; or against the lesser threat of inconvenient and unexpected lump sum outlays.

Primarily the savings bank was regarded as a barrier to misfortune, but sometimes as a means of achieving affluence. Some argued that through regular saving the worker might come in due course to own his house; to a degree, the savings bank foreshadowed the building society. At the very least, regular saving would enable the worker to buy a plot of land upon which some day he might be able to build. To some, money in the savings bank was even the means by which the worker could establish himself as an independent businessman.

To the most optimistic it seemed that this simultaneous curtailment of self-indulgence and provision for the future would transform the working class. In later years the most famous exponent of this view was Samuel Smiles, who composed two widely read treatises entitled *Thrift* and *Self-Help*. 'Any class of men that lives from hand to mouth', declared Smiles, 'will ever be an inferior class. They will necessarily remain impotent and helpless, hanging on to the skirts of society, the sport of times and seasons.' The frugal and prudent who accumulated savings would acquire a security and dignity denied to the profligate. They would cut themselves free from degrading dependence on charity, rising in society in their own and others' eyes. Tasting the good fruit of financial reserves, they would also tend to become more industrious and more responsible in their work habits.

Even the most pessimistic saw a ray of hope in savings banks. In 1798 Thomas Malthus, in his first edition of *An Essay on the Principle of Population*, presented a gloomy picture of a working class practically predestined to grinding poverty and early death. By the time of his sixth edition in 1826, however, Malthus had become less pessimistic, and one reason for this was the development of savings banks in the intervening years. 'Of all the plans which have yet been proposed for the assistance of the labouring classes,' he wrote, 'the savings-banks, as far as they go, appear to me much the best, and the most likely . . . to effect a permanent improvement in the condition of the lower classes of society.'

These were the aims and hopes, but why were *savings banks* necessary to achieve them? What alternatives were there? None, it was argued, at least none that was really satisfactory. Certainly friendly societies were long-established, and indeed had given birth to the savings banks, but they were ill-designed to encourage saving as such, since their subscribers recouped their investment only in the event of misfortune. The commercial banks at that time provided little accommodation for workers' savings. They were not interested in the small customer, and deposits were not yet a major part of their business. The determined saver might hoard his savings in the mattress or up the chimney, but there were obvious drawbacks to this form of saving. Always there was a temptation to draw on these readily accessible funds; there was a very real danger of loss by theft; and there was also the possibility that the secret of a man's savings would die with him. The mattress or chimney, furthermore, did not add interest to the funds received.

Savings banks of the early nineteenth century were the product of class society. They were designed by one class for another and therefore developed most where class structure was strongest; in the United States they thrived in the longer-established and stratified east coast states, but not elsewhere. The wealthy members of the community established them, and subsequently administered them without charging for their services. Their motives may have been partly self-interest, collective or even individual. Politically, the savings banks were favourable to the forces of establishment. 'Give a man something to lose', it was quietly pointed out, 'and he ceases to be a radical.' Financially, the savings banks were advantageous to the affluent members of society, since they reduced expenditure on charitable handouts. Some may even have coveted the funds accumulated by savings banks as loans to themselves. Yet first and foremost the affluent had a genuine philanthropic interest in the banks. As a class they were like the Launceston microcosm, vigorously religious in a practical manner, fervently devoted to worthy public causes. One such cause, self-improvement of the less-affluent members of society through savings banking, particularly captured their imagination.

The exact form and mode of operation of savings banks varied greatly, but there were certain common elements. Generally great value was placed on *regular* saving, on depositing some portion, however small, of the week's wages; banks opened, accordingly, at least once a week, particularly around pay day, and quite often on Saturday nights. Since a primary aim was to remove temptation, conditions of withdrawal tended to be restrictive; frequently there were provisions for refusing payment to a depositor in a state of intoxication, and also for graduated interest rates according to the duration of a deposit. Generally notice was required to withdraw funds, more notice being required for larger amounts. The rules and regulations usually also made it quite clear for whom the bank catered: sometimes savings-bank administrators had discretionary power to close accounts considered not truly working-class accounts; generally limits were imposed on the amount of money that might be deposited in any one year, or on the total size of the account. The composition of bank custom was also reflected in investment policies that gave primary attention to safety and security rather than high earnings; fear of the repercussions if depositors made capital losses often obsessed bank administrators. Finally, in the form of institution adopted, the savings banks were clearly philanthropic. There were no shareholders, and therefore all profits went directly or indirectly to depositors. Usually, and increasingly, the banks paid their officials, but over them were the unpaid decision-makers—the directors or executive committee, and the trustees, the moral and, in some instances, legal guarantors of the banks' funds.

Early Australian savings banks

If savings banks were a useful institution anywhere, there was particular scope for them in Australia in the early nineteenth century. Australian society was then tailor-made for self-indulgence. In Australia workmen were paid relatively high wages, frequently in large sums at long intervals; many rural workers, particularly, received regular subsistence but only one annual cash payment. At the same time, available outlets for surplus funds were very limited. While 'useful' outlets were almost non-existent, the sale of alcoholic beverages was a highly developed art. These same conditions, however, provided fertile ground for savings banking. The existence of a relatively wealthy working class prone to drunkenness was the challenge prompting the creation of many Australian savings institutions.

The establishment of such banks was all the more urgent because so many of the working class in Australia were convicts under sentence. To their credit, government officials and private employers regarded themselves as moral as well as legal guardians, responsible in a degree for the rehabilitation of their charges. Savings banking was one highly promising aid to rehabilitation.

Australia's first savings bank was founded in 1819, only six years after the Edinburgh Bank and three years after the Philadelphia Bank. In June of that year Robert Campbell, a dynamic and humanitarian Sydney merchant, established a savings institution later known as Campbell's Bank. It nearly failed. According to evidence given at the time by Barron Field before Commissioner Bigge, New South Wales had 'not arrived at the Period when the habits of Frugality and Economy in the Lower Orders can be said to be general so as to induce them to make Savings from their weekly wages.' Following a recommendation of Commissioner Bigge, Governor Brisbane began to deposit all funds of newly arrived convicts in the bank, and Campbell's institution survived. However, the amounts deposited were small. Furthermore, there was a strong backlash effect from identification of the bank with convicts' forced deposits. For some years the bank's scale of operations was very limited. Eventually in 1832 the bank was reconstructed by special legislation as a closely supervised institution with much wider appeal.

In Van Diemen's Land, savings banking dates from 1828 when Lieutenant-Governor Arthur received instructions to follow the New South

Wales practice of making deposits for convicts. Arthur arranged for the Derwent Bank to provide the appropriate facilities in Hobart. The scheme received modest sums of money for about twenty years, finally ending in 1849 when the Derwent Bank liquidated. Meanwhile, in 1831 the recently formed Commercial Bank established the so-called General Savings Bank, also in Hobart, and intended mainly for assignees and expirees. It apparently survived as a separate department of the Commercial Bank for some years, eventually merging with the general business of that bank.

Savings banking elsewhere in Australia may well have influenced the move for such an institution in Launceston, although direct evidence is lacking. Not only were models fairly well established in Australia, but in the months immediately preceding the Launceston meeting important developments occurred which may have spurred efforts in northern Van Diemen's Land. In New South Wales at the end of August 1834 a new Act came into force paving the way for a new phase of expansion in savings banking. The Act increased the number of trustees, raised the maximum size of deposits and allowed branches to be established at a number of country centres. In Van Diemen's Land a few weeks later the Derwent Bank for Savings was established as a savings institution, separate from the convict bank. The Derwent Bank for Savings aimed, like its Commercial Bank rival, at the broader class of depositor. Moves for a bank in the north of the island may in part have been Launceston's response to this second and more publicized Hobart institution.

However, two other factors probably influenced the moves for a Launceston institution. One was the formation in Launceston of the Tamar Bank, only days before the savings-bank meeting. The Tamar was a commercial bank, but unlike the rival Cornwall Bank, or most other commercial banks in Australia, it offered five per cent interest on deposits held at the bank for six months. Since there was a minimum requirement of twenty-five pounds, this was ill-suited to working-class saving directly. However, with a savings bank as intermediary, new opportunities existed. A savings bank could receive working-class deposits in small amounts and place the proceeds at interest in a consolidated account at the Tamar Bank. The latter eliminated any problem of investing funds, and it was probably more than coincidental that three of the eight sponsors of the Launceston Bank for Savings, Oakden, Gilles and Ball, were connected with the Tamar Bank, Gilles as managing director.

The other factor influencing Launceston moves was the changing position of the working class. While in general the workers of Van Diemen's Land were prosperous, for a time in the mid-1830s their position deteriorated, providing a sharp reminder of the benefits of 'rainy day' saving. Earlier, working conditions had perhaps been too good from this point

Isaac Sherwin

George Pullen

John C. Cathcart

Hardwicke Weedon

Launceston Bank for Savings, Pate son Street, Launceston (*left*); th first building owned by the Bank, was purchased in 1874 and occupie until 1900.

First Launceston Bank for Savings branch premises in Cattley Street, Burnie, adjoining Winter's Studio; a photograph taken in the early 1920s showing (*right*) Keith R. Westbrook, the branch manager, with a prospective client.

of view. When it was claimed that a workman could 'generally work only four or five days and spend the rest of the week in drinking', the advantage of saving for the future was perhaps not so obvious. By the mid-1830s this was no longer true. With an increasing rate of convict arrivals, wages sagged by a third during the first half of the decade. The years 1834 and 1835 were also less prosperous from other causes, particularly a bad harvest. Late in 1834 conditions were already serious enough to prompt moves for a benevolent society in the north. At a meeting on 30 September it was decided that the number of cases of distress in Launceston had increased sufficiently to merit action. The Launceston Benevolent Society duly came into existence.

This meeting was the forerunner of the gathering in January 1835 to establish a savings bank. Seven of the eight men at the later meeting were also active at the benevolent society meeting. Browne was chairman, Dowling moved the first resolution stressing the need for relief, and Oakden seconded that resolution. 'After the Meeting', recorded the *Launceston Advertiser*, 'a question rose as to the expediency of instituting a Savings Bank in this town, and from what fell from several gentlemen present, we have no doubt such an excellent Institution will speedily be formed.'

The establishment of the Launceston Bank for Savings

At the meeting in January 1835 two decisions were reached: one, to contact all who might be interested in supporting the venture, presumably as trustees; the other, to appoint a committee consisting of Oakden, Browne, Dowling and Whitcomb to draw up rules and make other detailed arrangements. The committee duly met on 2 February and delegated Browne and Dowling to consult with the two commercial banks and arrange for one of them to handle the business of the Launceston Bank for Savings. The bankers were interviewed four days later and given a fortnight to consider the matter. Arrangements were finally made with the Tamar Bank and on 9 March the committee reported to a general meeting held at Dowling's stationery warehouse. The meeting approved the banking arrangements and the proposed rules. It also appointed the Bank's Trustees and a Managing Committee.

The twelve rules were a model of simplicity. They provided for the deposit or withdrawal of money at the Tamar Bank on Tuesdays between twelve noon and three o'clock. As little as one shilling could be deposited, and five per cent interest was to be paid on the first ten shillings and every additional ten shillings, calculated on the minimum monthly balance. Anyone—rich or poor—might use the Bank. However, not more than fifty pounds could be deposited in a year, and the Managing Committee reserved the right to refuse any account.

The Bank had a long and impressive list of trustees. This was appropriate, since their main purpose was to impress. The Trustees had no legal responsibility, and their only administrative function was to meet annually to appoint a Managing Committee. Their role was essentially as moral underwriters, to instil confidence in the institution. The thirty-three men who undertook this duty included almost all the wealthiest and socially eminent of town and country, and represented a wide spread of interests. Seventeen were primarily businessmen in Launceston itself, mainly importing and retailing merchants, but there were also one or two manufacturers. Seven others were leading landowners in northern Van Diemen's Land, five were eminent government officials, and there were two lawyers and two doctors.

The Managing Committee consisted of Browne, Oakden and Dowling from the original group, and four newcomers but men of similar mould: twenty-eight-year-old Henry Reed, a successful businessman and a strong Wesleyan; thirty-year-old Henry Jennings, a solicitor by profession, and also a Nonconformist; twenty-seven-year-old Charles Henty, one of eight brothers who made their family's name one of the best known in Australia's history, managing director of the Cornwall Bank; and William Lawrence, perhaps northern Van Diemen's Land's most highly regarded immigrant at the time, a man of great wealth and social standing who had migrated for health reasons. In Van Diemen's Land, Lawrence settled comfortably into the life of landowner and merchant, with active philanthropic interests; at fifty-three he was the oldest member of the Committee.

The Launceston Bank for Savings had a quiet, unpublicized debut. Not until 19 March was it even mentioned in Dowling's own newspaper. Then in a five-line news item it was noted that the savings bank which had been long hoped for would open soon, and that much good was likely to result. A week later a small advertisement told readers that business would commence at the Tamar Bank on Tuesday 31 March and would continue every succeeding Tuesday. Perhaps this was one reason for the Bank's relative lack of publicity. Since the Tamar Bank provided the facilities and handled its day-to-day affairs, in one sense it was little more than an additional service provided by the Tamar Bank.

The establishment of the Bank for Savings, if a good deed done, was hardly a major preoccupation of its promoters. In his diary Browne, perhaps the most active of the organizers, recorded only the briefest references to attendance at meetings, usually after a long day of clerical and other activities. The rest of the Committee seems to have been currently more absorbed with leading public issues. At the time of the March meeting two major issues engaged the attention of most of them. On one, a flattering address from certain northern residents to Lieutenant-Governor Arthur, they were strongly divided. However, they all joined forces on the second issue, an address from residents of southern Van Diemen's Land to the Lieutenant-Governor against transportation. With Dowling's *Launceston Advertiser* as their mouthpiece they lashed at the southerners who 'club their heads together and talk nonsense in grandiloquent strain'; later at 'the crude and undigested out-pourings of a very small junta of the good burghers of Hobart Town'. Lack of representativeness rather than the particular views expressed was the real point at issue. That this Hobart junta could claim to represent Van Diemen's Land as a whole was nothing less than a 'bare-faced piece of presumption'.

Opening day for the Launceston Bank for Savings proved a major anticlimax. No one came along to deposit money. In view of the lack of publicity and lack of a really separate identity, this is not altogether surprising. The following week, however, four accounts were opened. Charles Collins, now only a name, had the distinction of opening the first account with a shilling.

CHAPTER TWO

The Fight for Survival 1835–1845

The boom of the late 1830s

In 1835 Van Diemen's Land's fortunes changed dramatically. Until then the island colony had looked to England spiritually and materially. Now, following the successful expeditions across Bass Strait, all eyes turned to the mainland of Australia. The settlement of Port Phillip became the preoccupation of Van Diemonians, particularly of northern Van Diemonians who were closest to the mainland. For three or four years Launceston was both spring-board and pipe-line for the new settlement.

The north's proximity to Port Phillip was not wholly a blessing. For a time the Launceston pipe-line resembled a drain which drew off manpower, livestock and supplies, and returned little. In the late 1830s hundreds of the north's most enterprising settlers left for the mainland, with servants, supplies and livestock. All told, perhaps a quarter of a million sheep were ferried across Bass Strait, and the value of all assets involved in this one-way transfer was at least half a million pounds—a sum greater than Van Diemen's Land earned from exports in a whole year.

Overall, however, such losses were probably more than counterbalanced by the sale of goods to the mainland. As settlers across Bass Strait became increasingly obsessed with raising sheep, they neglected other activities and instead imported their needs. When drought aggravated the mainland's deficiencies in the late 1830s, Van Diemen's Land sold vast quantities of food to the whole of New South Wales: potatoes, fruit, but above all, wheat and flour. Most of these products came from the north of the island.

A buoyant export trade brought booming prosperity to Van Diemen's Land, though mild when compared with the New South Wales boom of the late 1830s. Prices of property and livestock rose, capital flowed in from Britain and India, and credit was extended freely. Banking facilities particularly were greatly enlarged: first with the arrival of the British 'mammoth banks', the Australasia in 1836 and the Union in 1838; then with the establishment in 1840 of two new local banks, the Colonial in Hobart, and Archers, Gilles and Company in Launceston.

In Launceston employer and employee alike experienced good times. The shrewd and energetic with a little capital found it easy to become rich. Wages were rising, workers were comfortably off, and there was no unemployment. And despite the drain to the mainland, the population of Launceston increased from 5,000 in 1835 to nearly 7,000 in 1840. Prosperity and expansion transformed the town's appearance and character. In 1840 John Glover, son of the fashionable English painter, contrasted Launceston of the time with the primitive little settlement he had first seen in 1831: 'it was then about three parts small detached wooden cottages in $\frac{1}{4}$ acre or less paled gardens; it is now a little London of grand and continuous shops . . . of brick, stone or handsomly [*sic*] stuccoed, scarcely a quarter of the original cottages remaining.'

The Bank in an 'obscure and lethargic state'

Although times were favourable for a new savings institution, the Launceston Bank for Savings gave little cause for satisfaction in its early years. At the outset there was apparently trouble within the Managing Committee. At a meeting in April 1835 Charles Henty resigned, and in his place two new members were appointed: George Whitcomb, one of the original sponsors, and John Ward Gleadow, a thirty-three-year-old solicitor and another active Wesleyan. Possibly Henty resigned in protest against the decision to place the Bank's funds with the Tamar Bank, archrival of the Cornwall Bank of which Henty was managing director. However there is no direct evidence for this, and not even the exact date of the meeting is known.

Much more seriously, deposits were not coming in as anticipated. After the first four accounts were opened on 7 April 1835 no new accounts were opened for a month. By the end of the year still only thirty-two accounts were open, and six months later, when the Bank held its first general meeting (nearly three months after the scheduled date), the number had risen by a mere ten. The abysmally small number of accounts open fifteen months after the Bank commenced business reflected not merely a lack of new depositors but an alarming proportion of depositors who had already closed their accounts. No less than one-third of the depositors who opened accounts in 1835 had closed them by the time of the meeting in June 1836.

Apparently dismayed by the poor showing of their Bank, the Trustees at this meeting decided to take turns personally in receiving deposits on Saturday nights, provided Gilles at the Tamar Bank was agreeable. Gilles consented, and from August 1836 two trustees stood duty at Dowling's warehouse every Saturday between five and seven p.m. There they received but did not pay out money, depositing the sums collected at the Tamar Bank the following Monday morning.

Launceston's early efforts, if so far not very successful, at least stirred others to action. Late in 1836 Van Diemen's Land's second independent savings bank was established—at Longford, south of Launceston, centre of the rich Norfolk Plains. The driving force came from the Reverend Rowland Robert Davies, a colleague and friend of W. H. Browne since their Dublin days. Like Browne, Davies was Irish, energetic and evangelical, but rather more tolerant and good-humoured. He was a good minister, preaching 'beautiful' sermons, and earning from the Bishop of Australia the comment that 'the tillage of the Soil of the Norfolk Plains is not carried on with greater energy or success than the spiritual cultivation is conducted by its spiritual and able pastor.' Typical of his times, Davies was a man of many interests, most notably the Launceston Horticultural Society which he virtually founded, and presided over for many years. For a time the Longford Savings Bank was another of his interests. First advertised in November 1836, it was modelled after the Launceston Bank and most of its managers were connected with the senior institution. The Longford Bank operated until Davies temporarily left the colony in January 1840; the accounts were then transferred to the Launceston Bank for Savings.

Meanwhile the Launceston institution was rapidly sinking into an 'obscure and lethargic state'. As early as 28 October 1836 the Minutes refer cryptically to a meeting held to consider conducting the Bank 'as a distinct establishment'—presumably distinct from the Tamar Bank. On 12 June following, a meeting resolved briefly to continue paying into the Tamar Bank money received by the secretary, Henry Dowling. After that there was an official silence for nearly four and a half years. Possibly meetings were held but not recorded: more likely, meetings were simply not held. The Trustees and the Managing Committee seem to have lost interest in a rather feeble institution, particularly, and this may have been the real point, since it operated in practice as a minor branch of a commercial bank. The last Minute Book entries for 1836 and 1837 seem to indicate an unpopular but unchecked subservience to the Tamar Bank. As the Trustees and the Managing Committee lost interest, it was probably not long before the provision of the valuable facility of Saturday-night depositing at Dowling's warehouse lapsed.

Not only did the Bank for Savings become little more than an adjunct to a commercial bank, it became almost the personal concern of one commercial banker, Lewis Gilles. In 1838 the Union Bank absorbed the Tamar Bank and Gilles became Launceston manager for the new institution, taking the Bank for Savings' business with him. Gilles was, however, a strong, independent and able banker, and fretted at his shackles as a mere branch manager for a large British concern. Though many concessions were made to him, he eventually resigned to form his own banking business, Lewis Gilles and Company, in June 1840, again holding on to the Bank for Savings' business. In August 1840 he acquired as partners the wealthy landowning brothers, William, Joseph and Edward Archer, and their equally wealthy neighbour James Cox. The bank now changed its name to Archers, Gilles and Company.

Whatever the real reason, the Launceston Bank for Savings in its early years clearly failed in its primary aim of encouraging working people to save. As late as 1840 there was only one savings account for every twenty residents of the Launceston district, a dismal ratio, and total deposits in the institution still fell short of £5,000. Despite the support of Cox and the Archers, Gilles' own bank was apparently not highly regarded by the Bank for Savings' depositors; total accounts fell from £4,926 in August 1840 to £3,715 in November 1841.

By then public and promoters alike had largely forgotten the Bank for Savings. On 8 November 1841 Browne wrote to Van Diemen's Land's Colonial Secretary about the unsatisfactory state of the Bank's affairs. He claimed that not even the Managing Committee was 'in the smallest degree acquainted with the economy of the institution, what capital there is & how employed, what interest allowed, how the books are kept, what security is given, nor in fact anything about it.' Without realizing it, Browne underlined the point he was making when he claimed in the same letter that the Bank's funds totalled around £1,500; three days later in another letter he corrected that figure to £3,715.

This more accurate information Browne obtained at a meeting of the Managing Committee held on 9 November, the first recorded meeting since 1837 and apparently prompted by the departure overseas of the secretary, Henry Dowling, on a mission to recruit bounty immigrants to work for Van Diemen's Land settlers. At the meeting the Committee appointed solicitor Henry Jennings to act as secretary until Dowling returned. A Minute of the same meeting recorded that Henry Dowling senior had been contacted and had promised to look for the missing books and papers of the institution as soon as possible. The Launceston Bank for Savings was close to being literally little more than a memory.

The parlous condition of the Bank finally came to the notice of the *Launceston Examiner*,* a third local newspaper launched in March 1842 by a group of Congregationalists; among them the Reverend John West

* The *Launceston Examiner* rapidly became Launceston's leading newspaper. In 1847 it took over the *Launceston Advertiser* and ultimately, in 1880, the *Cornwall Chronicle*.

and two men later prominent in the Bank's affairs, James Aikenhead and William Stammers Button. Aikenhead, as editor of the *Examiner*, was soon to become an active critic of the Bank's management. On 25 June 1842 he launched the first of many vigorous attacks. 'So completely has its existence escaped the notice of the public,' he wrote, 'that the majority of those who pledged their names as collateral security to depositors, have we daresay forgotten the obligation.' Aikenhead claimed that the Managing Committee had not now met for two or three years, and concluded, 'We call upon the managing committee to assemble without delay. Let them either perform their duties or resign their office.'*

The need for legislation

Browne and Aikenhead both saw a solution to the problem, in legislation similar to that which operated in Britain or New South Wales. This had been the main subject of Browne's correspondence with the Colonial Secretary in November 1841. His first letter listed several points which might be incorporated in a savings bank Act, and when in the succeeding months the government procrastinated, he made further requests for action. Meanwhile Aikenhead had also become a strong advocate of legislation, in his newspaper contrasting the prosperity of well-regulated and maintained savings banks in Britain with the poor condition of Launceston's weakling institution.

Legislation, it was believed, would confer a range of benefits. The benefit of perhaps most immediate importance would be continuity of administration. An Act would establish formal procedures for appointing trustees and for trustees in turn to appoint an executive; this would guard against such a major and serious depletion of the Bank's administration, as had occurred. Aikenhead claimed that no less than four of the eight members of the Managing Committee were now either absent or dead.† He also claimed that fifteen of the original trustees, or again nearly half their number, were now dead, absent or bankrupt.

A savings bank Act would mean far more security both for those running and those using the Bank. As matters stood, the Trustees were in an invidious position—moral guardians of the Bank's funds but without real control over those funds. Apparently the problem so worried them that they announced publicly in the *Examiner* of 28 January 1843 that 'from this time, we decline all liability, even to the opinion of the public'. An

* This criticism was actually made in a letter to the editor from an unnamed correspondent, but since on 6 August an editorial remarked that some weeks earlier the *Examiner* itself had called attention to the state of the Bank, and there is no other report, comment or letter to which it could possibly refer, it is safe to assume that the unnamed correspondent was Aikenhead himself.

† Dowling, most notably, was still overseas on his immigration mission.

Act would have defined their position; if based on the English model, excluding them from any general responsibility while holding them legally liable in cases of wilful neglect or fraud. For depositors an Act would similarly mean greater security, in several ways: more systematic administration; careful regulation of the rules of deposit and withdrawal, and perhaps investment of funds; and government supervision of accounts, or at least compulsory publication of accounts.

Regular published returns would, it was believed, bring other benefits, in addition to more security. They would provide invaluable statistical information about the working classes; at a time when people were first becoming aware of social arithmetic and showing much philanthropic enthusiasm for its apparent scope, this advantage was held to be very important. Published returns would also be a very fine advertisement to attract new customers. With such publicity, Aikenhead claimed, ten times as much money might have been accumulated by the Launceston Bank for Savings alone. In addition, there would have been a strong chance of new savings banks or branches opening elsewhere in Van Diemen's Land.

The depression of the early 1840s

The case for legislation acquired greater urgency with the adverse turn of economic events. Van Diemen's Land's boom had reached a peak in 1840, and gave way in 1841 and 1842 to a period of depression. This was partly a reaction to excessive speculation at the end of the 1830s in livestock and real-estate markets, and in the import trade. But it also, and more seriously, reflected a marked deterioration in the position of Van Diemen's Land's leading exports—the life-blood of the colony. Whaling had reached its high point in the late 1830s, then declined as supplies of bay whales were depleted. Wool exports were well maintained in volume, but suffered severely from falling prices. Above all, the mainland food market collapsed, as New South Welshmen first imported more from elsewhere at the expense of Van Diemen's Land, then, spurred on by their own severe depression, produced more locally for their own needs.

Just as the north of the island had gained most from the boom of the late 1830s, now in depression it was worst hit. As wheat and other food markets on the mainland collapsed, northern farmers suffered acutely, and there was little that could be done. There were many advocates of greater efficiency or reduced costs, but such advice could evoke little enthusiasm among the hard-pressed farmers, even if there was scope for improvement. A proposal that New South Wales should discriminate in favour of Van Diemen's Land bread-stuffs while Van Diemen's Land discriminated in favour of New South Wales tobacco, raised hopes for a time but in the end came to nothing. Merchants experimented with shipments of wheat to

Britain, but could make little headway so long as the restrictive Corn Laws still operated.

Distress among farmers had widespread repercussions in a rural and urban community already weakened by its earlier speculative excesses. Insolvencies, which first became common in 1841, were widespread by 1842 and all but universal by 1843. On 30 June 1843 James Henty, one of Launceston's leading merchants, described the preceding half-year:

> a most miserable one it has been with reference to business matters. The embarassment [*sic*] amongst all classes engaged in Trade, Commerce Agriculture or Stock-holding exists in all its force and without some decided improvement in prices for produce of most kinds during the next six months it will be found impossible for many to stand up against the times. . . . The prospect is altogether most gloomy and for those who have families to educate and provide for distressing, requiring courage of no ordinary nature to bear.

Henty's comments epitomized the gloomy tone which pervaded contemporary accounts of that year. One commentator, the Reverend Robert Russell, went so far as to suggest that 'a general bankruptcy will be the best for all parties'.

While employers went bankrupt, workers became unemployed. Until 1841 wage-earners seem to have been relatively well-off. However, as the depression deepened and unfortunately-timed shiploads of bounty immigrants stepped ashore, their position deteriorated sharply. Unemployment and poverty mounted rapidly during 1842, and in the following year the position was so bad that the *Launceston Examiner* could argue *against* the introduction of a piped water-supply to the town, since so many needy people were finding employment carrying water from the Cataract Gorge.

The depression increased the need for savings-bank legislation in two important ways. Firstly, an Act was needed to brace up sagging deposits. In bad times, such as the early 1840s, depositors were inclined to withdraw money. This was to be expected and from one point of view commended, since it meant the Bank was fulfilling one of its stated objectives. For the Launceston Bank for Savings, however, a general economic decline could not have been worse timed, and bolstering legislation would be very welcome. As it happened, the new publicity given to the Bank's affairs in the local press won for it far more funds than the depression lost, but this could hardly have been foreseen.

Secondly, legislation was needed as a buffer against the real possibility of insolvency among those conducting the affairs of the Bank. Statements about such matters were always guarded, but there seems to have been a growing uneasiness, especially about the position of Archers, Gilles and

Company and its manager, Lewis Gilles, who controlled the Bank for Savings' funds. Fears may have been partly allayed when in November 1842 the Trustees accepted a guarantee from the firm for the deposits held by Gilles, and assurance that the firm would continue to handle the affairs of the Bank for Savings in the event of Gilles' death. Uneasiness persisted, however, and perhaps increased in January 1843 when Archers, Gilles and Company formally proposed to take over the Bank for Savings as a private venture. The *Launceston Examiner* strongly attacked the proposal to make the Bank 'a mere private concern', and the Trustees firmly rejected the offer.

The fears of the Trustees were not unfounded, for by the middle of 1843 it was known in Launceston's inner financial circles that Archers, Gilles and Company was in considerable financial difficulty. Further, personal animosity towards Lewis Gilles may have aggravated suspicion about his financial stability. Like most ambitious men Gilles made enemies, as became particularly apparent later in the same year when he presumed, without consulting his fellow citizens, to prepare the address of welcome when Lieutenant-Governor Eardley-Wilmot visited Launceston. Gilles thus incurred the wrath of Richard Dry, soon to become one of Tasmania's most distinguished politicians. In a maliciously eloquent piece of exaggeration Dry described Gilles as:

> a person who has spent his life in creating broils and quarrels, who has disturbed every society with which he has been connected, and every meeting in which he has taken part, who loses his temper whenever he is contradicted, and seldom speaks without insulting those who may differ from him, who has secretly defamed his neighbour's reputation, and when detected in his falsehood, shrunk from the responsibility of his misdeeds, who has been branded a liar, posted as a coward, and suffered his character to sink so low that a jury of his acquaintances valued it at a farthing.

In the latter part of 1842 and for most of 1843 considerable efforts were made to obtain savings-bank legislation. Apart from the *Examiner*'s campaign, the Bank's Trustees themselves were now officially active. At a meeting on 1 November 1842 Browne, Gilles and Gleadow were deputed to draw up a memorial to Lieutenant-Governor Franklin. Subsequently, in March 1843 a deputation from the Bank met the Lieutenant-Governor in Hobart, following extensive preliminary groundwork. During May, Franklin was planning legislation, and the matter was considered in the Legislative Council. However, nothing eventuated, even though new penal arrangements made public in the following month greatly increased the need for such legislation. Under these new arrangements probationary convicts were graded according to the proportion of their wages they were allowed to retain. For two of the three grades one-third and one-half of their wages respectively was to be paid into a savings bank. Now the *Examiner* considered legislation 'indispensable', but still nothing happened. In August the campaign received a major setback when Franklin was recalled, and a new Lieutenant-Governor had to find his feet.

Nevertheless, more progress might well have been made if savings-bank legislation had received general and active support from the north's men of influence. This, it seems, was lacking. In practice there was only a small group of activists, while a large majority of the Trustees and others outside the Bank were apathetic. Originally Launceston's leading citizens had eagerly promoted the Bank. Now things were very different. As a class they were inactive in a time of need. Their original enthusiasm for a worthy cause had clearly waned. This becomes more understandable, though perhaps not excusable, in the light of the Bank's very indifferent performance since its establishment.

One cannot fail to notice in this time of crisis the striking contrast between the Launceston Bank for Savings and the Launceston Mechanics Institute. In March 1842 prominent men had met with great enthusiasm and publicity to promote a Mechanics Institute. Its lectures, library and other facilities were to be the new panacea of the workers, calculated, according to one promoter, 'to make the office of the police magistrate a sinecure'. From the start the Institute attracted widespread attention among working men and, in the early months at least, was lavishly patronized by the more affluent classes in a blaze of publicity. The Mechanics Institute had everything on its side—novelty, success and publicity. The Bank for Savings had only the publicity.

Reconstruction as an independent establishment

The Launceston Bank for Savings entered a critical phase in its history when on 9 December 1843 Archers, Gilles and Company announced their intention to relinquish banking business. Later it was revealed that the Company was hopelessly insolvent. Archers, Gilles and Company was probably the most important victim of the depression to that time. Gilles, the active member of the firm, had to sell up and leave the colony. On 3 February 1844 auctioneer Charles James Weedon announced for sale 'The whole of the valuable household furniture, plate, plated ware, glass, china, horses, carriages, etc. etc., the property of Mr L. W. Gilles who is about leaving the colony.' Gilles retired to Victoria where he became a moderately successful public servant. The Archers were left to pay the firm's outstanding debts of £70,000; in due course these debts were honoured, but not without bringing the family close to bankruptcy.

The failure of Archers, Gilles and Company posed the greatest challenge to date for the Bank for Savings. Fortunately, if lacking wide support, the Bank had a core of active workers well able to meet the challenge. Its founding trio, Oakden, Browne and Dowling, were still very much involved in its affairs, and they had strong support from lawyers Jennings and Gleadow, and the now exceedingly wealthy businessman Henry Reed. At the end of 1843 the Managing Committee was perhaps stronger than it had been for some time, particularly with the return from overseas of Henry Dowling. Arriving back early in November, Dowling quickly became secretary again, providing a meeting-place and also, it seems, supplementary depositing facilities at his warehouse. Although Dowling was soon to become embroiled in libel cases about supposed fraud and his misconduct as immigration agent (later proved to be without foundation), such distractions seem to have had little effect on his devotion to the Bank's interests.

When Archers, Gilles and Company announced on 9 December that their doors would be closed, the immediate problem was to rescue the Bank's funds. Apparently no time was lost, for the Minutes of a meeting of the Managing Committee two days later noted that the funds were already supposed to have been paid over to the Bank for Savings. On 13 December the Bank advertised that the money had been received and that business would continue for the time being at Dowling's stationery warehouse.

Rescuing the funds was only the first of many problems, however, and it was perhaps with these in mind that the Trustees on 13 December gave the Managing Committee virtually blanket powers to 'take such steps as may be deemed requisite for the future carrying on of the Savings Bank'. One particularly pressing problem was how to maintain the five per cent interest which Gilles had paid to depositors since the Bank had opened. The two British banks, the Australasia and Union, were consulted in the hope of obtaining from them five per cent on deposits without the three months' notice of withdrawal normally required. On 23 December the Union and Australasia each accepted £2,300, but apparently without making the hoped-for concession. The Bank for Savings therefore had to retain part of its funds as a liquid reserve, and having idle cash was forced to reduce interest paid to depositors to four per cent; this new rate operated from 1 January 1844.

Meanwhile it was decided to appoint a paid part-time manager to conduct the day-to-day affairs of the institution. Three candidates offered themselves: Gilles, Dowling, and Isaac Sherwin, one of the Bank's original promoters. The election took place at a full meeting on 29 December 1843 attended by eleven of the remaining trustees, with Thomas Walker, a retired government official, now landowner, in the chair. Since Gilles was hardly in the running, the contest was between Dowling and Sherwin. Five voted for Dowling, and five for Sherwin. The chairman gave his casting vote to Sherwin.

Dowling's impressive record of service to the institution makes his defeat for the position a little surprising. Perhaps the result was influenced by a clash of personalities. Browne and Dowling later were bitter enemies, and there may have already been some antagonism between them at this early date; however, direct evidence is lacking. Another possible factor may have been that Sherwin was a professional banker, while Dowling was at best a conscientious amateur. For his services rendered, which included provision of office space at his own expense and daily opening for depositors, Sherwin was to receive surplus profits up to a maximum of £100 per annum.

At the same meeting of 29 December 1843 eleven new trustees were appointed in place of those who had died or left the colony. By profession and standing they were similar to those on the original list. While, as before, Launceston businessmen were easily the largest single group, landed interests, the government and professions were all well represented.

Now operating as a genuinely independent establishment, the Bank intensified its efforts for legislation. On 17 January 1844 a fresh deputation was organized to interview the new Lieutenant-Governor, Sir John Eardley Eardley-Wilmot.* The deputation visited Hobart where Wilmot promised to make himself familiar with the matter and see them on his forthcoming visit to the north. On 20 April the Trustees met Wilmot at Launceston and were asked to prepare heads of a Bill for submission to the official law officers. A sub-committee consisting of Browne, Dowling, Gleadow and Charles Henty, now again on the Managing Committee, was established for the purpose.

However, a more urgent issue now intervened. On the day that the Trustees met the Lieutenant-Governor, it was made known that the Australasia and Union Banks were no longer to pay interest on three-month deposits. Presumably interest was to be paid for the next three months, since a full meeting of trustees was arranged only for 2 July. A few days before that meeting was to be held the legislation sub-committee wrote to the Lieutenant-Governor, partly to explain that delays in preparing the draft Bill had occurred because copies of the current New South Wales Act had not yet arrived, but also to remind Wilmot of a suggestion he had apparently made for the government to take the Bank's funds at interest. On 9 July the Bank formally offered £6,500 to the government for three months at six per cent. Apparently Sherwin interviewed the Treasurer who informally

* Usually referred to in contemporary documents as Wilmot.

agreed to the proposal, but the government took no action. By the end of the month the sub-committee was getting desperate: 'The whole of the funds of the depositors are now lying in the banks here *without interest*,' it wrote despairingly to the Treasurer on the 29th, 'and we are unwilling to place them out upon private securities if the Government will close the arrangement made by you with the Accountant.' The government now refused to take the Bank's funds.

Having no other alternative, the Trustees took immediate steps to lend out the funds on private security. On 3 August 1844 the Bank advertised that it had £7,000 to lend in minimum amounts of £100 at interest not exceeding seven and a half per cent. Applications should be submitted by 14 August. Several applications were duly received and on 15 August the Trustees met to consider these and formulate general principles for lending. In his diary Browne made a rare departure from his usual entry 'Attended Savings Bank meeting,' to record, 'Engaged at Savings Bank all day.' Browne chaired the meeting, and at least thirteen other trustees took an active part in its proceedings.

In addition to approving several loans, the all-day meeting of 15 August established guide-lines for future lending. Caution was their keynote. Loans, it was decided, would be made up to one-third of the value of the collateral security only; a proposal had even been made to lend only to the extent of one-quarter. Mortgage loans could be terminated by either party at six months' notice, and the initial rate of interest was to be seven per cent. New loans could only be made at full trustee meetings, attended by at least five trustees, in addition to the manager. Mortgage loans were to be issued in the names of three specially appointed trustees, Oakden, James Henty and James Robertson, another leading merchant.

Caution was also evident, perhaps understandably, in the pattern of loans actually made. Initially most loans were to highly reputable and established parties, in particular to businessmen in the town itself, loans which presumably the Trustees could keep an eye on without much difficulty. About three-quarters of the funds lent in 1844 and 1845 went to urban interests, the rest to nearby landowners. None of the loans was particularly large, £1,200 being the largest in the first two years, and loans were made for as little as £100 and £120.

While caution is evident in most of the principles the Bank adopted and in actual loans made, there was a striking lack of caution in the total proportion of funds lent out. Doubtless with the depositors' rate of return in mind, the Bank lent as much as it dared as rapidly as possible. At the meeting of 15 August three-quarters of the total funds had been set as the limit for mortgage lending, a much higher proportion than the one-third permitted by law in New South Wales. By October 1844 the total amount lent was only £250 short of that limit, and it was not long before the Trustees decided that the limit was too restrictive. In April 1845 the proportion to be retained was changed from one-quarter to £1,000, which at the time meant little more than one-eighth of all funds. In October 1845 this was further reduced to a mere £500. Interest on deposits was thus maximized, but with virtually no liquid assets the Bank for Savings would be at the mercy of the commercial banks in the event of even a moderate setback.

A few weeks after mortgage lending had begun Isaac Sherwin resigned as manager for personal reasons. During the depression members of Sherwin's family had suffered losses, particularly his brother on the family property in southern Van Diemen's Land. Sherwin now retired to manage the property, but in such reduced circumstances that he sought a gratuity from the Bank before his departure. Dowling now became acting manager, and on 16 October a meeting of the Trustees was held to elect a new manager, now re-styled 'actuary'. There were two candidates, Dowling and James Down, a Launceston merchant who had recently pioneered wheat shipments to Britain. Dowling was the unanimous choice. Even Browne voted for Dowling, though not, it would seem, with great enthusiasm. Browne's diary entry for the day merely mentioned in passing his attendance at a meeting of the Bank for Savings. By contrast he wrote at length and with great concern about his 'poor and valuable horse so injured by fall when Justin [his son] was riding as to require his knees to be sewn up'.

The Bank under fire

In an eventful ten months the Launceston Bank for Savings had made remarkable progress. It had weathered a major crisis, and in doing so had become a truly independent and soundly based savings institution. Yet just as its troubles seemed over, the Bank had to face one last challenge. Soon after Dowling became actuary the Bank became the target of perhaps Australia's most ferocious newspaper editor of the day, William Lushington Goodwin. Goodwin, a journalist of seafaring background, had started the *Cornwall Chronicle* in Launceston in 1835 and rapidly became famous for his vitriolic attacks, which earned him a string of libel suits. One of those he maligned condemned him as a 'scurrilous and oft-convicted libeller'. Likewise the *Chronicle* was dismissed contemptuously by the *Examiner* as 'a FLASH newspaper' and 'a vile press'. Unfortunately for Goodwin's opponents, there was too often a disconcerting grain of truth in his diatribes. Furthermore, he won strong support in principle for his anti-establishment stand on most issues. Goodwin was much feared as well as hated.

Launceston, *c.* 1848; drawing by Margaret Black

Launceston wharves, *c.* 1850; water-colour by Frederick Strange

Longford township, 1837; painting by William Pritchard Weston

Brisbane Street, Launceston, *c.* 1850; water-colour by Frederick Strange

At the time of the Bank for Savings' reorganization one of Goodwin's favourite enemies was 'the Brisbane Street clique', said to be a tight-knit group of establishment men who ran everything and perverted everything. In a slightly manic editorial a few days after Dowling became manager of the Bank for Savings Goodwin attacked this 'combination of wicked men, who, under the *pretence of religion* and to *benefit the community* practised every species of extortion upon it, set family against family, and severed the bonds of friendship between man and man'. In the idyllic days before 'the clique' took over, Goodwin continued, there were few parsons but more religion, no teetotallers but less drunkenness, no Horticultural Society but more private gardens, no fire insurance companies, but then there were no fires. Now 'the clique' had a stranglehold, with at least two or three of its 'obnoxious members' strategically implanted in almost every institution.

As a child of 'the clique' the Bank for Savings was ripe for attack, and Goodwin aimed at its most vulnerable spot—the credit-worthiness of its managers. All three of the Bank's managers so far, Gilles, Sherwin and Dowling, had been victims of the depression. Gilles had gone bankrupt in a spectacular manner. Sherwin had suffered serious losses and retreated south. Now, as Dowling took over, it was widely known that he was informally insolvent, and offering to pay only two shillings in the pound, but so far this offer had been rejected by his creditors. These facts Goodwin published with relish in February 1845. Dowling, Goodwin conceded magnanimously, was not likely to use the Bank for Savings' funds for his own purposes, but some day a manager in financial difficulty might. The only solution, Goodwin asserted, was the strictest regulation by the government. A few months later, on 20 September 1845, Goodwin returned to the attack along broadly similar lines.

Shortly after this further onslaught a rumour was apparently circulating the town about certain malpractice by the Trustees. The exact nature of this rumoured malpractice is unknown, but it was serious enough to bring a threat of resignation from Browne and some urgent scurrying to and fro to get at the bottom of the matter and to persuade Browne to withdraw his resignation. There was talk of a run on the Bank. In the event the Bank came through unscathed, Browne stayed and there was no run. The *Launceston Examiner*, now the Bank's loyal spokesman, pointed out, perhaps a little smugly, that during the crisis only one family had withdrawn their money, and that was for the purpose of buying cattle. Goodwin was condemned as a 'notorious liar' and a 'moral bandit'.

CHAPTER THREE

The 1848 Act and the Bank's Customers

Political and economic affairs 1845–1850

The 1840s were years of crisis not only for the Launceston Bank for Savings but for the whole colony of Van Diemen's Land. The early part of the decade was dominated by economic crisis. Later, while the economy slowly recovered, came perhaps the greatest period of political crisis in the island's history.

During 1845 a long-smouldering financial dispute between Lieutenant-Governor Wilmot and his Legislative Council flared, and before it was settled six members of the Council had resigned, thus writing themselves into history books as the 'Patriotic Six'. Not long after, a greater and more prolonged issue developed over transportation. Local colonial opinion was strongly and increasingly against its continuance. The system was universally condemned on social grounds, and now there were powerful economic arguments against it. Transportation, it was maintained, did not augment the labour supply, as might be imagined, because it increased the exodus of those free to leave for neighbouring Port Phillip; transportation was also a strong deterrent to free immigrant labour. Convict labour, in any event, was hardly worth having. One contemporary, James Scott, believed convict labour was 'perfectly worthless'; female convicts, he said, for example, would rarely remain with an employer for long, and if compelled to do so had effective means of retaliation; 'they think nothing sometimes of letting fall a whole dinner or tea service, which is a general practice to get turned away', Scott commented despairingly.* From 1848 agitation against transportation was an organized movement, strongest in the north, and until news of its abolition arrived in 1853 transportation was the outstanding political issue. Meanwhile, in 1850, the third major political conflict in five years arose over the Imperial Act for the Better Government of the Australian Colonies, which conferred on Van Diemen's

* The letters of James Scott, surveyor, of 'Bowhill', Glen Dhu, Launceston, to his elder brother, Thomas, who had retired from Van Diemen's Land to Scotland in 1836, constitute a well-informed and detailed commentary on current events from 1846 to 1855.

Land and other colonies a two-thirds-elected Legislative Council such as New South Wales had had since 1842. What might have been cause for celebration, however, became a major source of grievance when Lieutenant-Governor Sir William Denison, already out of favour for his pro-transportation views, postponed its implementation.

Van Diemen's Land made slow economic progress in these years. Apart from the dislocating effects of depression and constrictions imposed by transportation, Van Diemen's Land suffered from the continued lack of a market for grain and the continued low price of wool. These years also, and perhaps more seriously, revealed certain basic limits to the island's natural resources. Whalers continued to work out sources of supply and by the close of the decade 'fishery' exports were negligible. Above all, the best open farmland was now almost all taken up. Cultivation could no longer be easily extended; there was no longer a large supply of readily exploitable land to attract immigrant settlers, and therefore little money from land sales to finance immigrant labour.

Nevertheless, conditions were a little better than they had been earlier in the decade. Already on 24 July 1844 the *Launceston Examiner* could comment about the sick Van Diemen's Land economy that 'the patient is fast approaching convalescence'. Perhaps this was rather too optimistic, for in September another informed observer, George Russell, manager of the Clyde Company, reported that almost every employer was still in an 'exceedingly precarious' position, and the economy still in a 'critical state'. However, certainly from 1845 conditions were improving. Bankruptcies were fewer, though the sensational failure of James Henty in 1846 was a major setback for a time. In some directions important advances were now being made. Grazing, after years of relative stagnation, extended during the second half of the 1840s into the central highlands and the Deloraine area. As a result there was an increase in sheep from about 1.25 million to 1.75 million, and wool exports rose by one-half. In urban centres lower costs and unemployed resources encouraged manufacturing development, most notably in shipbuilding. Overall during the 1840s Van Diemen's Land became much more self-sufficient. Despite a fifty per cent increase in the island's population during the decade, imports were lower in value in 1850 than in 1840.

The Hobart Savings Bank and the 1848 Act

Against this rather mixed background the Launceston Bank for Savings made striking progress in the second half of the 1840s. Earlier it had benefited from publicity, though at times the publicity may have been two-edged, and had managed to double total deposits during the depression years 1841 to 1844. After 1844 the continuing campaign for legislation kept the Bank in the public eye. With a paid actuary and regular daily openings, it now offered improved facilities to depositors. Strengthened further by a slow but definite economic recovery, and the fact that commercial banks no longer paid interest on deposits, the Bank also managed to double its deposits between 1844 and 1848. During this period surplus funds helped to force down interest rates to three per cent on deposits and six per cent on mortgages, and encouraged larger individual loans on lower security. Late in 1846 the maximum permitted loan was increased from one-third to one-half of the value of the security, and on these new terms individual loans of up to £3,000 were made. Enlarged business in turn permitted some relaxation of the Bank's stringent administration policies. The Bank now acquired its own furniture, increased Dowling's salary to a maximum of £250 per annum, and even paid a small gratuity to Sherwin for past services.

In March 1845 a new phase in the campaign for savings-bank legislation began with the formation of the Hobart Savings Bank. Largely the creation of George Washington Walker, a recently arrived shopkeeper of strong Quaker convictions, the Hobart Savings Bank opened on 1 March 1845 with the support of a group similar to the Launceston Bank for Savings Trustees. Initially it shared a corner of Walker's drapery shop with the Total Abstinence Society, perhaps appropriately, since Walker regarded drunkenness and saving as opposite sides of the same coin. At the time he claimed that the Bank was vital, 'now that hundreds, nay thousands, are discontinuing their visits to the public house, and begin to find that money remains in their pockets'. Later, when the Hobart Savings Bank occupied separate premises, Walker maintained the connection with appropriate posters.

> I have adopted a new method of silently advocating the cause [he wrote to his son in 1855] by exhibiting some of the most striking prints and placards, depicting the evils of intemperance and the contrasted benefits of total abstinence, in the office window of the Savings Bank. I am just now making even the moderate drinkers tremble, at the graphic illustrations . . . of the injuries which even these may sustain by indulgence in daily potations.

Despite its strong moral background, the Hobart Savings Bank was unmistakably business-like—more so perhaps than its northern counterpart. In its stated objects the Hobart Bank cordially appealed not only to the working classes but 'to all who chuse to avail themselves of its advantages'. From the outset it had not only a part-time manager but a paid clerk, something the Launceston Bank for Savings lacked until 1853. The Hobart Savings Bank also paid interest to depositors as a dividend varied according to actual earnings, rather than at a rate guaranteed in advance as the Launceston Bank for Savings did.* The Hobart Savings Bank was very successful. On its first day as many accounts were opened as in the first six months at Launceston, and within three years its deposits already exceeded those held by the northern institution.

The Hobart Savings Bank was as eager for legislation as the Launceston Bank for Savings, yet still for the time being little progress was made. On 10 January 1845 the government published the draft of a Bill in the *Hobart Town Gazette*, but its clauses were too restrictive to be acceptable. Provisions for making loans were particularly severe: the draft Bill limited individual loans to £500, specified a minimum interest rate of six per cent, required an elaborate and expensive system of registering mortgages, and permitted loans to be made only at quarterly trustee meetings. The 1845 Bill has been explained as really an attempt to bolster the commercial banks rather than assist the savings banks. It was strongly opposed by both savings institutions and withdrawn.

Nearly three years elapsed before any further action was taken by the government, despite persistent badgering from the Hobart Savings Bank. Eventually Walker himself prepared a draft Bill, but still the government delayed. On behalf of his trustees Walker wrote to the Colonial Secretary on 8 April 1848 expressing 'extreme disappointment and regret, that no notice has hitherto been taken' of his Bill. He hoped that 'the Lieut[t] Governor will be good enough to allow no time to be lost in confirming the same by Legislative Enactment'. The Bill finally received official approval and was passed by the Legislative Council on 22 September 1848.

Modelled largely on British and New South Wales legislation, the 1848 Act to Encourage the Establishment of Banks for Savings in Van Diemen's Land formalized rather than changed savings-bank practices. Trustees were now re-named managers and had to number between ten and thirty. Their liability was limited to wilful neglect or default, and their responsibilities to two meetings a year, at which they were to determine general lending policy and rates of interest and elect an executive committee. The powers of the executive committee were to be defined by the managers. Depositing conditions also conformed broadly with established practice, particularly the maximum limit on which interest could be paid, fixed at £150 per depositor.

Among the few new practices envisaged by the Act was the accumulation of reserve funds. A savings bank under the Act could allocate up to ten per cent of earnings from interest to a reserve fund annually; and such a reserve fund could accumulate up to one-quarter of total deposits.

* Notwithstanding its stated principles, in 1849 it would have nothing to do with the large number of uneconomically small convict accounts until then administered by the Derwent Bank.

Another important new practice was the regular publication of bank returns. Earlier this had been one of the major arguments for such legislation.

The 1848 Act was particularly notable for its liberal lending provisions; in this it contrasted with the 1845 Bill and to some extent with legislation operating elsewhere. Under the Act loans could be made at any time by the executive committee, with no restriction on the size of individual loans or their security, and no limit to the total proportion of funds lent on mortgage. In Britain, all normal savings-bank deposits had to be invested in government bonds; only special funds could be invested, within limits, in private mortgages. In New South Wales, mortgage loans at the time were restricted to half the total of all deposits.

On 12 December 1848, three months after the passage of the Savings Bank Act, the Trustees of the Launceston Bank for Savings met and decided to operate the Bank within the new Act. In June 1849 detailed arrangements were made, including the drawing up of a complete new list of managers, and in September the Bank finally came within the jurisdiction of the Act.

The Bank's depositors

The decision of the Launceston Bank for Savings to register under the 1848 Act marks a turning-point not only in the Bank's administration but also in the historian's knowledge of its affairs. From 1849 it becomes possible to build up some sort of picture of perhaps the Bank's most important facet—its depositors. Section 16 of the Savings Bank Act required every new depositor to give his or her name, business profession or calling, and place of residence. The Launceston Bank for Savings recorded all these details, along with the signatures of depositors, in volumes called new-account books. These new-account books, with the individual depositors' ledgers which had been carefully maintained from the day the first account was opened in 1835, tell us quite a bit about the Bank's depositors, their characteristics and savings habits.

A sample of new accounts opened between September 1849 and the end of 1850* establishes clearly the type of people who used the Bank at that time. Nearly two-fifths of all depositors were unskilled wage-earners, principally general labourers and domestic servants. Something over one-quarter were from a variety of other occupational groups, mainly artisans and mechanics, but with a sprinkling of white-collar and miscellaneous occupations. The remainder, about one-third, appear to have had no formal occupation; they were almost entirely children or married women. Their social status is not recorded, but almost certainly they were pre-

* A sample including every third depositor, 189 altogether.

dominantly working class, particularly since many of the women were illiterate and a large proportion of the children had very small accounts. As with British savings banks for which information is available, depositors overall appear to have been overwhelmingly from the classes for which the Bank was intended.

Perhaps most striking at this stage was the predominance of unskilled workers, particularly the common labourer and female domestic servant. Unskilled workers accounted for nearly three-fifths of new depositors with stated occupations. Such people were numerous of course in the community as a whole, but certainly did not account for anywhere near three-fifths of all occupation groups. Furthermore, being the lowest-paid workers one might have expected them not to be good savers. The most likely explanation for their prominence is one that has been advanced by historians writing of British savings banks, namely that a large proportion of these workers 'lived in' and were therefore very susceptible to persuasion by their employers. In Van Diemen's Land where the convict system reinforced the master-servant relationship, patronage of this almost feudal kind was particularly strong. In many instances new accounts record the employer's name instead of the actual address. Frequently employers opened accounts directly on behalf of their employees, sometimes as trust accounts over which they kept control.

This same sample for 1849–50 also shows clearly where the depositors lived. Overwhelmingly they came from the town of Launceston itself, or its 'suburbs'. While Launceston accounted for only about one-third of northern Van Diemen's Land's population at the time, it supplied nearly three-quarters of the Bank's depositors. Almost all the rest lived near to the town, on the Norfolk Plains or along the River Tamar. The more distant centres of population in the Midlands, along the north-west coast, or even the Deloraine area, were barely represented. This is perhaps not surprising given the shortcomings of the postal system.

At the time new accounts were first recorded, about one-fifth of all depositors appear to have been illiterate. Since they were unable to sign their names they posed a major problem of identification and, to overcome this difficulty, Dowling and later actuaries recorded brief personal descriptions in the new-account books, alongside the crosses of these 'marksmen'. Sometimes identification was easy, as with the Longford carter who sported a tattooed man and woman on the left arm, a mermaid on the right, or the 'esquire' with rings in his ears. Occasionally it was not so easy. One labourer had to be described painstakingly as a 'native of Sheffield, peculiarly formed face, long, sunken cheeks, projecting lower part', while a miller had to bare his chest every time he visited the Bank to reveal the identifying deep scar. Usually, though, a depositor had some visible scar or deformity, a broken nose, missing finger or limb, pox marks or other imperfection by which he or she could be identified. The frequency of such major blemishes is perhaps graphic evidence of the still primitive and hazardous state of life in Van Diemen's Land.

The pattern of saving

While the new-account books throw light on who the depositors were, the individual ledgers tell us something of their savings habits. Most strikingly, they show that very few of the depositors were in practice long-term savers. Of some 900 accounts opened in September 1849 only about 100 had been open for more than five years; these were the sole survivors of around 1,500 accounts opened up to 1845. Again, of the original thirty-six accounts opened in 1835 only three now remained, and two of these existed simply because their owners had died or forgotten them; these 'orphans' were the first of the so-called dormant accounts which were to be an accounting nightmare for generations of bank officers.

While only a small minority of depositors kept their accounts for any length of time, an even smaller number resembled at all the ideal saver as conceived and encouraged by savings-bank promoters. Almost no one made regular weekly deposits, and even by the most liberal definitions of steady saving habits* the steady saver seems to have been a rarity. A one-in-ten sample of all accounts which were open some time during the first twelve months of the Bank's operation under the Savings Bank Act shows that of 125 depositors only five saved regularly. Another fifteen depositors were accumulating money, but in a very irregular manner. Nearly all the remaining 105 accounts showed few or no additions during the twelve-month period.

The predominance of short-term accounts and sparsity of genuine savings accounts shows up even more clearly in a rather different type of sample that records the *complete history* of *new* accounts opened shortly after the Bank came under the Act. Of some seventy-seven accounts in the

* Savings accounts for this and later samples have been classified as follows:

1. 'ideal' or 'steady' savings account: at least twelve deposits in a year, and at least twice as many deposits as withdrawals.
2. 'irregular' or 'semi-savings' account: from four to eleven deposits a year, and at least twice as many deposits as withdrawals.
3. 'running-down' account: at least four withdrawals a year, and at least twice as many withdrawals as deposits.
4. 'current' or 'active' accounts: at least twelve transactions a year, excluding accounts in categories 1 & 3.
5. 'semi-current' or 'semi-active' account: from five to eleven transactions in a year, excluding accounts in categories 2 & 3.
6. 'idle' or 'store' account: not more than four transactions a year, excluding accounts in categories 2 & 3. Inevitably the divisions are arbitrary, but in practice they are very useful, in particular because almost all the accounts sampled during any one year fall clearly into one of the categories; there are very few borderline cases.

sample* thirty-one, or approaching half, were closed within twelve months, and fifty-seven, or about three-quarters in all, were closed within three years.† Of the forty-six accounts still surviving after twelve months not one at any time showed any tendency towards regular weekly or monthly deposits, and only seven could be regarded as the accounts of successful, though highly irregular savers. Typically, new accounts were opened with lump sums, though these varied greatly from a few shillings to the maximum allowable of £150. As a whole, they showed only a moderate tendency to increase the longer they remained open, and much of this growth was due not so much to new deposits as to accumulation of compound interest.

The pattern of withdrawals also diverges markedly from that expected of the 'ideal' saver. In the philanthropists' vision savings were accumulated for the 'rainy day', chiefly unemployment or sickness, when the prudent family would withdraw regularly in small amounts to make up for the missing wage. This seems to have happened rarely at the Launceston Bank for Savings during the mid-nineteenth century. In the first sample mentioned, only five depositors out of 125 were running down their accounts at fairly frequent intervals. In the second sample, only two out of the seventy-seven accounts examined were run down in this manner at some time during their history.

Interpretation of these deposit and withdrawal patterns must be to a large degree conjectural. However, certain suggestions can be made. Clearly on the face of it the model or ideal saver, defined according to either depositing or withdrawing habits, was virtually non-existent. It is certainly quite possible that infrequent lump-sum transactions concealed habits which in reality were closer to those of the model saver. Lump-sum deposits may to some extent represent gradually accumulating private hoards, placed at the Bank when the sum reached 'respectable' proportions—a practice not recommended by savings-bank promoters, but not too far removed from savings-bank philosophy.‡ Similarly, lump-sum withdrawals may to some extent represent a gradual running down of assets in times of unemployment or sickness, since some families perhaps found it convenient or reassuring to make large, and therefore infrequent withdrawals. In any event, large withdrawals are not entirely in conflict with a 'rainy day'

* One in ten new accounts opened between September 1849 and February 1851.

† Very few of these closures can be accounted for by the exodus of Van Diemonians to the mainland goldfields. Only twelve of these fifty-seven closed accounts were those of adult males who closed them after the discovery of gold had been publicized.

‡ Lump-sum deposits may to some extent reflect also the annual-wage payment system fairly common in Australia's early history. However, since this system of payment was primarily for bush workers, and the vast majority of the Launceston Bank for Savings' depositors were from the town or neighbouring district, such a possibility is not likely to explain many lump-sum deposits.

savings philosophy, since the latter clearly allows for unanticipated large outlays for funerals and other contingencies.

Perhaps some of the Launceston Bank for Savings' depositors were regularly but privately putting money aside to be banked occasionally as a safeguard against disaster, but it is unlikely that there were many of this kind. The extreme irregularity and infrequency of deposits suggests rather the sudden acquisition of money, which may reflect a variety of factors: seasonal fluctuations for those connected with the land; the highly variable incomes of many tradesmen and other independent workers; repayment of debts owing or sale of assets; inheritances, and a whole range of other windfall gains. To its depositors the Bank for Savings most likely served primarily as a repository for suddenly or irregularly acquired money which was not to be spent at once; and it was in most instances a very temporary repository.

To sum up, the Bank's depositors around the mid-nineteenth century seem to fall into three main groups. One group, the largest, consisted of those who simply deposited lump sums for a relatively short period of time. The actual amounts varied greatly, but they were rarely added to, and usually withdrawn in their entirety, frequently within a few months of depositing. For such depositors the Bank was simply a glorified safe and the interest earned of trivial importance. A second important group were the longer-term inactive depositors. Their accounts also ranged widely in absolute amounts, were also rarely operated on, but over the years accumulated a considerable amount of interest, and one may reasonably suppose that interest earned was an important consideration in their continuation. Within this group, however, there were a not unappreciable number of long-term savers by default, those who held dormant accounts. The third group were the more active depositors, and included a wide variety of types. Some operated what were virtually current accounts, particularly the charitable institutions which received special consideration from the Bank. Some held what one might call semi-current accounts, accounts which depositors found useful for periodic large payments or receipts. Some clearly held accounts which were meant to be savings accounts but in practice were added to very irregularly. A few, but very few, were regular savers.

CHAPTER FOUR

'Great Things for the Fair City of the North' 1850–1860

The gold discoveries and their effect

On 31 May 1851 the *Launceston Examiner* announced that gold had been discovered near Bathurst in New South Wales. Although it was only the first of many sensational discoveries, within days of this announcement the wider implications of a golden age were already being discussed. The *Examiner* believed that Van Diemen's Land would on the whole benefit greatly. In the immediate future the island might suffer dislocations as people left for the diggings. Many of those leaving would, however, be of the undesirable convict type and well rid of. Furthermore, the mainland diggings would bring vast numbers of enterprising migrants from Europe, many of whom would eventually settle in Van Diemen's Land, attracted by a 'fertile soil, a salubrious climate, and an organized and advanced state of society'. In any event, it was believed, gold would very likely be discovered in Van Diemen's Land also. Within a month of the first mainland finds a party had set out to investigate promising quartz country at the headwaters of the Derwent River.

Early assessments were rather optimistic. Soon gold was discovered in the much closer colony of Victoria and, as finds there became larger and more frequent, the exodus of people from Van Diemen's Land grew alarmingly. During 1851 and 1852, 13,000 more people left the colony than arrived there in the same period, a number equal to one-fifth of Van Diemen's Land's population when gold was first discovered. The depletion of the *work-force* was much greater, since most of those who left were adult males, while most arrivals were women and children; Lieutenant-Governor Denison estimated that no less than half of the adult male population left the island in these early years of the 1850s. It was little wonder that the government now campaigned vigorously in Europe for immigrant workers. In an alluring pamphlet it attempted to show just how great were the opportunities. The island, it claimed with a considerable degree of truth, had 'a *most urgent necessity* for ordinary working people of all kinds'.

Little could be done about the loss of population. Select Committees met, and immigration agents recruited, but funds were sparse and immigrants assisted to Van Diemen's Land were inclined to leave for the diggings as soon as practicable: it was the old problem in accentuated form. Moreover, the anticipated backwash from the mainland failed to materialize. The government tried to help the flow by sending an agent to Melbourne with funds to subsidize fares for those willing to go to Van Diemen's Land. It also offered Crown land to new settlers on extremely favourable terms, hoping in particular to settle the undeveloped but potentially rich north-west coast. But to little avail. Neither expatriates nor 'new chums' were much attracted to the island. The total net gain from immigration between 1853 and 1860 fell far short of the net loss by emigration in 1851 and 1852.

Hopes for gold in Van Diemen's Land also came to nothing. After early exploratory expeditions failed, a public meeting in Hobart offered £500 to the discoverer of gold. Possibly resenting this southern initiative, the *Launceston Examiner* now felt 'upon mature consideration, after revolving the subject in our minds, and viewing it in every aspect', that perhaps gold should not be discovered in Van Diemen's Land. Two months later, when gold was finally discovered in the *north*, near Fingal, only one day's hard ride from Launceston, the *Examiner* made another about-turn. The first results, it now claimed, were more promising than those of Victoria, and the development of goldfields on the island would now, it believed, be a good thing. However, the Fingal diggings belied their apparent promise, and for another twenty years remained an unfulfilled hope.

If Van Diemen's Land had neither migrants nor gold, she could at least sell to those areas that had both. During the 1850s the island shipped large quantities of goods to the mainland, as it had done in the late 1830s, but now more extensively and continuously. Initially, as demands and prices sky-rocketed, almost anything useful to gold-diggers found a market—butter, boots and shoes, horses, carts and hay, as well as the traditional export commodities. For two years, timber was in particularly great demand and ships carried it to Victoria from almost every inlet of the island. More lasting was the export trade in foodstuffs—grain, fruit and vegetables. From the middle of the decade mainland farming expanded rapidly in response to demands, but it had a long way to go to catch up with the ever-expanding market.

In addition to these large export shipments to the mainland, the overseas wool trade was reviving; in part this may have reflected the general stimulus of Australian gold on world commerce. Certainly in the 1850s the trend of wool prices was strongly upwards and resulted in a substantial rise in total earnings from wool, though the volume exported did not rise. In 1860 wool still accounted for two-fifths of the island's exports.

During the early 1850s Van Diemen's Land experienced simultaneously a great loss of population and a great rise in the standard of living of those remaining on the island. The rest of the decade brought no basic change in this new position. Population again increased as the outward flow of gold-seekers halted, but it was not a dramatic increase. The standard of living drifted from the heights of the early 1850s, but for some time only gently. In 1855 Van Diemen's Land's new Governor, Sir Henry Young, considered his people extremely prosperous. Exports from the island, although declining after 1853, in 1860 were still much higher per head of the island's population than they had been in 1850.

Material prosperity during the 1850s was accompanied by major political progress. During 1852 citizens of Hobart and Launceston at last saw their towns declared municipalities, after years of campaigning for the privilege of determining and financing their own public-works programmes. In Launceston the first council elections were held on New Year's Day of 1853 amid great rejoicing and optimistic comment about the future. In May 1853 there was even greater rejoicing when news arrived that transportation to the island had finally come to an end. This had been widely anticipated since the discoveries of gold, but it was good news nonetheless. Two years later, in 1855, new constitutions for self-governing Australian colonies were at last completed, and in 1856 the first truly responsible colonial government was elected. Perhaps symbolic of this new political maturity of the island was its change of name from Van Dicmen's Land to Tasmania in the previous year, a change long sought and now widely acclaimed.

Economic and political advancement alike were most apparent in the north of the island. At the start of the decade Launceston had exuded an air of despondency. Depression had then still not been quite shaken off, and the government, it was widely believed, aggravated the problem by neglecting northern interests. Trade with California had given some stimulus, but, according to one commentator, 'this gold fever is not, however, likely to last very long, and, when abated, the prospects of the Launcestonians, in all probability, will become as gloomy as ever.' The discovery of gold in Australia and subsequent developments described above, transformed the north's fortunes. As in the late 1830s, the north benefited more than the south because of its proximity to the mainland and its greater agricultural potential. With the development of rapid steam communication, it now became still more closely linked to the mainland. In 1853

James Scott commented that 'people now think nothing of going over to Port Phillip & back again in a few days, merely for a pleasure trip'.

Politically also, the north was the chief beneficiary of new developments. Municipal autonomy in 1852 helped to weight the political scales more evenly between north and south; according to the *Launceston Examiner* it was 'the first step towards breaking up that centralization of government from which Launceston has long suffered by neglect on the one hand, and rapacity on the other.' If the north was so hard done by as claimed, then parliamentary government also, since this meant representative government, would further have helped to rectify injustices. It is possible that the changing political balance of power in the 1850s helped to account for the decline in Hobart's population during the decade, through the decentralization of government expenditure.

Descriptions of Launceston in the mid-1850s contrast strikingly with those before gold was discovered. By 1854 Launceston, once a place of gloom, was described by H. B. Stoney as:

> a large and busy town:—hundreds of vessels crowding the wharves; steamers and ships hastening to or hurrying from the port;—all is life and bustle, with crowded streets in all the turmoil of daily toil and traffic.

After describing in some detail the amenities and facilities of Launceston, Stoney concluded with a most optimistic assessment of its prospects: 'a very few years will no doubt improve this city wonderfully . . . and as the go-ahead principle prevails, we prognosticate great things for the fair city of the North.'

Stoney's prognostications were at least partly borne out by events. In civic affairs the years immediately following those of which Stoney wrote brought a host of achievements, perhaps not matched in any similar period of time in Launceston's history. Most notable perhaps, at long last in 1857, was the provision for the municipality of a piped water-supply, a major engineering work financed by debentures and regarded by historian Dr Michael Roe as probably Australian local government's greatest achievement to that time. In the same year the Marine Board was created. In 1858 two fire brigades began operation, and the Mechanics Institute completed fund-raising for a large new building which eventually opened in 1860. In November 1890, by an Act of Incorporation, the Mechanics Institute was renamed the Launceston Mechanics Institute and Public Library. Regrettably, the building was demolished in 1971. Also in that year, 1860, Launceston acquired a gas supply, a Volunteer Rifle Corps was formed, and a new building for the general hospital started. Meanwhile Launceston had become the headquarters of a powerful movement for

Tasmania's first railway, projected to link Launceston with the rich farmland westward to Deloraine.

Booming business for the Bank

No class in northern Tasmania gained more from the prosperity of the 1850s than the ordinary working men. As they crossed Bass Strait in their thousands the labour force dwindled alarmingly, yet at the same time demands for labour increased as Tasmanian produce found new markets on the mainland; those who remained virtually dictated their own wages. Their prosperity was further enhanced by the many who made good in Victoria and returned to enjoy their wealth in Tasmania. Naturally some of the new-found wealth was dissipated. In September 1852 James Scott complained bitterly that 'in Launceston the *Gold diggers* spend their money most foolishly—for instance hiring cabs & having a band of music with them in the cabs driving through the streets—purchasing the best of everything, & [he added] most insolent sometimes.' Even servants, he commented, went round better dressed than their masters or mistresses; they also were most insolent.

Much of the new-found wealth, however, found its way into the Bank for Savings. During the 1850s thousands of new accounts were opened at the Bank, and the number of accounts open more than doubled between 1849 and 1854. Over the same period the north's population certainly did not increase and may well have declined. Initially, an even larger proportion of new depositors than earlier was from Launceston itself, perhaps reflecting the immediate boost of gold to urban activities. As time passed and farming expanded, the proportion of new accounts from rural districts rose. As before, working-class depositors predominated, but there were some variations in the pattern, again mostly reflecting economic fluctuations. At first the more skilled workers, such as bootmakers, predominated among new depositors, perhaps because they gained most from mainland markets. Later, with the growing general labour shortage, unskilled workers re-established their dominant position, despite a marked and understandable reduction in the number of domestic servant depositors.

The average size of depositors' accounts also greatly increased. In 1849, the last pre-gold year for which information is available, the average size of all accounts was less than £20. By 1853 they averaged more than £30, and during the next two years were over £40. Certainly prices rose at the same time, but the growth of average account size was much greater and lasted much longer than price inflation.

Although accounts expanded greatly in number and size, their character otherwise remained virtually unchanged. There was still a high casualty rate, for a time greater, if anything, than before. The vast majority of accounts also still failed to show real saving characteristics. In a sample of 141 accounts operating between 1852 and 1854 only one qualified fully as a genuine savings account, and another twenty-two were of the semi-savings variety. Lumpiness still characterized both deposits and withdrawals, although the lump sums paid in or taken out were now larger.

Relatively, the Launceston Bank for Savings made more progress in important respects than other savings banks in the 1850s. In 1850 it had compared unfavourably with its counterparts in both Melbourne and Sydney. Per head of urban population Launceston had considerably more savings-bank depositors than Melbourne and slightly more than Sydney. However, the average size of depositors' accounts was far lower in Launceston, and total funds deposited per head of population were lower; this comparison would be still less favourable if allowance were made for Launceston's relatively more developed hinterland. By 1854 the average total deposit was still low in Launceston, but the number of accounts per head of population had risen greatly, so that Launceston then had twice as many depositors *per capita* as Sydney, and about five times as many as Melbourne. Now Launceston saved appreciably more per person than either Sydney or Melbourne. This reflects the affluence of Launceston's working classes and, perhaps more importantly, the relatively even spread of prosperity within its ranks.

Launceston's advance was particularly marked compared with that of Hobart. By 1850, despite its more recent establishment, the Hobart Savings Bank had forged ahead of the Launceston Bank for Savings in every respect. For example, Hobart then had one account for every ten urban residents, Launceston only one for every twelve. The average total-deposit size was also greater in Hobart than in Launceston. By 1854 the position had been decisively reversed. By then Launceston easily led, both in the number of depositors' accounts per head of population and their average size. With still less than half the population of the capital, Launceston now had practically the same amount of funds in savings-bank accounts as Hobart. This rapid transformation is some indication of how much more northern Tasmania gained from the gold rushes than the south.

During the first half of the 1850s, funds held by the Launceston Bank for Savings increased four and a half times, from around £20,000 to £90,000. This great expansion enabled it to operate more efficiently, and in particular to reduce the margin between the rate of interest charged to borrowers and that paid to lenders. In practice, it allowed the Bank to maintain the mortgage rate at not more than six per cent while increasing the rate paid to depositors from three per cent to generally around four per cent. On the other hand, the greatly increased size of its business strained the Bank's administration to the limit. In January 1853 the Execu-

Family Drapery Warehouse,

OPPOSITE THE SAVINGS' BANK,

BRISBANE-STREET, LAUNCESTON.

W. GRICE,

MOST respectfully acquaints the Ladies of Launceston and the Country Districts that he has made arrangements for a constant supply of family and individual requisites.

CALICOS, HABERDASHERY, and SHOES always of the very first qualities.

HAWKERS AND SETTLERS PROVIDED ON LIBERAL TERMS.

Family Drapery Warehouse advertisement
Wood's Van Diemen's Land Almanack, 1852

tive Committee appointed a permanent clerk for the first time, to assist a very much over-worked Dowling. On 8 March 1853 several new managers were appointed to spread the work of the Executive Committee among more men; at this stage service on the Committee was by rotation in alphabetical order. A few days later the Executive Committee, still not happy with its burden, instructed Dowling to ask inactive country managers to retire. Dowling wrote accordingly to one country manager:

> The Managers are sensible of the importance of country gentlemen in favor of such an Institution & feel the value of such names as your own on the list of Managers but the work falls so heavily on the Town residents at present that this application becomes imperative.

By 1854 the routine work of the Bank had so increased that further clerical assistance was necessary.

The great increase in business enhanced the prestige of the Bank in the eyes of the people of northern Tasmania. Perhaps more indicative of its new status than a host of flattering *Examiner* editorials was the simple advertisement of a family draper who informed readers that his shop was now to be found in Brisbane Street 'opposite the Savings' Bank'.

The problem of investments

In the deposit boom of the early 1850s the Bank for Savings experienced a new type of crisis—a surfeit of funds. During 1852 and 1853 particularly, deposits mounted so rapidly that they could not all be put to good use. This was a fairly common phenomenon at the time. In 1852 the Hobart Savings Bank similarly experienced an embarrassment of funds, and many other banks around Australia, commercial and savings, found themselves in the same position.

In Launceston the surplus of funds was greatest in the closing months of 1852. Then, according to James Scott, the Bank was refusing to open accounts for many people. Despite this fairly drastic step, the balance-sheet for 31 August of that year revealed that no less than one-third of the Bank's funds were lying idle in the Bank of Australasia and in the Union Bank. At the general meeting on 4 September 1852 the Managers for the first time refused to commit themselves to a predetermined rate of interest on all deposits, in view of the extent of idle funds. They adopted the Hobart system of a retrospective rate depending on profits earned; this new policy was retained for forty years. On accounts closed during the next half year, however, they would pay three per cent, half a per cent below the previous rate. They also reduced the minimum mortgage rate from six per cent to five per cent.

The real problem was perhaps not the rapid accumulation of funds as such, but rather the limited scope for their investment. Had there been a developed investment market a sudden growth of deposits would have posed no great problem. This, however, did not exist at the time. The colonial government was not yet an extensive borrower of funds, and municipal governments were only now being established. The commercial banks did not pay interest on deposits, and had not done so for a number of years. Private mortgages alone provided a profitable investment outlet. Investment in mortgage loans, however, was a fairly slow process, ill-adapted to absorb a sudden spate of deposits. Furthermore, since funds generally were so abundant, the Bank had to compete with many other prospective lenders for the business of the relatively few would-be borrowers. At the time of the September meeting James Scott commented that 'it is now a *hard matter* to find *safe* and *profitable investments* for money'.

This was an unhealthy situation, quite apart from the risk of investing in assets all of one type. There was a very real danger that mortgages would be arranged too quickly, particularly that the investigation of collateral security might not be thorough. Alternatively, there was the danger of erring on the side of optimism in assessing the value and risks of a particular security. There was also the danger that the terms on which mortgage loans were made might be too lax. In an effort to gain mortgage business the Bank for Savings not only advertised extensively but greatly liberalized the conditions of its loans. In July 1852 it advertised that it was now prepared to lend for a fixed period of some years as well as the normal indefinite period terminated by six months' notice; subsequently business was done in this manner. Later, at the September general meeting, it was also decided to relax the rule that security must be twice the value of the loan; this rule was no longer to apply to loans of more than £1,000.

The Bank for Savings' lending policies and procedures were all the more vulnerable because of high real-estate prices. The abundance of money which encouraged adventurous lending practices by the Bank at the same time inflated the prices of real estate, the security upon which the Bank's loans were made. Scott had commented on the trend as early as February 1852 when he noted that allotment prices had already risen by fifty per cent. In September 1852 he reported that '*land is now rising every week*—in fact people are afraid to sell, or do not know what to ask for land.' By February 1853 the land boom had become, in Scott's opinion, a mania that was likely to turn sour once gold ceased to be so abundant. These were the times when the Bank was looking around most actively for investments. In the two and a half years from March 1852 to September 1854 its mortgage loans rose in value by nearly £50,000. Little more than half this amount was added overall in the next six years.

While there were certainly obvious dangers it is difficult to see how, with a pressing need to invest funds and a limited range of outlets, the Bank could have avoided them. Furthermore, for the time being all seemed safe. Values in fact did not collapse, and even Scott soon became optimistic again about the future. In addition, the Bank at least appeared to have done well in its mortgage business. It clearly preferred to lend primarily in large amounts to wealthy long-established settlers and, broadly speaking, succeeded in doing this.

A significant portion of the funds lent, particularly in the early part of the boom, were on large urban businesses and properties. In 1852, for example, John Thompson, a manufacturer and merchant with extensive property near the wharf, borrowed £4,000 from the Bank. In the following year James Robertson, one of the town's leading merchants and an ex-trustee of the institution, raised a loan of £5,000. Other large mortgage loans included £4,000 to a Mrs Lukin, on a large brewery complex, and £3,200 to a Mr Williams, on stores and residential property.

Most of the loans, however, especially from 1853, went to rural borrowers and included some of northern Tasmania's largest landowners. Thomas Field, one of several Fields whose properties sprawled along the fertile valley of the Meander River west of Launceston, borrowed £2,500 from the Bank in 1851 and another £3,000 in 1859. Thomas Parker, a prominent landowner in the Longford and Deloraine districts, borrowed £5,000 in 1853. The wealthy doctor Matthias Gaunt, pioneer settler, flour-miller and vigneron on the east bank of the Tamar, borrowed £5,000 in 1854. Mrs Landale, widow of the doctor-landowner Thomas Landale and sister of Richard Dry, raised three loans on her rural properties between 1852 and 1854, totalling £7,500.

Smaller borrowers absorbed only a minor part of the Bank's funds but they included some interesting and notable individuals. Among them was Jesse Pullen, widely known for his Baptist missionary work in the Deloraine district and the north-west; Jesse Pullen was the father of George Pullen, the Bank's new clerk and later actuary. James Barnard was an eminent amateur scientist, Government Printer in Hobart, and in fact the only borrower living in southern Tasmania. The Reverend R. R. Davies, back from England, had been recently appointed Archdeacon of Launceston and was by then undoubtedly northern Tasmania's most famous gardener. His parsonage, which provided part of the security for a loan, was a horticultural showpiece; one visitor commented that the greenhouse alone contained '18 varieties of Fuschias, & more rare flowers than I have seen even in the Govt. Garden.'

Perhaps most distinguished of all the Bank's borrowers was Ronald Campbell Gunn, eminent botanist and talented administrator. In a career which took him to many parts of the island Gunn had won great public regard; few could have matched his collection of presentation purses, plate, and snuff-boxes, an impressive tribute to his services. Now in the 1850s he had finally settled in Launceston as the government jack-of-all-trades: he eventually accumulated no less than seven official posts. In 1854 Gunn acquired a fifty-acre estate on the outskirts of town and here built, in 1856, the stately and elegant Newstead House. In 1857 Gunn borrowed £2,000 from the Bank for Savings, presumably to fund these outlays; the estate and house provided the security for his loan.

The Bank's leaders

The Launceston Bank for Savings was perhaps more closely linked with the fortunes of the town and immediate district in the 1850s than at any other time in the nineteenth century. Already by the middle of the decade there was one account at the Bank for every five urban residents; even allowing for the rural accounts this averaged about one account for every urban working family. The funds deposited had been used to finance much of the area's development, in Launceston itself, but even more in the surrounding country. And the directors of the Bank's affairs were also, by and large, the directors of northern Tasmania's affairs. With the resignation of Browne in 1850 and the death of Oakden in 1851 the Bank lost the services of two eminent citizens, but there were many more who were willing to take their places. The Bank now had the security of an Act and the prestige of a booming business.

Henry Dowling personified the bond between the Bank and the district it served. During the 1850s Dowling continued as actuary of the Bank, running its day-to-day affairs and no doubt greatly influencing its major decisions. By then he was also one of the outstanding public figures in northern Tasmania. Dowling had been particularly active in the anti-transportation movement, as secretary of the Australasian League which spearheaded the campaign, and eventually received a presentation gift of 250 guineas in appreciation of his services. With the institution of local government Dowling threw himself into municipal politics. According to Dr Michael Roe, Dowling was the dominant personality on the town council in its early years, and was mayor between 1857 and 1861, one of the most creative periods in Launceston's history. In the 1860s he rounded off a distinguished public career as the chief promoter of Tasmania's first railway project, the Launceston and Western Railway.

For all his political activities, Dowling still found time for the philanthropic causes which were so dear to him. During the 1850s, for example, he maintained his links with immigration as secretary of the Immigration Aid Society. He was also treasurer of the Launceston Town Mission and a trustee of the Launceston Cemetery Company. The Baptist Church also continued to engage much of his attention; in 1856 he was the one to take an unfortunate lady to court for drunken disturbance during a church service.

Meanwhile Dowling retained his private business interests, though little is known of them. Apparently he recovered from his financial embarrassment of the 1840s, retaining his stationery and printing business until 1854 when he sold out and went into the drapery business with a Mr Swain for a number of years. In 1862, with the Bank and public affairs proving too much of a burden, and perhaps having accumulated the means for a comfortable retirement, he disposed of the business to Melbourne interests.

Many other influential men were closely linked with the affairs of the Bank for Savings, although their individual influence was limited by the system of a rotating Executive Committee. Perhaps most notable, apart from Dowling, was William Stammers Button. A devout Nonconformist, like so many of his contemporaries, courteous and modest yet with a fierce determination, Button in many ways resembled Philip Oakden. From 1853 he was a trustee of the Bank and in this capacity served on the Executive Committee more often than most of his fellow managers, frequently chairing its meetings. When the committee membership ceased to rotate in 1862 Button served on the Committee continuously for the next ten years, usually as chairman.

Button rivalled Dowling as the leading public figure in northern Tasmania. He was the first mayor of Launceston, serving in that capacity from 1853 to 1857, during which time most of the work of acquiring the town's water-supply was accomplished. From 1856 to 1862 he was a member of the Legislative Council of Tasmania, and later for a time chairman of the Launceston and Western Railway Company. If anything, Button had even more numerous and diverse interests than Dowling. The first *Walch's Almanack* of 1863 records an impressive accumulation of positions: trustee of the Launceston Building and Investment Society, the Cemetery Company and Public Library; treasurer of the Cornwall Hospital and Infirmary, and the Colonial Missionary Society, director of the Launceston Gas Company and Cornwall Fire and Marine Insurance Company; and vice-president of the Horticultural Society. He also served on innumerable committees.

By profession Button was a brewer. Although involved in a number of business ventures, his main interest was the brewery which he ran in conjunction with his half-brother and fellow Congregationalist, Jonathan Stammers Waddell. Button was the first but by no means the last brewer associated with the Bank. Brewing and savings banking were strange bedfellows, and Button's active promotion of the Bank's affairs is perhaps indicative of a willingness, probably widespread, to sacrifice private wealth in the public interest. Button's position resembled that of an English brewer, also a savings-bank trustee, who, hearing how well his bank had done, is reputed to have exclaimed ruefully, 'Well, that represents thirty thousand pints of beer *not drunk*.'

Many other leading public figures regularly served on the Executive Committee. John Ward Gleadow, a committee member since 1835, was now one of Tasmania's most influential politicians; he was the Bank's solicitor and frequently chaired the general meetings. Adye Douglas was another eminent lawyer-politician, later Premier of Tasmania and Agent-General in London. James Aikenhead was the editor of the *Launceston Examiner*, the leading and eventually only local newspaper; when membership of the Executive Committee became more permanent in 1862 he served continuously until a few months before his death in 1887. Joseph Gellibrand Jennings, brother of Henry Jennings, was manager of the Union Bank in Launceston, and had earlier been closely associated with the formation of the Hobart Savings Bank. Among the innumerable businessmen who served on the Committee were Thomas Corbett, the ironmonger, later a trustee and member of the permanent Executive Committee, merchant Richard Green and builder Robert De Little, both also to be members of the permanent Executive Committee; and auctioneer Joseph Cohen, leading figure in Launceston's Jewish community.

During the 1850s the Bank's Managers became much more closely associated with the Launceston business community, at the expense of other groups. In 1853 thirteen new managers were appointed, and in 1858 eleven new managers, together equal to five-sixths of the total numbers permitted. In accordance with deliberate policy they were all residents of Launceston. Furthermore, except for one solicitor and two doctors, they were all businessmen. In these ways the Bank became almost wholly identified with the town's establishment, or, to the Goodwinites, 'the Brisbane Street clique'. Perhaps symbolic of this identification, during the 1850s the Bank began to hold its general meetings in the Town Council Chambers.

The Launceston establishment was then at the height of its power and influence. The men who composed it were now predominantly in early middle age, young enough to have retained the energy and restlessness that brought them to Tasmania, but old enough to have acquired experience and authority. Economic conditions were also propitious. Tasmania had emerged from the gloom of the 1840s, but had not yet encountered that deep stagnation which was to characterize the 1860s. For a few years Launceston, its ruling elite, and the savings bank it controlled, enjoyed good times.

CHAPTER FIVE

'Come, Take Your Money to the Post'
The 1862 Crisis

The establishment of agencies

For all its new-found prestige the Launceston Bank for Savings of 1850 served a town rather than a region. Well under half of northern Tasmania's inhabitants then lived in Launceston, yet almost three-quarters of the Bank's depositors at that time came from the town or suburbs. Nearly all the rest lived within a radius of about twenty miles of Launceston, at places such as Longford or Westbury. In more distant centres, such as Campbell Town, George Town or Deloraine, there were very few depositors. In the most distant centres, like Stanley, there were practically none.

After 1850 northern Tasmania's population became still more dispersed. While Launceston's population stagnated, elsewhere population continued to grow, especially in the more distant areas of the north. One of these areas was the Deloraine region. Already developing rapidly in the late 1840s, it received a further boost from mainland demands of the 1850s and added crops, especially oats, to an already important livestock industry. By 1861 it supported a population of more than 3,000. Still more rapidly developing was the coastal country north-west of Deloraine, a land of wide rivers, immense forests and deep fertile chocolate soil. Until the 1850s the dense forests effectively checked settlers' attempts to exploit the area's fertility. The gold rushes, however, created a new demand for timber, a large export trade sprang up, and on the cleared land farmers settled to produce food for the mainland. In time the north-west's timber trade led to the making of furniture, and to shipbuilding, and the ports which developed also came to be used as ports of call. Practically uninhabited before gold was discovered, the north-west boasted a population of more than 5,000 by 1861. By then the Deloraine district and the north-west together had almost as many residents as Launceston itself. Along with other rural areas they now accounted for three-quarters of northern Tasmania's population.

The further people lived from town the more need in important respects they had for savings-bank facilities. In the more remote rural areas many workers still received wages in annual sums, and there was little financial or social outlet other than the public house; many farmers also received large seasonal payments for which they had little immediate use. Yet the further people lived from town the less likely they were to have accounts at the Bank for Savings. Few among the working classes owned horses, or could afford the luxury of a coach ride. They travelled on foot, and unless they lived within a few miles of Launceston, rarely came to town. In theory, savings-bank business could be conducted by post, but this was slow and costly; unless packages were registered at further cost, it was also risky. From time to time branch banks had been advocated, but even with the expansion of the 1850s the rural population was still too dispersed for these to be profitable.

Southern Tasmania faced a similar problem. There the rural population, if not so large relatively as that of the north, was more dispersed from an earlier date. In 1847 the Hobart Savings Bank had seriously considered opening branches, but deferred the matter pending savings-bank legislation. In 1850 Isaac Sherwin suggested to his friend George Washington Walker, still the Bank's actuary, that a branch might be established at Bothwell, where Sherwin then lived; however, no action was taken. Again, in 1853, the branch issue was considered by the Hobart Savings Bank, only to be dropped once more because of the practical difficulties involved.

On 6 July 1854 Charles Octavius Eardley-Wilmot, son of the late Lieutenant-Governor, put forward a rather different suggestion. In a letter to the Colonial Secretary, Wilmot, then police magistrate at Sorell, east of Hobart, proposed that police magistrates might act as savings-bank agents. Police magistrates were then the principal government officials outside Hobart and Launceston, and one more public duty would make little difference to them. The Colonial Secretary referred the matter to Walker, who gave his cautious approval, and soon afterwards Wilmot put the idea into practice at Sorell. The results were sufficiently encouraging for Wilmot to recommend in June 1855 that the scheme be applied generally.

Wilmot's enthusiastic comments, ultimately published as a pamphlet, provide perhaps the ultimate exposition of that nineteenth-century ideal—guided self-improvement within the class structure. Stage by stage Wilmot demonstrated in the pamphlet how, with the assistance of their superiors, labouring men could learn to save, how their drunkenness and other crimes would disappear, and how they could become 'sons of the soil, freeholders . . . gainers in position, influence and respectability'. He concluded with an impassioned plea to his equals:

Let each *impress* upon the poor fellows who have so many temptations, and so few resources, how the Savings' Bank system may make them happier and better; and let the Magistrates gladly welcome the *little extra trouble* this Savings' Bank system may entail from them as their happy contribution to the cause of morality and virtue. The trouble is but slight—the results may be very great in proportion.

Wilmot's suggestions were circulated to police magistrates throughout Tasmania, who to their credit were uniformly favourable in their replies. The Hobart Savings Bank approved the scheme, even though the government was unwilling to accept responsibility for funds in transit; and by the end of 1855 police magistrates in southern Tasmania were receiving deposits for the Hobart Bank. The scheme was a failure, however. Depositing facilities were little used, perhaps because the process was slow and indirect, perhaps because the police magistrates themselves were not well liked. When in the early 1860s the whole police magistrate system was abandoned rural depositing quietly disappeared.

Northern Tasmania, meanwhile, followed its own line. While the government was communicating with its police magistrates, Walker had written to Dowling suggesting that police magistrates in the north might receive funds for the Launceston Bank for Savings. The Executive Committee greeted the proposal without enthusiasm. The risks, it believed, were too great, and when the government refused to take responsibility for funds in transit, the Managers rejected the scheme at a special general meeting on 11 October 1855. Nevertheless, they appointed a committee to investigate the position of country depositors. Possibly they were disturbed by the prospect of northern money being remitted to Hobart through the police magistrates.

The special committee quickly decided that private agencies were the answer. Although they would involve added expense in commission and cost of postage, private agents could be more easily controlled than government officials, and the Bank could more reasonably risk taking the responsibility for funds in transit. The recommendation was put to a special general meeting on 1 November 1855 and accepted. Early in February 1856 the Bank formally announced that agencies would soon open for business in five country centres. The *Launceston Examiner* greeted the news with great enthusiasm and with the usual strong affirmation of its belief in savings-bank principles.

The provision of five country agencies went some way to meet the needs of potential depositors outside Launceston. Agencies at Longford and Westbury catered for long-established and populous districts relatively close to town, while agencies at Ross and Campbell Town catered for the large Midlands district. The fifth agency was located at Deloraine in recognition of the area's growing importance. The major omission was the north-west coast, apparently still too remote and with still too fluid and dispersed a population to merit consideration. Most, if not all, of the agents were leading storekeepers.

Deteriorating fortunes

The second half of the 1850s was not the most favourable time to launch a new scheme. If not at the time the agencies opened, certainly soon afterwards there were signs that prosperity was on the wane. Fewer Tasmanians now returned to the island enriched by gold. More seriously, mainland markets for Tasmanian produce were now shrinking. For some time the timber trade had been declining. Now the markets for farm produce were beginning to show a slow but definite decline. These reductions were only partially offset by rising values for wool. Increasingly there was talk of stagnation and difficult times ahead.

The Launceston Bank for Savings reflected the uncertainty of the times. In 1855 the growth of business had come to an abrupt halt. After that the level of deposits drifted, despite the opening of agencies, lending ceased and some loans were called in as a precautionary measure in August 1856. These were the first loans recalled by the Bank. Two months later, perhaps in an effort to attract deposits, the Bank once more opened on Saturday nights. Briefly the trend of deposits was reversed, and new loans were again made in 1857 and 1858, only to be followed in the latter part of 1858 by the calling in again of some loans. Meanwhile interest paid on deposits had fluctuated according to the Bank's ability to pay, without much apparent effect on deposits.

For a brief period in 1859 and 1860 the Bank seemed to regain some of the buoyancy and optimism of the early 1850s. In September 1859 the Managers felt confident enough to change the Bank's own bankers—quite a major decision, since the Bank for Savings made no pretence of having liquid funds and depended completely on its commercial bankers in an emergency. The Bank for Savings now transferred its business accounts from the Australasia and Union Banks, its bankers since 1844, to the three local Tasmanian banks, the Commercial Bank of Tasmania, the Bank of Van Diemen's Land and the Bank of Tasmania. Then, as if to test the new alliance, the Executive Committee proceeded to lend out freely again, running down the Bank's liquid assets to a negligible figure, and increasing loans to a new peak of almost £100,000.

In this brief phase of optimism the Managers and the Executive Committee also seriously considered acquiring a separate building for the Bank. Perhaps with this in mind the reserve fund, until then neglected in favour of maximum returns to depositors, had been rapidly built up since 1857. Now reserves approached £3,000 and the Executive Committee considered it appropriate for the Bank to have its own premises. The old Union Bank building was on the market, but the price of £2,500 sought was considered too high. Instead, Dowling agreed to reconstruct the Bank's premises at his store into a distinct building with a separate entrance. For this the Bank paid an annual rental of £100, with twelve months' notice required from either side of termination of the agreement. The reconstructed premises opened in March 1860.

The Bank's apparent faith in the future was ill-founded. Between March 1860 and March 1862 total deposits declined from a peak of £99,000 to only £83,000. Mainly this reflected the degeneration of an economy that was stagnant into one clearly depressed. However, some part of the decline in deposits might be attributed to the departure of many would-be miners, with their funds, to the newly discovered goldfields of New Zealand, and some to the reintroduction of interest-bearing deposits by commercial banks in the late 1850s. The fall in deposits forced yet another calling in of loans, the third and largest in six years.

On a smaller scale the Bank's fortunes were also reflected in its newly created agencies. In the first full half-year to 31 August 1856 the five agents collected more than £2,000 in deposits. What might have seemed just a good beginning, however, turned out to be a typical level of business. At their peak in the half-year ending August 1858 total deposits received by the agencies still amounted to less than £3,000. Although the areas they served then had far more inhabitants than the town of Launceston, the agencies could at their best achieve little more than ten per cent of the business conducted at Head Office. The reasons for the unpopularity of the private agents are probably much the same as for the unpopularity of the police-magistrate system. Their facilities for depositing were inevitably slow and indirect, and they were not full-time specialist bankers; local storekeepers could hardly provide the efficient and confidential service of the Bank itself. Furthermore, if in theory the agents served large communities, many in these communities were so distant from the agents that their existence was little improvement on the one central bank in Launceston.

Whatever the reason, the agencies failed to attract custom. Commission and postage made them costly at the best of times, and by 1861 when their business fell sharply they were barely worth continuing. Early in 1862 it became known that the agent at Ross had been embezzling Bank funds. The amount was only £60 and was ultimately repaid by the agent's sureties, but the episode was enough to seal the fate of the agencies. In February 1862 the actuary recommended that the agencies be discontinued, the

Executive Committee agreed, and the Managers confirmed the decision at their general meeting in March.

By then the Bank had other problems as, with the onset of depression, its whole condition became increasingly unsatisfactory. For the first time in twenty years business was declining sharply. Among other problems this meant a relative increase in administrative expenses, since these were not easily reduced in proportion. Further, since many borrowers were finding increasing difficulty in paying interest, income was declining more than assets. Together these factors made it necessary to widen the margin between the mortgage and deposit rates of interest. Apparently it was considered unwise to lower the deposit rate, so the mortgage rate had to be raised. At the general meeting in March 1862 it was proposed to increase the mortgage rate to seven per cent, higher than at any time previously, except briefly from 1844 to 1846. The proposal was accepted, though in the face of much opposition from a number of managers.

The move also met with public opposition. On 1 April 'A Borrower' wrote to the *Launceston Examiner*. Quoting the letter sent to mortgagors by Dowling, he maintained that the Bank was no longer serving its true purpose. Many of the depositors, he claimed, were essentially investors seeking a high rate of return, and it was to these that the Bank now bowed. In fact, the Bank's ledgers and new accounts give very little substance to the claim, but the *Examiner*'s readers were not to know that. In retrospect 'A Borrower' 's letter also has special significance as the first shot in a campaign that was to bring the Bank close to liquidation.

The post-office savings bank controversy

In May 1861 legislation came into operation in Britain to provide savings-bank facilities at post offices. This important new development followed a short but enthusiastic campaign, initiated by an enterprising North Country banker, William Charles Sikes, and led in Parliament by William Gladstone. Post-office savings banks were an immediate success. Within four months facilities were established at 300 post offices, to the accompaniment of a great wave of revived philanthropic fervour. Such facilities, it was argued, would be far more extensive than those of the existing trustee savings banks, available for much longer hours, and virtually foolproof against fraud and default. In their honour London's *Punch* composed a lengthy and entertaining piece of doggerel. Its first verse set the tone:

> The savings bank, the savings bank,
> Bland Gladstone's best and latest boon,
> Come, use it, folks, of every rank,
> You cannot get your books too soon.

Display the common sense you boast
And take your money to the post.

Later verses advised the 'tight-built smiling servant girl' to save rather than buy crinoline, and exhorted 'Pale wife' to take from her 'tipsy spouse'

. . . what his pot-house treats have left,
Lodge it in that receiving house,
Some day he'll thank the kindly theft.
Some day twill give you boiled or roast,
Come, take your money to the post.

The post office was also recommended to those of greater means: to the young lady, Miss Rose, who should not spend on rings but save for her wedding which 'Alphonso Briggs may soon propose': and to Mamma, whose husband's cheques, if saved,

Twill help that month M'm on the coast,
Come, take your money to the post.

Within a few months post-office savings banks had strong advocates in Australia, and perhaps nowhere so strong as in Tasmania where the two savings banks were freer from government control than in any other colony. Beginning with an editorial on 17 April 1862 the *Launceston Examiner*, hitherto the Launceston Bank for Savings' loyal supporter, launched a vigorous campaign for the establishment of the new system in Tasmania. The *Cornwall Chronicle*, now no longer so vitriolic following the retirement of Goodwin but still firmly anti-establishment, was an even stronger advocate. Most active of all was the Reverend Doctor Browne. With his long interest in savings banking, his hostility since 1850 to the Launceston institution, and, he claimed, first-hand knowledge of British developments* Browne quickly spearheaded the campaign.

The first public meeting in Launceston to discuss post-office savings banks was held on 4 July 1862. Over 300 people attended, and after introductory remarks by Isaac Sherwin, now living again in Launceston, Browne 'came forward amidst loud cheers' to expound the virtues of the new system. At the close of the meeting he had the satisfaction of seeing a motion passed unanimously in its favour. On 30 July the *Cornwall Chronicle* announced the formation of an action committee composed 'of most intelligent citizens', and plans were made for a massive campaign in rural areas, to be led by Browne. During August, Browne addressed in-

* However, as Browne had not been in Britain since 1855, and the post-office savings-bank movement had developed only from 1859, he could not have had first-hand knowledge of the new movement.

numerable meetings as far away as Deloraine and Oatlands. Their success varied. At some he encountered considerable opposition, at others none. Some were well-attended, others poorly attended, and still others, since they were scheduled but not reported, one may suspect were cancelled for lack of attendance. Yet overall, support in Launceston and in the country seems to have been widespread and active; many petitions were sent to Parliament.

Ostensibly the proposed new system was not designed to destroy the old, but rather to be complementary. At the July meeting Browne claimed that the Launceston Bank for Savings was not hostile to his proposals. A few days later the *Launceston Examiner* stated that only gradually and over many years would the existing institutions in Launceston and Hobart be superseded. A month later the *Examiner* further claimed that all the Executive Committee members of the Launceston Bank for Savings favoured the post-office scheme. The claim cannot be discounted lightly, since Aikenhead, still editor of the *Examiner*, was a member of the Committee.

In reality, an early demise of the Launceston Bank for Savings was seriously contemplated, if not by supporters of the post-office savings-bank movement in general, certainly by Browne, its leader. From the start Browne did his utmost to discredit the existing institution. More than once he made comments directly about worthless securities held by the Bank. However, his main line of attack was less direct and probably more effective: he emphasized just how susceptible trustee savings banks in general were to fraud and failure, while at the same time hastening to add, perhaps with subtle malice, that he had every faith in Tasmania's existing savings banks. At a meeting at Longford on 15 August, for example, Browne opened his remarks by discussing how in principle and despite the best endeavours of their trustees, such banks were intrinsically vulnerable to fraud. He went on to demonstrate how in this respect the post-office system was completely infallible. Having established the argument, Browne proceeded to enumerate the more spectacular examples of failure among trustee savings banks in England, and, at his eloquent best, declared that only honour and honesty maintained the existing system. However, he added, he had no doubts about the safety of the Launceston and Hobart institutions!

Browne and some of his supporters attacked not only the Launceston Bank for Savings but its actuary, Henry Dowling. Browne and Dowling were long-standing enemies, though just why is not clear; letters from Browne referred to but not reproduced in the Minutes of Executive Committee Meetings, and a public denial by Browne that he had no personal quarrel with Dowling, hardly clarify the matter. However, one issue certainly became clear: Browne resented Dowling's ability to use his influence as a Member of Parliament against legislation to set up post-office savings banks. On 30 July the *Cornwall Chronicle* first commented critically that the government was not likely to prejudice its support in Parliament, notably from Dowling, by introducing such legislation. The *Chronicle*'s suggestion was effectively substantiated when on 16 September the Tasmanian government introduced into Parliament a Bill for special concession rates on the postage of savings-bank books,* clearly as a counter-measure to plans for post-office savings banks as such.

Now Browne came out into the open. In letters published simultaneously by the *Examiner* and *Chronicle* on 20 September he denounced Dowling, the Premier and the Treasurer for blocking the institution of post-office savings banks and trusted 'that a power will be brought to bear on the subject, which . . . will prove stronger than individual and interested influence'. For good measure the *Chronicle* threw in comments of its own about Dowling's 'ministerial jobbery' and his 'secret Star Chamber Savings' Bank'. Dowling responded with self-righteous indignation. In a letter published by the *Examiner* on 27 September he wrote:

> my efforts in various public directions in this colony for 32 years have been given cheerfully at the cost of much personal ease. Misrepresentation, falsehood, slander, I have accepted as the penalty of public service in a new country, colonised under peculiar social circumstances; but when I find a clergyman of the Church of England taking advantage of an assumed difference of opinion—the assumption being his own—and descending from the high and holy position of a minister of peace and good-will, to malign and slander, I begin seriously to consider if we are not drifting into a condition of utter public degradation, from which it becomes the duty of all men, desiring to secure their own personal and domestic quiet, at once to dissever themselves.

By now Aikenhead and the *Examiner* had made a complete about-turn, abandoning their earlier stand in favour of post-office savings banks to defend the existing system. Originally perhaps annoyed by continuous insinuations about the Launceston Bank for Savings, later attracted by the alternative legislation, and ultimately enraged by attacks on Dowling, the *Examiner* now launched perhaps the most scurillous attack in the whole disreputable controversy. On 30 August 1862 news of a sensational triple murder at Longford had made the headlines in the local press, and subsequent investigations were reported in great detail. By the time Browne's letter attacking Dowling appeared the circumstances of the murders had been at least partially clarified, and on 23 September an extraordinary editorial appeared in the *Examiner*. The murders, it claimed, could ulti-

* See p. 63.

Mechanics Institute, Launceston

Customs House, Launceston

Exhibits at the Tasmanian International Exhibition, 1891-2

Duck Reach hydro-electric power-station, Launceston

mately be traced to the withdrawal of some £300 from the Launceston Bank for Savings by a Mrs Hill, who feared for the safety of her money because of the current controversy. She had lent the money to her brother, who had spent part of it getting drunk, boasted about the rest, and had ultimately been robbed and murdered for it; to avoid recognition the thieves had also found it necessary to kill his housekeeper and an aged neighbour. The editorial concluded: 'it is certain that if Dr Browne had not been so indiscreet less money would have been spent on liquor, and there would have been no murders at Norfolk Plains.' On 25 September the *Examiner* published Browne's reply which, naturally enough, flatly denied that such an inference could be made. In any event, Browne claimed, the *Examiner* had got its facts wrong. Sliding from defence to attack, Browne queried the reason for the newspaper's suspiciously sudden change of opinion, commenting suggestively, 'Has the screw reached the *Examiner* office that it now argues against government security!!' An editorial comment on the same day summarily dismissed Brown as 'afflicted with monomania' and declared in grandiloquent fashion, 'We treat with thorough contempt the insinuation that any one, high or low, can put a screw upon the *Examiner*.'

A run on the Bank

The campaign for post-office savings banks and the venomous brawl into which it degenerated spelled near-disaster for the Launceston Bank for Savings. Even before the campaign began in earnest, deposits had been dwindling in response to a worsening economic situation. Now funds were withdrawn and accounts closed at an alarming rate. Notice required to withdraw large sums—one month for sums over £50, and two weeks for sums between £10 and £50—only seems to have delayed the run. The first major withdrawals occurred in August, reflecting the launching of the campaign in the previous month. In September there was a lull in the rate of withdrawals, but following the recriminations of the same month a greater and more prolonged run on the Bank occurred during October and most of November. Overall, in the four months from the end of July to the end of November total deposits fell from £80,000 to £63,000.

A sample of those depositors who withdrew money or closed their accounts during these four months clearly shows, perhaps a little surprisingly, that in most respects they made up a reasonable cross-section of depositors. There is little evidence that newer depositors panicked more than older depositors, that any occupational group was less trusting than another, or that there was any significant difference in reaction between urban and rural depositors. The only major deviation from this cross-section pattern is that a significantly higher proportion of women depositors withdrew their funds than men.*

The Bank's Managers reacted to the crisis in three main ways: by calling in loans, by asserting officially and unofficially that the Bank was sound, and by seeking assistance from the commercial banks. In retrospect it is very easy to be critical of their behaviour, yet one cannot help wondering if in the first two respects there was an element of misjudgement. Anticipating a fall in deposits, the Managers had already by 1 August issued to certain borrowers notices to recall loans worth close to £20,000. However, since this money was not legally payable for six months, it could do little to offset a run on the Bank in the meantime; on the contrary, news that such notices had been issued may have considerably reduced the public's already waning confidence in the Bank. Similarly, while official reassurances seem to have been restrained and prudent, unofficially many of the Bank's Managers and supporters may have done more harm than good by over-reacting to the post-office savings-bank campaign. Browne and the *Cornwall Chronicle* were quick to point this out. The former claimed that great damage had been done to the Bank's reputation by its supporters who followed Browne in the streets, abusing him for causing an alarm which would lead to a run and suspension of payment. Such claims can by no means be discounted simply because they came from the enemy camp, and at least one long-standing supporter of the Bank, J. W. Gleadow, agreed that the Bank's friends had done it more harm than its enemies.

The key to the Bank for Savings' fortunes in these critical months lay in its close relationship with the three local commercial banks, the Bank of Van Diemen's Land, the Bank of Tasmania, and the Commercial Bank of Tasmania. Over the years one of the Bank for Savings' most consistent and basic policies had been to retain negligible liquid assets, thus enabling the highest rate of return to depositors, and to rely on the commercial banks for accommodation if the need arose, using its mortgage loans as security. As early as 20 June 1862 the Bank for Savings had anticipated a possible withdrawal of funds, and at least forewarned them of the possible need for overdraft facilities. By the end of July, as notices of withdrawals accumulated, formal arrangements were made for overdraft facilities to the extent of £6,000. This amount proved adequate to meet the first run in August.

By the beginning of October the run had become much more serious. At a special meeting of the Managers held on 6 October the Executive Committee grimly reported:

* One other point of interest is that George Pullen, the Bank's accountant, was among those who withdrew funds; however, since Pullen operated his account virtually as a trading account, his withdrawals may have been for reasons unconnected with the soundness of the institution.

> Not only is the question one of great importance to this Institution but it may affect seriously the larger one at Hobart Town, and the Building Societies of both Towns, each of which Institutions will be imperilled by even a temporary suspension of the payments of this bank. Not only would the benevolent labours of many years be frustrated, but every monetary interest of the colony most seriously affected, if the two Savings Banks . . . are to be injuriously affected.

On the following day a meeting was held with the managers of all five commercial banks represented in Launceston. Now accommodation of £20,000 was sought until March, when loans on mortgage would fall due for repayment. Much to the relief of Dowling and his colleagues, the commercial bankers accepted the proposals in principle, each agreeing to lend £4,000. The extra accommodation re-established the Bank on a secure basis, and the crisis was all but over. Fears may have revived when both the Australasia and the Union later in October demanded personal security from four of the wealthier managers, and subsequently withdrew from the agreement.* However, each of the three local banks now increased its accommodation to £5,500, making £16,500 in all available to the Bank for Savings. This proved ample. During November the run petered out. By early December the Bank's position was sound enough for Dowling to take a fortnight's break in Melbourne.

Meanwhile the campaign for post-office savings banks had been largely undermined by the special postal legislation. Under its provisions, packages of up to four ounces containing savings-bank books and money could be posted as registered mail at a cost of only one penny; the return of such books similarly would cost only one penny. Previously the cost had been fourpence per package, plus an additional shilling if registered; understandably, few savings-bank transactions had taken place by post. Now, with the final passage of the legislation on 20 October, to become operative from 1 November, depositors outside Launceston could operate accounts cheaply and safely by post. The advantage of formal savings-bank facilities at post offices was greatly reduced, if not wholly eliminated. Two days before the Act came into operation Browne and his supporters held a last, slightly desperate meeting. By now the movement had virtually collapsed and little more was heard of it. Hopes revived briefly when in July 1863 a Parliamentary Select Committee investigated and recommended the institution of post-office savings banks. However, the government took no immediate action. In 1865 an Act was passed enabling the establishment of post-office savings banks, but was never implemented, and the issue remained dormant for nearly twenty years.

* Their less co-operative attitude is perhaps understandable, since the Launceston Bank for Savings had ditched them only three years before.

When the Launceston Bank for Savings held its general meeting on 6 March 1863 the Executive Committee could report with some satisfaction. The mortgage loans called in had been, or were being, repaid. Depositors who had withdrawn funds and, according to the Executive Committee, buried them in their gardens, were now busily digging them up and replacing them with the Bank. A few weeks after the meeting the Bank's overdrafts were paid off in full. By the time of the next general meeting in September 1863 the total direct cost of the crisis, in terms of interest, legal expenses, etc., was calculated at a mere £408 14s 1d, and was written off against the reserve fund. The indirect costs of the crisis were another and very different matter.

CHAPTER SIX

'Perilous Financial Seas'
The Depressed 1860s

Tasmania in the 1860s

The decade of the 1860s was undoubtedly the gloomiest in Tasmania's history. Already by 1860 there were unmistakable signs of less prosperous years ahead. By the time the Bank for Savings experienced its crisis in the second half of 1862, depression prevailed over most of the colony. Until at least the end of the 1860s, deep stagnation and a profound sense of hopelessness paralysed the island's community. Tasmania had, for the time being, become one of the 'backwaters in the mainstream of Australian progress'.

Most striking and perhaps most significant evidence of depression was the slump in Tasmania's import trade. Imports, which for Tasmania provided most of the consumer goods for a high standard of living and most of the capital goods and materials for economic expansion, declined from a level of around £1.25 to £1.75 million in the mid- and late 1850s to a mere £0.75 million by 1865; there was no significant increase from this low level until well into the 1870s. Unemployment was widespread and chronic, though in the absence of figures one cannot even attempt to calculate its magnitude. Wages for those fortunate enough to retain their jobs were sharply reduced; W. A. Townsley estimates a reduction of thirty-five per cent in wage levels between 1857 and 1870, much greater than the fall in prices over the same period. Not surprisingly there was a large exodus of workers to the mainland. Despite strenuous efforts to promote immigration, first through generous bounties and later through the offer of free land,* departures from Tasmania exceeded arrivals over the whole decade. By the late 1860s many houses were unoccupied and large areas

* Under the latter system, agents recruited not only British migrants but in the late 1860s Anglo-Indians and Germans, with in each case disastrous consequences. The settlement at Castra of retired Indian colonels, who expected the quiet comfort of 'happy English homesteads' but instead found themselves wielding axes and saws in wild bushland, was one of many social tragedies of the period.

of farmland abandoned. Charles Dilke wrote in *Greater Britain*, published in 1868, of his trip from Launceston to Hobart:

> It is disheartening . . . in an English colony, to see half the houses shut up and deserted, and acre upon acre of old wheat-land abandoned to mimosa scrub. . . . Since leaving Virginia I have seen no such melancholy sight . . .

Southern Tasmania was reputedly the worst hit. The Melbourne *Argus* of 1865 is quoted as saying, 'In the south the hopeless stagnation of life depresses the mind like an evil dream.' Yet there is little evidence that the north fared much better. While settlements in parts of the undeveloped north-west continued to grow in the 1860s, this was hardly a sign of prosperity. Many of the north-west's pioneer settlers, it was reported, were experiencing physical destitution of the 'most painful description'. In Launceston and on the northern plains unemployment and poverty prevailed. The *Launceston Examiner* frequently claimed that the depression was comparable in intensity to that of the early 1840s but was much more serious because the community was so much larger.

The immediate cause of the slump was the collapse of Tasmania's export trades, especially to the Australian mainland, on which Tasmania had come to rely so heavily. From the mid-1850s the mainland became progressively more self-sufficient. Timber was the first Tasmanian export industry to suffer; already by the early 1860s this once thriving trade was all but extinguished. The decline of Tasmania's grain exports was a more prolonged process but in the end almost as complete, and because of their greater importance to the economy, much more serious. Reflecting this trade's decline, wheat production during the decade fell by more than one-third. Meanwhile, overseas markets provided no relief. Whaling, already by 1860 a much reduced activity, declined still further in the 1860s. Exports of wool continued at a high level, but given the island's physical limitations no significant increase in production was possible. In the late 1860s sheep farmers suffered two major reversals: a sharp fall in wool prices, and a serious spread of the disease known as fluke.

On 21 August 1868 the Tasmanian Legislative Council appointed a Select Committee 'to enquire into the present depressed state of the Pastoral and Agricultural interests in this Colony'. The Committee found, as everyone knew, that such interests were very depressed, but complaining that the time allowed for its investigations had been very short, made no recommendations except that a Royal Commission should be appointed. No Royal Commission was appointed, no solution was offered, and no relief came. At the lowest point, in 1870, Tasmania exported produce to the value of only £649,000, compared with an average in the mid-1850s of about £1.5 million annually.

One factor accelerating the decline of Tasmanian exports was the imposition of import duties by Victoria, Tasmania's 'big and cruel sister' in the words of Anthony Trollope. In 1865 and again in 1866 the Victorian government raised tariffs both on overseas manufacturers and on farm produce from other Australian colonies. Victoria was Tasmania's largest mainland market. In 1867 the Tasmanian Government Statistician, whose commentary on the yearly published statistics was normally rather staid and formal, lashed out at the new duties 'as a matter of notoriety', and argued at length in favour of free trade. In the following year he advocated in some detail a customs union with the rest of Australia to overcome the problem. The idea was a popular one at the time, and chiefly on Tasmania's initiative delegates from the various colonies met at Melbourne in July 1870 to discuss the matter. No agreement was reached. The *Cornwall Chronicle*, searching desperately for an alternative solution, two years later seriously advocated a political union with Victoria.

Tasmania's proximity to the mainland, in many respects and at many times an advantage, proved in the 1860s to be a major disadvantage. While Tasmanian exports there were dwindling, mainland interests on the other hand increasingly came to dominate Tasmania's import trade. Shipments direct from the mainland increased, most notably shipments of livestock, and Tasmania's overseas imports came to be handled more and more by Melbourne merchants. Tasmania was rapidly becoming a commercial adjunct to the big city. Proximity to the mainland was also a disadvantage in another more serious respect: it facilitated the departure of those who could have done most to solve Tasmania's plight. At only slight cost and inconvenience, the young and the enterprising were easily able to escape across Bass Strait to follow their fortunes in other colonies.

Despite all these problems, many believed that progress could still be achieved. Farmers, the Government Statistician argued, for example, could re-establish themselves if only they were to show enterprise and adaptability; historians were later to endorse this view. Minerals, it was also widely believed, would be found in abundance if only active searches were to be made. In neither respect do the efforts seem to have been made. Outsiders believed Tasmanians had only themselves to blame for their misfortune. The Melbourne *Age* claimed that 'the apathy and sleepy-hollowism of Tasmanians are proverbial'. In similar vein Dilke commented scathingly that 'The curse of the country is the indolence of its lotus-eating population'. The judgement was a harsh one. If enterprise and energy were lacking, much of the explanation lies in two elements inherent in Tasmania's condition at the time. One, just mentioned, was the inevitable tendency for those with initiative to leave for larger and currently more prosperous mainland colonies. The other was Tasmania's convict legacy

—'a fearful drawback' according to one commentator. Thousands of ageing and aimless ex-convicts seriously degraded the quality of the colony's labour force and thus undermined the efforts of the few with initiative and enterprise. They also proved a major drain on the public funds which could otherwise have been used for more productive purposes.

Tasmania's government could do little to solve the colony's economic and social problems. If funds had been available they could have been usefully employed to provide better transport facilities, promote land settlement and perhaps provide assistance to manufacturing industry. But in the depressed conditions of the 1860s and with much of the public revenue needed to support ex-convicts, funds were not available. On the contrary, the outstanding problem which confronted governments in the 1860s was how to find enough revenue for even the most basic expenditure. Successive ministries proposed increased customs duties, property taxes and taxes on incomes, but could never find a parliamentary majority to implement them. Government financial policy came to mean little more than negative retrenchment. As if to compensate for their helplessness, politicians turned their energies to personal feuds and rancorous factionalism; Dilke dismissed them contemptuously as 'Lilliputian'.

One of the few important and progressive movements of the 1860s was towards the building of Tasmania's first railway-line. As early as 1855 the Legislative Council had made preliminary investigations into the possibility of building railway-lines from Hobart to Launceston and from Launceston west to Deloraine. The Hobart-Launceston scheme was quickly dropped, but the second proposal came soon to be taken up in earnest. In August 1857 a large meeting in Launceston, chaired by the mayor, Henry Dowling, formally launched a movement which, as it developed, proposed to build a line from Launceston to Deloraine via Longford and the rich Norfolk Plains. The proposed line would service a rich agricultural and pastoral area and create opportunities for further development. As time passed, the case became in some respects still stronger. To the northern farmer the need for cheap railway transport to maintain a hold on mainland markets became increasingly urgent. Among the residents of Launceston the railway came to be seen as a solution to depression; once it was built, wrote a correspondent to the *Launceston Examiner*,

> Launceston, aroused from its torpor, would become redolent of life: activity would take the place of lethargy, prosperity the place of depression, and men being healthfully employed, . . . our position as a people . . . would rapidly improve.

The movement was powerful and highly organized; in Henry Dowling, Richard Dry and W. S. Button it had outstanding leaders; the newspapers, most notably the *Examiner*, campaigned strongly on its behalf; and there seems to have been widespread popular support. Yet in spite of all this, it was not until January 1868, more than ten years after the movement had been launched, that construction of the Launceston-Deloraine railway actually began.

The explanation of this extraordinary delay reflects much of what was wrong with Tasmania in the 1860s. The primary obstacle was capital. About £400,000 would be needed to build the railway, according to the experts. On the one hand, however, local residents with their limited and rapidly dwindling resources could certainly not raise the funds. On the other hand, successive governments were, given their precarious finances, unwilling to raise a loan for that purpose unless the local residents would in effect underwrite that loan. Given their own financial situation, however, local residents were not prepared to do so on terms satisfactory to the government.

Despite this apparent impasse the railway-line might still have been built earlier but for other complicating factors. One was general political instability; each time a government fell from power, negotiations were interrupted and had to recommence under changed conditions. Again, the issue became clouded by the revival of north-south rivalries. Southern politicians saw no reason why they should commit themselves to a project which would only benefit the north; in a fit of pique the *Launceston Examiner* countered by suggesting that it would be preferable for the north to secede as a separate colony. To complicate matters still further, the north itself was not wholly unanimous. Many farmers on the northern plains were hostile because the proposed route by-passed them, or was too far away for their liking. More seriously, residents of Deloraine and the north-western districts had their own alternative and competing proposal, for a tramway from Deloraine to Latrobe, the deepwater port on the Mersey; this they argued would be a cheaper means of getting northern farm produce to the mainland markets. The whole issue was certainly not clarified by suggestions that the Deloraine-Latrobe scheme was inspired by malicious southerners.

The bogging down of the Launceston-Deloraine railway proposals was one of the tragedies of the 1860s. Had Parliament come to terms when the line was first proposed in 1857, and had the line been built by, say, 1860, the gains would have been large. In the short run the benefit of cheap transport would have offset some of the forces making for depression, at least in northern Tasmania. In the longer run it is conceivable that the railway would have enabled many northern farmers to retain a foothold in mainland produce markets. As it was, by the time construction of the railway commenced (and it took more than three years to complete) these markets were lost.

The Bank's financial troubles

As for Tasmania generally, so for the Launceston Bank for Savings the decade of the 1860s was undoubtedly the gloomiest in its history. After the 1862 crisis the safety of the Bank was, perhaps understandably, no longer taken completely for granted. People of modest means with surplus funds no longer automatically placed them with the Bank. In addition, those with more substantial sums of money who sought a safe longer-term investment, never more than a small minority of *depositors*, but between them accounting for a major portion of all *deposits*, now had alternative opportunities. From the end of the 1850s, as already noted, commercial banks throughout Australia revived the practice of paying interest on term deposits, something they had not done since the mid-1840s; for a time, particularly in the mid-1860s, interest on three-month deposits offered by commercial banks exceeded the maximum the Launceston Bank for Savings was able to pay.

In these ways the Bank for Savings' deposit business suffered. But above all it suffered because of the depression. Whereas in the 1850s wage-earners as a class had benefited most from prosperous times, now in the 1860s they suffered most. As a result the rate at which new accounts were opened declined sharply from an average of about 1,000 a year in the mid- and late 1850s to a low of only about 400 a year in the late 1860s. The fall was particularly marked among those depositors with formally stated occupations, because of widespread unemployment and the drift to the mainland. Earlier these had accounted for about two-thirds of new depositors, but now in the 1860s for less than half; now most new depositors in the 1860s were married women, children, or others not earning incomes.

The depression adversely affected not only new accounts but established accounts. In the 1860s very few accounts showed a tendency to increase, but many were closed or reduced as depositors drew on their reserves. The history of a sample of ninety-two accounts opened in 1859–60 establishes the trend very clearly. While retaining many of the basic characteristics already described for earlier years, they showed three significant differences. Firstly, there was a markedly higher early closure rate.* Secondly, many of the accounts at some time in the 1860s were run down in, broadly, the classic fashion, that is, moderate amounts were withdrawn at frequent intervals; excluding the very temporary accounts, nearly half the sample

* However, part of this might be attributed to the unusual conditions created by the 1862 crisis.

showed this characteristic. Thirdly, only two of the ninety-two accounts clearly accumulated funds in any manner.

At the start of the decade total deposits in the Bank had exceeded £99,000. Just before the crisis of 1862 they had declined to £80,000, and during the crisis fell sharply to £63,000. Under normal conditions a marked revival should then have taken place as ex-depositors returned their funds, but this seems to have occurred to only a very slight degree. Indeed the longer-run tendency was for a further fall in deposits. At their low point early in 1868 they amounted to only £55,000, little more than half the peak at the start of the decade.

With so many pressures making for a reduction in deposits, it is perhaps surprising that they did not fall even more. The reason is undoubtedly that the sagging fortunes of the Bank received some boost from the penny-postage legislation of 1862. From the early 1850s the proportion of rural accounts had been rising gradually, but on the eve of the legislation still accounted for only about one-third of new accounts. With the provision of the new postal facilities the proportion of rural depositors jumped sharply, to well over half the total. Many of them were farmers who tended to have larger, though more fluctuating, surplus funds than most urban depositors.

While deposits were a major problem for the Bank, its investments were an even greater problem. Already at the start of the 1860s the need for an overhaul of investments was a matter of some importance. Following the 1862 crisis it became a matter of urgency. The crisis made the Bank acutely aware that it should keep more of its funds in relatively liquid form. This required the calling in of more loans, which in any event was necessary as deposits showed a persistent tendency to decline. But above all the Bank had to do something about its non-paying investments. While these as such were a direct reflection of depression, their *proportion* of all investments had risen sharply when during the crisis the Bank had been forced to call in loans which it considered safe to recall, the better loans, well covered by their collateral security and paying interest regularly. In March 1866 the Executive Committee revealed to the Managers that nearly one-third of the Bank's securities were producing an average annual yield of only one per cent.

The Bank's preference in the 1860s was for central or local government bonds or debentures. As early as June 1859 it had applied for municipal water-works debentures, shortly afterwards had applied for more, and in the early 1860s the Minutes of the Executive Committee and the Managers' meetings make several references to local and colonial government securities. In 1864, when private mortgage loans and government securities were first formally distinguished in the Bank's accounts, the latter totalled some £23,000, mostly in Tasmanian government stock yielding six per cent per annum, compared with some £45,000 in private mortgage loans. By then preference for government securities was the formally stated policy of the Bank, and new private mortgage business had long since been abandoned. Yet for the rest of the decade the Bank was unable to increase its holdings of government stock beyond the £23,000 recorded in 1864.

The great stumbling-block was the Bank's inability to terminate its non-profitable mortgage loans without incurring capital losses. From 1863 this was referred to constantly at Executive Committee and the Managers' meetings, though details were rarely given. In fact, their subsequent history recorded in the Loans Books shows that nine mortgage loans were in this category, three on rural properties, six on urban properties. Seven out of the nine loans had been made in the boom years of 1852 to 1855 and two in 1857. Altogether their loan value totalled more than £20,000, or nearly half of all private loans. After selling the foreclosed properties, mostly in the 1870s, the Bank sustained a total capital loss in excess of £9,000. This was in addition to the loss of interest before final disposal, which was probably nearly double the capital loss.

Outstanding among these nine loans were those made on two large city properties adjacent to each other along the North Esk wharf. One was a large brewery complex on the site now occupied by the Monds Affleck flour mill. There, in the 1830s, George Lukin had built one of Launceston's first breweries. Following his death, the brewery and adjoining inn and cottages passed to his wife who, in 1855, borrowed £4,000 from the Bank for Savings on property then valued at £12,000. In 1861 the Bank foreclosed because of non-payment of interest, and ultimately disposed of the property in 1874 for a mere £1,200, one-tenth of its original valuation. The other property, on the site now occupied by Boags brewery, was owned by John Thompson, a flash-in-the-pan merchant with interests at the peak of his fortunes in flour-milling, grain and produce, groceries, wine and shipping. On the strength of his flour-mill, house and land on the wharf Thompson raised loans from the Bank in 1852 and 1854 totalling £6,000. By 1858 he was already unable to pay interest, the Bank foreclosed, and eventually sold the property, also in 1874, for only £3,000, incurring a capital loss of £3,000.

Perhaps the real dilemma facing the Bank for Savings in the 1860s was that it was unable to cut its losses on such loans because it lacked reserves against which to write them off. In this respect at least the Bank's policies of the 1850s had clearly lacked foresight. By force of circumstances it may have been unable to avoid making the loans it did make in the early 1850s, but it could certainly have built up reserves to guard against possible losses on their account. Active accumulation of reserves did not begin until the late 1850s, long after the boom had passed, and by 1862 amounted to only £5,000, less than the value of the Bank's largest single loan, and totally inadequate to cover losses that might be sustained on the sale of even some of its non-paying assets. If all nine bad securities had been sold at the time, the Bank would have been at least technically bankrupt. It is little wonder that the Executive Committee and the Managers vacillated in their attitude to the problem loans. They wanted to sell and on many occasions came close to doing so, but generally backed away, or fixed a high reserve price at the amount of the original loan.

Once the basic problem was recognized, reserves could in theory have been built up, and there is ample evidence that the Executive Committee and the Managers were well aware of the need. In practice, however, it was almost impossible to do this. Accumulation of reserves could only occur at the expense of interest paid to depositors, but this, it was rightly realized, presented serious dangers. The Executive Committee believed that it was vital to maintain interest at four per cent, otherwise many deposits would be lost to competing institutions. Four per cent was a modest return—the Hobart Savings Bank regularly paid four and a half per cent—but was the maximum the Bank could afford, because so many of its investments were unprofitable. The attempt to maintain interest at four per cent, and even this could not always be achieved, left little available for allocation to reserves. At their peak in 1867 these still fell short of £7,000.

The vicious circle was thus complete. There could be no improvement in the interest rate on deposits, which might have attracted more funds, without a major overhaul of investments. Such an overhaul was impossible until more reserves had accumulated, but reserves could not be accumulated except by paying a lower rate of interest on deposits. A lower rate of interest on deposits would almost certainly have lost deposits, and this was the last thing the Bank could afford, since it then would have been necessary to sell some of its remaining *good* investments, thus further lowering the rate that could be paid to depositors. The Bank was in a highly precarious position. A second run on its funds, even if much smaller than the first, could easily have brought it close to liquidation.

Caught in this vicious circle the Bank had little room to manoeuvre. As far as possible it put on a bold front, making sure, for example, by selling government bonds if necessary, that it never showed an overdrawn account on its balance sheet. Twice it juggled the funds a little, by allocating expenses in the balancing month to the next accounting period, in order to maintain the four per cent return. It cut back on administrative expenses, so far as it was able, mainly by sacking the third and most junior official, Ambrose Dowling, even though he was Henry Dowling's cousin. And to avoid realizing further assets it allowed cash in hand to run down to almost nothing. Yet essentially it was a matter of sitting tight, waiting and hoping for the economic revival which alone could solve the problem, by increasing deposits and perhaps restoring some of its bad investments to a paying basis.

The 1860s marked the low point in the Bank for Savings' fortunes. It is some indication of its acute problems and the condition to which it had been reduced that by then it had been far outstripped by its southern counterpart. Although Hobart had fared no better economically than Launceston and perhaps even worse, its savings bank had gone ahead while Launceston's slid back. In the mid-1850s they had had almost equal total deposits. By the end of the 1860s the Launceston Bank for Savings' deposits were well under half of those of the Hobart Savings Bank.

Administrative reorganization

At least, in retrospect, there was one bright side to the Bank for Savings' affairs in the 1860s. During the course of the decade its administration underwent a major reorganization which was to place the Bank on a much sounder basis in the future. There was no sudden or spectacular change; gradually the Bank became a less personal and in some respects a less philanthropic institution, more organized, and certainly more business-minded, while retaining its basic aim of providing all possible facilities for saving by low-income groups who received directly or indirectly all profits of the institution. The changes occurred partly by chance and partly by force of circumstances.

The first significant change came early in 1860 when the Bank formally became more independent of its dominating figure, Henry Dowling. For fifteen years Dowling had had sole control of the Bank's day-to-day affairs, had operated it in his own business premises, and as one of Launceston's most powerful public figures had no doubt largely guided its major decisions. In March 1860 the first step away from what was virtually a one-man organization occurred when Dowling's premises were rebuilt to provide the Bank with its own distinct quarters and separate entrance, in effect a building of its own, though still owned and rented to the Bank by Dowling. At the same time, the two junior officers in the Bank became formally responsible not to Dowling, the actuary, but to the Executive Committee. The senior of the two clerks, George Pullen, a full-time employee since 1863 and by now widely recognized as an efficient and valuable officer, was officially promoted to the position of accountant.

There is no reason to believe that Dowling was displeased with the changes. By then, aged fifty, suffering at times from ill-health, and increasingly absorbed with other issues, he seems to have been happy to play a less active role in the institution. Dowling was still mayor of Launceston, and although his term of office ended in 1861, in that year he was elected to the House of Assembly as a member for Launceston and immediately became immersed in parliamentary affairs. Increasingly, however, it was the Launceston-Deloraine railway which engaged his attentions. Dowling undoubtedly gave more of his time to the project, and perhaps exerted more influence on its behalf, than any other person. When in October 1865 the Launceston and Western Railway Company was formally projected, Dowling sought and obtained six months' leave of absence from the Bank to promote the cause. Most of the six months he spent actively canvassing the areas through which the railway would pass. When the Launceston and Western Railway Company was finally registered in March 1867 Dowling became its secretary. A few months later, negotiations with the government were successfully concluded and construction work began early in 1868. Now devoting most of his time to railway affairs, Dowling took another three months' leave of absence from May to June 1868, and on 30 July, in order to give his full time to railway company affairs, he announced his retirement as actuary of the Bank for Savings.

There was never any question about Dowling's successor. George Pullen had given excellent service to the Bank over fifteen years, and was the automatic, unanimous choice of the Executive Committee. Pullen, except that he shared Dowling's Baptist faith, was fundamentally different from his predecessor. Unlike Dowling, Pullen had wandered round Australia for a long time before he settled down. He had perhaps the same streak of restlessness as his father, Jesse Pullen, who ranged far and wide through north-western Tasmania as a Baptist minister, and had become one of the district's celebrated figures. Not until he was aged thirty-five did George Pullen finally stay in Launceston to work for the Bank for Savings. From that time, however, he was a completely changed man. Although he developed some outside interests, these were minor compared with Dowling's, and minor compared with his own devotion to the Bank. Warm-hearted but shy and retiring, married but without a family, Pullen progressively came to identify himself with the Bank. Overall, Pullen, the professional dedicated banker, was perhaps as appropriate for the institution during his term of office as Dowling, less professional and less fully committed but still very enthusiastic and with great public standing, had been earlier during the Bank's formative years.

The 1860s also mark a major growth in the stature of the Bank's Executive Committee. To some extent this would have occurred anyway, as Dowling's interest waned, but it also stemmed from a fundamental change in the method by which committee members were selected. Since 1849, when the Bank came under the 1848 Act, managers had simply taken turns to serve on the Committee, seven at a time, generally following a simple alphabetical sequence, except that one of the three trustees of the Bank was always included. On 26 February 1862 the Executive Committee decided to replace alphabetical rotation by outright election at the Managers' meetings. In practice membership was decided in advance.* Membership became permanent or semi-permanent, and the Committee acquired a definite Chairman, though informally at first; W. S. Button served in this capacity from 1862 until his retirement from the Committee ten years later. Continuity of membership meant that the Committee had much greater familiarity with, and a longer-run interest in the Bank's affairs, while a regular and recognized chairman made proceedings more efficient and provided the Bank with a second leader. While there is little direct evidence, this new-style Executive Committee almost certainly greatly increased its role in the Bank's affairs, both in relation to the actuary and in relation to the Managers, to whom it was formally responsible. For the rest of the nineteenth century at least, the Executive Committee was the key policy-making body.

This was undoubtedly a major advance. To some extent the troubles the Bank encountered in the 1860s might be attributed to the deficiencies in administration in the 1850s. Except for Dowling, and to a very limited extent the three trustees, no one then had a really continuing interest in or close knowledge of the Bank's affairs. Rotating membership was certainly partly to blame for the absence of a long-term policy of building up reserves. It may also have made for errors in lending policy; it so happened, for example, that in the six months when most money was lent out, from September 1852 to February 1853, only three of the seven members of the Executive Committee were businessmen. Again during the final phase of heavy lending, March 1854 to February 1855, a majority of Executive Committee members were new managers appointed in 1853 and serving on the Committee for the first time.

The new form of the Executive Committee eliminated such weaknesses and dangers. Furthermore, as it developed, the Executive Committee came to be composed almost entirely of experienced businessmen. First the rural interests, then the professional men dropped out. In 1866, for example, the Committee consisted of W. S. Button, the brewer, James Aikenhead of the *Launceston Examiner*, Richard Green, a long-established and now leading Launceston merchant, Robert De Little, a Launceston builder since the 1830s, James John Hudson, who had acquired Dowling's stationery and book-selling business in the 1850s and had founded and now managed the Northern Tasmanian Permanent Building Society, and Isaac Sherwin,

* Rarely were there more candidates than positions to be filled.

Main Street, Zeehan, *c.* 1900

King Street, Scottsdale, 1917

Emu Bay Railway locomotive crossing trestle-bridge over the Que River now prominent again in Launceston business circles as secretary of the Gas Company, a director of the Bank of Van Diemen's Land and Launceston agent for the Australian Mutual Provident Society.

The progressive development of more professional administration and business-like direction was characteristic of savings banks throughout the world. In many instances, and this would certainly apply to the Launceston Bank for Savings, such changes partly resulted from the almost inevitable decrease of philanthropic fervour after the excitement of promotion had passed, and the loss of one or more dominant personalities. Generally though, savings banks appear to have changed in character because of their rapidly growing size and the need for a more professional full-time administration which developed a vested interest of its own. In Launceston this clearly was not the case. Essentially a more business-like administration came in response to the challenge of increasing problems rather than increasing size. Increasing size came only later, and then was only to reinforce a form of administration already well established.

CHAPTER SEVEN

'The Tide has Turned for Tasmania Now'
Revival and Boom 1870–1890

The first railways

On 15 January 1868 Prince Alfred, Duke of Edinburgh, paid a brief visit to Launceston as part of his official tour of the Australian colonies. Launcestonians eagerly awaited the Duke's arrival, not only because he was their first Royal visitor, but because one of the highlights of his day in Launceston was to be the turning of the first sod of the Launceston-Deloraine railway. A special stand was erected for the occasion, with tickets selling from one shilling for standing room up to ten shillings for the most favoured seats. Local craftsmen produced, and displayed for some days beforehand, an elaborately carved wheelbarrow and silver spade with which the ceremony was to be performed. The Duke, attended by the Premier, Sir Richard Dry, and most of Launceston's notables, duly turned the first sod, though the occasion was marred by bad weather and an overcrowded schedule, then proceeded with the rest of his itinerary, climaxed by a sumptuous banquet in the hall of the Mechanics Institute. Meanwhile, for the paupers of the town the Benevolent Society turned on special rations of bread, meat, suet, raisins and spice.

Despite this auspicious beginning, the Launceston-Deloraine railway-line took more than three years to complete. Some months elapsed before the government raised funds in London to allow real construction to commence. Then followed delay after delay, and argument after argument. To some extent these were the inevitable fumblings of a small colony building its first railway-line. Mostly, however, problems arose from the poor organization of the construction work, which permitted no less than four parties to wrangle and battle interminably: the Launceston and Western Railway Company, which was to operate the line; the construction contractors, Overend and Robb; the Tasmanian government, which raised most of the funds; and special commissioners appointed by the government to supervise construction. To make matters worse, the commissioners disagreed between themselves. It was little wonder that Anthony Trollope was to refer to the northern railway tangle as more complicated than the old Schleswig-Holstein question. With costs mounting, the government had to raise an additional loan. Then, just as the line approached completion in the winter of 1870, came severe floods. Work had to be abandoned for a time, and when the floods receded much damage was discovered, particularly to some of the embankments. It was not until February 1871 that the Launceston-Deloraine railway-line finally came into operation.

With the opening of the line, new problems arose. In its first months of operation the Launceston and Western Railway Company sustained major losses. While this was not unusual for a new railway-line and no real indication of its long-run value, for the Launceston and Western Railway Company it spelled disaster, since there was no reserve to meet such losses. In June 1872 the company was forced to suspend operations and, after urgent negotiations, sold out to the government in August. In the circumstances, the government's terms were generous. Capital was refunded to shareholders, and northern landowners were asked to pay an annual levy of only £15,000, less than half the amount originally accepted as payable if the need arose.

The levy encountered fierce opposition. Landowners, it was argued, had to pay indiscriminately, whether they benefited from the line, were unaffected by it, or adversely affected. Even more vehemently it was argued that the government, controlled by southerners, was discriminating against the north. It insisted on landowners paying a levy in the north, but made no such provision in an agreement recently signed with the Main Line Railway Company, promoted in the south, which planned to construct a line north from Hobart to extend eventually to Launceston, for which the government guaranteed five per cent interest on capital. The levy, some declared, was a 'mad crusade against the only little bit of progress Tasmania can boast of'. But the government still persisted and appointed its faithful and distinguished servant, R. C. Gunn, to the difficult task of collecting the money. Gunn was refused point blank by innumerable landowners and, in protest against the government's obstinacy, some twenty-six northern justices of the peace resigned their commissions; conspicuous among them was Theodore Bartley, one of the founders of the Launceston Bank for Savings and a late commissioner for construction of the railway. The government replied by dispatching police from Hobart and by placing advertisements in the northern press which explained to readers the implications of the Riot Act. The goods of some of those refusing to pay were seized and arrangements made for their sale by auction in February 1874. Launceston's irate residents countered by systematically disrupting the auctions with loud jeering and whistling; some burned effigies, and a few broke the windows of those believed to be 'scabs'. The incidents hardly deserve the name 'railway riots' by which they were later known, but there is no doubt about the bitter and explosive state of north-south relations. Wisely, the Hobart government, although in the end it succeeded in collecting most of the unpaid levy for 1873, made no attempt to collect levies in later years.

During the six years that the Launceston-Deloraine railway project staggered from crisis to crisis the southern Main Line project had its own quota of problems. First brought to the attention of British financiers in 1869, it was not until March 1872 that final agreement was reached between the Tasmanian government and the London-based Main Line Railway Company. By that agreement the government guaranteed interest at five per cent on £650,000 spent by the company. Since the estimated expense of building the line considerably exceeded this figure, the agreement was no more than a partial insurance policy and still left the company with major problems: how to build the line at minimal cost, particularly in view of the hilly terrain over at least the southern half of any possible route; and how to pass through a sufficiently large number of developed or developing areas to provide adequate traffic, without making the line unnecessarily long. Controversy over the choice of route made for considerable delays in construction, and was only finally settled in 1874. Meanwhile the company had decided to use the narrow three-foot six-inch gauge, as against the five-foot three-inch gauge of the Launceston-Deloraine railway, to ensure the lowest capital cost per mile. With such a gauge the railway could be wound and twisted around the contours, requiring a minimum of expensive cuttings and embankments and only one short tunnel. Capital was thus saved, though at the expense of speed, operating efficiency and the comfort of passengers. Early in 1876 the 122-mile railway, three times as long as the Launceston and Western Railway, finally extended to Evandale, where it met the northern line. Before the end of the year a narrow-gauge line had been built over the remaining eleven miles to Launceston, parallel to the Launceston and Western Railway broad-gauge line.

The construction of Tasmania's two first railway-lines created immense problems and bitter controversies which seemed to drag on interminably. Yet there is no doubt that they gave a considerable boost to the colony's fortunes. During construction they provided welcome employment for a depressed community in which many were unemployed. Once completed they proved invaluable in many respects. The Main Line, especially, brought benefits to the whole colony in terms of society and defence, even ultimately the island's politics, as well as great economic benefits to the country it traversed between Hobart and the northern plains. The Launceston and Western Railway, sweeping in a wide arc south then west through much of northern Tasmania's richest farmland, brought major improvement to a depressed farm community. The widely-held belief that railways offered one of the best prospects for lifting Tasmania from depression was not entirely without foundation.

The development of mining

Apart from railways, one of the chief hopes for Tasmania's revival and renewed prosperity in the late 1860s lay in the exploitation of mineral wealth. Some minerals were already known to exist, and others, it was believed, would be discovered if searches were made. Eventually mining was to become the dominant force in the island's economic recovery, and ultimately brought to Tasmania prosperity and sustained continuous development previously unknown. Unfortunately, as with the construction of railways, such benefits were to be achieved only after years of failure, disappointment and frustrating delays.

Gold was the first mineral to attract systematic attention. After the spectacular successes of gold mining in New South Wales and Victoria, and now from 1867 in Queensland, this was hardly surprising. Furthermore, since 1852 gold had been found, though rarely in payable quantities, in various parts of Tasmania. From 1869, it seems, prospectors were becoming active again, particularly in the Fingal area on the upper South Esk, where most of the earlier finds had been located, but also at Nine Mile Springs (later known as Lefroy) to the east of George Town, and in the remote north-east, near Waterhouse Point. Promising finds were made in all three areas and by 1870 a reputed ninety gold-mining companies were operating amidst considerable publicity. But the boom was short-lived. Despite sustained encouragement from the press, only two important mines survived, one at Fingal, the other at Nine Mile Springs, and in each of the six years from 1870 to 1875 exports of gold amounted to less than £20,000.

With gold a disappointment, great hopes were now held out for the exploitation of iron ore, long known to exist at various places in the north. On 17 May 1872 the *Cornwall Chronicle* brought to the public's attention the 'mountains of iron ores of the finest quality yielding from 60 to 85 per cent of pure metallic iron' which existed on the west bank of the Tamar close to the mouth of the Estuary. At the time several attempts were being made to establish iron-smelting works on the mainland. Whether the *Cornwall Chronicle*'s reminder was coincidental or was prompted by mainland developments, conditions were favourable for the development of the Tamar deposits. In a little over eighteen months three companies were established to mine and smelt iron ore in the area. All were based in

Victoria and largely financed from Melbourne, though in each case with considerable assistance from Launceston interests. Most prominent of the three was the Tamar Charcoal Iron Company, formed at the end of 1872, and later reconstructed, rather hopefully, as the British Tamar Charcoal Iron Company. Operating intermittently over five years, it ultimately had smelting capacity exceeding that of any other Australian ironworks in the nineteenth century, and overall more than half a million pounds was spent on the venture.

None of the three Tamar iron companies succeeded. The immediate reason seems to have been the presence of chromium oxide in the ore, which made the pig iron too brittle for most purposes. Yet one may suspect that even if this had not been the case the Tamar companies would still have failed, like their mainland counterparts, because of competition from the incomparably more advanced and large-scale producers overseas. After 1874 no further attempts were made to exploit the Tamar deposits, and within thirty years the extensive works of the British Tamar Charcoal Iron Company were so overgrown as to be barely visible.

During 1872, when the Tamar iron deposits first began to receive great publicity, two short items appeared in the *Cornwall Chronicle* about the discovery of tin. On 1 May the *Chronicle* reported that the well-known geologist Charles Gould had left for Sydney hoping to establish there a company to mine tin in Tasmania at a so far undisclosed site. Later, on 8 November, the *Chronicle* reported, again very briefly, that samples of alluvial tin had been brought from an area inland from Bridport, on the north-east coast. Neither item seems to have aroused much interest, in striking contrast to the constant publicity given to gold and iron. Tin was a novelty, outside the long-established ideas of mining prospects in Australia.* Tin, however, was to be the critical factor in the return of prosperity to Tasmania.

Gould's visit to Sydney may have been related to the discovery of tin at Mount Bischoff. In December 1871 the veteran prospector James 'Philosopher' Smith had discovered the Mount Bischoff field and in the succeeding months made considerable efforts to enlist the necessary capital support. Gould had long been familiar with the wilds of western Tasmania and was subsequently to establish a tin mine close to Mount Bischoff. Whether Gould's visit to Sydney was on behalf of Smith's project or some other scheme is uncertain. If the former he was apparently unsuccessful, for in 1873 Smith was still hawking his claim around Launceston. Eventually Smith succeeded in gaining the support of the solicitor William Ritchie, a partner in the firm which handled the Launceston Bank for

* Although on the mainland such ideas were being dispelled by the new alluvial tin fields of New England.

Savings' legal business. In August 1873 Ritchie floated the Mount Bischoff Tin Mining Company, taking over Smith's claim for cash and shares. Operations commenced in the following month and were quickly to confirm that Mount Bischoff was one of the world's richest tin mines. Launceston was soon alive with high hopes for new ventures that were taking up land adjacent to the mountain itself over which the Mount Bischoff Company had a secure hold. A few at least were successful—one promoter proclaimed ecstatically that 'you can see the ore in the wash dirt . . . as thick as the currants in a rich bridecake'—but most fringe ventures failed dismally. The history of Mount Bischoff was virtually the history of one company.

Perhaps spurred on by the Mount Bischoff sensation, following the initial discoveries south of Bridport in 1872 prospectors quickened their searches in the north-east. During 1874 rich deposits of alluvial tin were discovered around and to the east of Scottsdale, particularly in the Ringarooma district. In the following year Launceston spawned another crop of companies to exploit these discoveries in the north-east.

Promising as they were, both Mount Bischoff and the north-east tin fields were severely hampered in their early years. Firstly, there were no local smelting facilities. Smelting at the mines was generally considered impracticable and to export ore or concentrate to smelters in Britain was uneconomic, even for the rich Mount Bischoff deposits. To meet the problem the Mount Bischoff Tin Mining Company began to build smelters at Launceston in 1875. By 1876 three were in operation, handling ores not only from Mount Bischoff itself, but from the north-eastern fields. In 1878 Messrs Gardner and McKenzie opened independent tin-smelting works in Launceston, financed largely by Sydney interests.

The other problem was transport of the ore or concentrate from the mines. Mount Bischoff was nearly fifty miles from the coast, and the north-eastern fields a similar distance from Launceston. Roads were virtually non-existent, and although successive Tasmanian governments attempted to raise funds for road construction, efforts were consistently vetoed by the Legislative Council, until the end of 1877 when £140,000 was finally allocated for expenditure on roads to mining fields. The north-east benefited greatly as a result, the Mount Bischoff field very little, since by 1878 the problem had been solved privately. As it happened, all but three miles of the route from the mine to the coast lay on the vast freehold property of the Van Diemen's Land Company. Quickly seeing the opportunities for a lucrative mine traffic, as well as the development of its own timber resources, in 1875 the Van Diemen's Land Company began to build a wooden tramway over the forty-five miles from Emu Bay (later Burnie) to the edge of its property, close to the Mount Bischoff mine. The tramway opened on 1 February 1878, and horses began to haul truckloads of ore to the new port at Emu Bay. Later, the Mount Bischoff Company completed the three miles to the mine after buying out the farmer who owned the land in between at an exorbitant price. In 1884 the tramway was finally replaced by a proper iron railway.

As tin mining overcame its initial problems, gold mining revived. In the mid-1870s major discoveries were made at both the Fingal and Nine Mile Springs goldfields. More important still was the discovery of a quite new field at Brandy Creek (later Beaconsfield), close to the Tamar iron deposits. First discovered in 1876, the Brandy Creek field became really important from 1877 with the formation of the Tasmania Gold Mining Company. The 'Tasmania' was to be one of Australia's most profitable gold mines.

The boom of the 1880s

During the second half of the 1870s the colony was again unmistakably on the road to prosperity. Perhaps the first clear sign of this was that people no longer left for the mainland. After fifteen years of losing population, Tasmania began from 1876 to record a definite, if modest, excess of arrivals over departures. Contemporaries commented increasingly on the transformation. For example, on 21 January 1878 the *Cornwall Chronicle* wrote for its 'home' readers, with its customary dig at southern political domination:

> The colony is, in fact, in a transition state from premeditated, wilful and prolonged stagnation to one of vigorous action, which has already led direct to unprecedented prosperity, with fair promise of its steady annual increase.

Edward Braddon, later Premier of the colony, commented in the same year that 'the tide has turned for Tasmania now; Victoria tempts no more.' Compiling his *Under the Southern Cross* at about the same time, Henry Cornish wrote in similar vein. Cornish hoped that Anglo-Indians seeking a place for retirement would continue to come to Tasmania, as they had done for many years, despite some recent disasters. The island, he believed, had many advantages, the major disadvantage, at least for retiring Anglo-Indians, being the lack of good servants; Tasmanian servants were 'a poor dirty lot . . . mostly thieves, degenerate families of convicts'. This was one of the last fleeting references in contemporary literature to the fast-disappearing convict element which had for so long hindered the colony's progress.

The mainspring of Tasmania's revival in the late 1870s and the continuing prosperity which followed was undoubtedly mineral wealth. From the late 1870s tin and gold provided directly or indirectly a vast amount of employment. Mining companies paid lucrative dividends to their predominantly Tasmanian shareholders. Some were of fabulous proportions: the Tasmania gold mine paid over £0.75 million in dividends during its lifetime, and the Mount Bischoff Tin Mining Company had already handed out over £1 million in dividends by the end of the 1880s. Minerals dominated a rapidly growing export trade. Already by the end of the 1870s tin and gold exports together surpassed in value the established staple, wool. During the 1880s, when exports overall earned around £1.5 million annually, or more than twice as much as in 1870, minerals consistently accounted for a third or more of the total.

Mining was the dominant but not the sole factor in Tasmania's renewed prosperity. In a less spectacular manner farming made some notable advances. Under legislation passed in 1870 wool-growers successfully eliminated the widespread disease of scab; by the early 1880s, when Tasmania was declared scab-free, major increases in production had been achieved as a result. Meanwhile fruit growing was becoming firmly established, particularly the apple orchards of southern Tasmania. During the 1880s the acreage under fruit increased four-fold, and by the end of the decade exports to the mainland exceeded £100,000 annually. Almost as important was the revival and expansion of potato growing, particularly in the newly developing country to the north-west. By 1890 exports of potatoes to the mainland also exceeded £100,000 annually.

Encouraged by the new-found prosperity and easy availability of funds in London, the Tasmanian government borrowed freely, and in increasing amounts to build up an imposing railway network. This was a vital factor in the continued affluence of the 1880s. With loans of £300,000 in 1881, £500,000 in 1883, £800,000 in 1884 and £1,000,000 in 1886 the government more than doubled the length of railway-line during the decade to nearly four hundred miles. An active railway building programme provided good employment for the unskilled and, as lines were completed, new opportunities for development. In 1885, for example, the Launceston-Deloraine line was extended to the port of Formby (later Devonport), opening up the rich Mersey valley and providing an alternative outlet for farmers in the Deloraine district; and by 1890 this line had been extended west to Ulverstone. In 1886 an important branch line was completed along the valley of the South Esk to St Mary's, providing farmers with cheaper transport and enabling exploitation of the extensive coal deposits around St Mary's; as a result, by 1890 Tasmania was producing 50,000 tons of coal annually, which met most of its own rapidly growing requirements. Perhaps the most valuable of all the new lines was that from Launceston to Scottsdale, opened in 1889. Not only did this line revitalize the tin mines of that area, but its completion marked the real beginning both of a large timber industry and a new farming area.

On the mainland the 1880s saw perhaps the greatest boom in Australia's history, a boom which benefited Tasmania in several ways. A rapidly increasing population and rising living standards greatly helped the revival of Tasmania's export trade in farm products to the mainland. Continuous heavy borrowing by various colonial governments greatly facilitated the Tasmanian government's own loan programme. Similarly, the influx of private capital from overseas, although directed primarily to the larger colonies, meant overseas funds were much more readily available for private development in Tasmania, either directly, or indirectly via mainland enterprises. Perhaps the least obvious at the time, but in the long run of very great importance, boom conditions on the mainland firmly established tourism as one of the island's major income earners.

From the time the first explorers set foot on the island, Tasmania had been renowned for its scenery and for its climate, the vital ingredients of a successful tourist industry. However, until means of communication were sufficiently developed, and more particularly until solid affluence established the holiday-making habit, the potential remained unexploited. In 1869 H. Thomas's *Guide for Excursionists from the Mainland to Tasmania* appeared on the market, the first published description of Tasmania intended solely as a tourist guide. During the 1870s, if recorded departures and arrivals are any indication, thousands of people visited the island annually, and towards the end of the decade the tourist trade was beginning to attract considerable publicity in the local press. But it was during the succeeding years of prosperity and rapidly improving railway facilities in Tasmania that tourism finally arrived. After 1880 Thomas's pioneering effort was reproduced in a score of variations by individual writers, tourist organizations and steamship companies. By 1890 Tasmania recorded more than 20,000 arrivals and departures annually, most of whom were probably tourists.

The most lasting and important result of Tasmania's prosperity from the late 1870s was a major increase in population. Although it could barely compete with mainland colonies in attracting migrants from overseas, Tasmania had a consistent excess of arrivals over departures in every year from 1876 to 1889; much of this can undoubtedly be attributed to the influx of miners from the mainland, where mining was a dwindling occupation. Net immigration, added to natural increase, greatly accelerated the rate of population growth. Whereas in the fifteen years from 1861 to 1876 Tasmania's population had risen from only 90,000 to 105,000, in the next fifteen years to 1891 it increased to 147,000.

Launceston, centre of the boom

Launceston shared more than fully in the progress and prosperity of these years. Like other parts of Tasmania it benefited from the revival of farming, from the influx of capital and influx of tourists. But in two particular respects Launceston gained more than elsewhere, especially as compared with the capital, Hobart.

First and most important, Launceston was from the start the mining capital of Tasmania. Partly because of geography, partly perhaps because of the initiative shown by certain of its residents, Launceston became the focus of Tasmanian tin- and gold-mining industries. The overwhelming majority of new companies were floated and directed in Launceston and a large proportion of shareholders were Launcestonians or resided in the district. The rewards were great, although at times there were disadvantages: the failure of many tin-mining enterprises floated in 1873 and 1874 resulted in quite a major though temporary commercial crisis towards the end of 1874. Similarly, tin smelting came to be concentrated in Launceston. Hobart eventually established smelting works, but they were hardly comparable with those of Launceston. Further, because of its relative proximity to the chief mining areas, Launceston became both a major supply base for the mines, and a social centre for miners in search of congenial surroundings to spend their wages.

Secondly, Launceston undoubtedly gained more than Hobart, or any other urban centre, from the pattern of railway construction in the 1880s. Although some branch lines were constructed in southern Tasmania, they were much less important than the three northern lines built to St Marys, Scottsdale and Ulverstone. The first two of these greatly enlarged and strengthened Launceston's hinterland. On balance this may also have been true of the line to Devonport and Ulverstone, even though this directed some trade away from Launceston. With a concentration of railways in northern Tasmania, focussing on Launceston, the town naturally tended to become the chief railway-engineering centre of the island.

Rich, buoyant and expanding, Launceston made notable advances from the mid-1870s in manufacturing. Apart from the new tin smelters and railway-engineering shops, the town acquired a whole range of new industries and factories. Among these were Salisbury's large foundry and engineering works, still in existence, a pottery works, and Launceston's first woollen mill, all initially established in the mid-1870s, but in each case enjoying real success and undergoing major expansion only later, with the growing prosperity of the late 1870s and 1880s. These later years also saw the establishment of a chemical works, a factory to make galvanized-iron products, Tasmania's first specialist biscuit factory, and the beginnings of Launceston's now best-known manufacturing concern, Boags brewery.

Boom conditions and abundant funds brought a great wave of new building activity which transformed the appearance and size of the town.

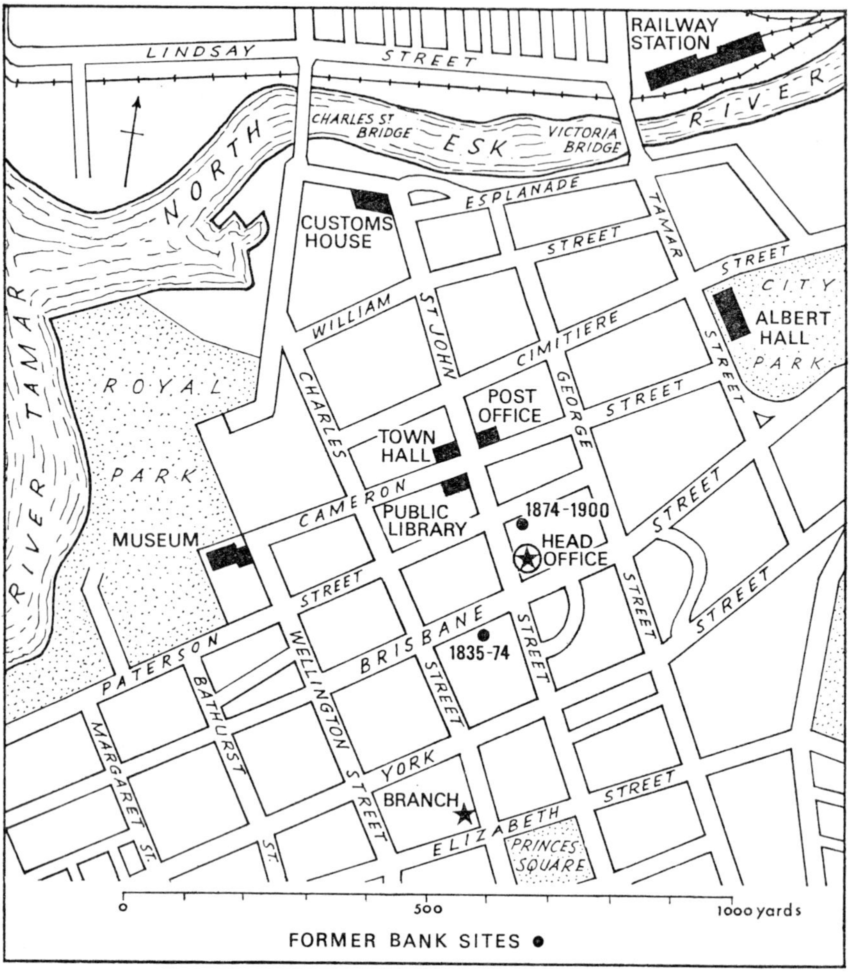

City of Launceston

In the commercial heart of Launceston the simple Georgian and early-Victorian buildings were engulfed by buildings that in their grandeur and ornateness were unmistakably high-Victorian; the earlier styles survived chiefly on the outer fringes of the commercial centre. Many of Launceston's most imposing public buildings were erected in these boom years: most notably the Customs House, the Post Office, the Queen Victoria Museum and, at the very end of the period, the grandiose Albert Hall. With a seating capacity of more than 2,000 this was claimed to be the eleventh largest hall of its kind in the world. Meanwhile in the ever-extending suburbs cast-iron lace and fancy brickwork became the dominant theme.

The extent of Launceston's growth during the 1870s and 1880s can be seen best in terms of total population. Whereas between 1851 and 1870 census figures show a slight decline in Launceston's population, between 1870 and 1891 it rose from 10,668 to 17,208; in addition, many Launcestonians now lived in suburbs beyond the census boundaries. By 1891 Launceston, the self-styled commercial capital of Tasmania, had nearly three-quarters as many people as the political capital. In recognition of the town's increased size and status Parliament had formally designated Launceston a city as from 1 January 1889.

If a city's enterprise, maturity and civic pride are measured by the exhibitions it holds, the new Launceston scored highly. During the summer of 1886–7 Launceston staged an Industrial Exhibition, a special feature of which was a display of Launceston's own products. Reports state that even many local residents were amazed at the variety and quality of local wares, which included, among other things, a wide range of ironmongery, sewing-machines, furniture, tobacco, pottery, jewellery, and excellent tomato sauce. The Industrial Exhibition was so successful that shortly afterwards a second and far more ambitious exhibition was planned. Early in 1888 a powerful committee was formed for that purpose. With the support of Parliament, the public, and the local council which built the Albert Hall specially for the occasion, the committee schemed, planned and prepared for nearly four years to see its vision finally come to fruition on 25 November 1891 with the opening of the Tasmanian International Exhibition.

Local reports naturally gave considerable attention to the Tasmanian part of the exhibition—to the mineral arch at the main entrance, the fernery inside the entrance, resembling 'some quiet cool sylvan glade in the depths of the forest primeval', to the displays of polished Tasmanian woods, and dazzling collections of minerals from Mount Bischoff and elsewhere. Yet the real importance of the exhibition was its size and genuine international character. No less than three acres of pavilions in the City Park behind the Albert Hall displayed the products of seven overseas countries and four other Australian colonies. Two ordinary bars, one colonial wine bar and one temperance bar catered for the thirst of the visitors who, by the time the exhibition closed after nearly four months, numbered 262,059 altogether, or nearly twice Tasmania's population at the time.

CHAPTER EIGHT

'Quiet and Steady Progressiveness' The Bank 1870–1890

Revival and expansion

The initial revival in the fortunes of the Launceston Bank for Savings resembled that of Tasmania generally, beginning modestly at the close of the 1860s, with recovery proceeding slowly and fitfully for several years. The first clear sign of improvement came in 1869; largely because fixed-deposit rates paid by the commercial banks dropped sharply, deposits in the Bank for Savings rose sharply. This was sufficient for the Executive Committee to risk selling off some of its bad securities and advertise that it had funds for investment in mortgages. In 1870, however, fixed-deposit rates increased again, the rise in the Bank for Savings' deposits ended and with it new lending. No further progress or new mortgage business was recorded until 1873, despite a further fall in fixed-deposit rates towards the end of 1871. Lasting recovery clearly depended on general economic recovery and in northern Tasmania this really became marked only from 1873 and 1874. Reflecting better conditions the Bank's deposits then rose strongly to reach nearly £80,000 in 1874, or about the level current just before the 1862 crisis.

The year 1874 was a major landmark in the Bank's fortunes in other respects. With deposits booming and reserves now in excess of £7,000 the Executive Committee at long last sold its remaining foreclosed properties, including the two largest, those of Mrs Lukin and John Thompson, although in the process reserves were reduced to a precariously low £1,500. In the same year, despite the large capital losses sustained on these sales, the Executive Committee decided to acquire its own building, vacating the premises it had rented from Henry Dowling for some thirty years. In August 1874 the Executive Committee accepted an offer of a property in Paterson Street, strategically placed between two major thoroughfares, George Street and St John Street. The purchase price of £1,600 was confirmed at the half-yearly general meeting in the following month, and after extensive building alterations the Bank for Savings eventually transferred business there in June 1875.

The next fifteen years were prosperous. The Bank encountered no major crisis, and as a whole experienced a large increase in business, reflecting essentially the growing size and wealth of the community, particularly that of Launceston itself. By the early 1880s deposits reached a new record level, and by 1890 exceeded £150,000, or nearly double their level of 1874. The Bank's expansion, though hardly spectacular, was certainly very satisfying, especially in the light of its erratic record to that time. On 9 March 1886 the *Launceston Examiner* described the Bank for Savings' performance over the previous six months as one of 'quiet and steady progressiveness'. The description would fit just about the whole fifteen years.

Progress might have been rather more than quiet and steady if the Bank had not to face strong and almost continuous competition for deposits. In striking contrast with the position in, say, the 1830s and 1840s, working men and their families of the 1870s and 1880s had a variety of outlets for surplus funds. For those willing to see their savings locked up for twelve months, the commercial banks offered a rate of interest generally higher than the Bank for Savings paid. For those prepared to gamble in the hope of large profits, the Launceston Stock Exchange offered a wide range of mining shares. And for those who preferred the liquidity, flexibility and safety of a savings-bank account, alternative facilities were available from the early 1880s. In 1881 the Tasmanian Parliament finally passed post-office savings-bank legislation with surprisingly little controversy or publicity. Under the legislation savings facilities became available at nearly all major post offices in July 1882.

Post-office savings banks presented at least a potential threat to the Launceston Bank for Savings, and to the Hobart Savings Bank. At the time, however, they seem to have caused little concern. Possibly one reason was that the rate of interest paid by the post office was below that paid by the trustee savings banks throughout the 1880s. No counter-measures were instituted or even discussed by the Executive Committee or the Managers of the Launceston Bank for Savings, and broadly their confidence seems to have been justified by subsequent events. Although in the eighteen months to February 1884 deposits at the Bank for Savings declined, the fall was not great and much of it might be attributed to sharply rising interest rates paid on commercial bank fixed deposits. From 1884 the upward trend in deposits resumed, little checked by the existence of the post-office savings banks. In 1890 post offices in northern Tasmania held about £22,000 of depositors' funds, which was only about one-seventh the total held by the Bank for Savings. The main area of encroachment was, as one might expect, outside Launceston itself, particularly in more distant country districts, but even there it was not yet serious.

The general policy of the Bank for Savings in these years of steady expansion was one essentially of caution, reflecting both past experience and a recognition of the institution's basic aims, though tempered by a degree of flexibility and business opportunism one might expect of those conducting its affairs. For example, while striving in every way possible to make the facilities at Paterson Street attractive and efficient, the Executive Committee never seriously considered establishing branches or agencies, even when the Melbourne Savings Bank in Victoria showed that this could be done successfully, and when the creation of the post-office savings banks in Tasmania enhanced their potential value. Similarly, in the distribution of earnings, though aware of the desirability of paying high returns to depositors, the Bank was distinctly conservative. Throughout the period it continued to fix the rate of interest retrospectively. Whenever possible it added to reserves rather than paying the maximum rate to depositors and, in addition, instituted a second 'reserve' fund in 1880 in the form of a profit and loss account. By 1890 total 'reserves' approached £16,000, or about ten per cent of deposits, compared with a maximum reserve ratio before 1862 of little more than five per cent.*

From the 1870s the Bank for Savings acquired a degree of pride in its affairs which had not been evident since the early 1850s. At times it was almost aggressively proud. When in 1880 the Bank received a circular from the Tasmanian Colonial Secretary which implied that it was just an ordinary commercial enterprise, Pullen, the actuary, replied with the utmost indignation. The Bank's aim, he declared, was simply the 'encouragement of provident habits among the operative portion of the population'; depositors received all profits, there were no shareholders, and the Bank did not issue notes or discount bills. 'The impossibility therefore', Pullen concluded, 'of answering the questions proposed in the printed form, arising from their utter irrelevancy, will be at once apparent.' More commonly, pride in the Bank's affairs took a quieter form. The Executive Committee's half-yearly reports regularly referred in modest language to the Bank's satisfactory, or sometimes highly satisfactory record, and the half-yearly general meetings became routine, pleasant gatherings. During the whole period there is no suggestion of major dissension among the Managers or Executive Committee members.

As business expanded, the Bank gained increasing public esteem. Before the late 1870s the Bank for Savings rarely got into print, except for its own advertisements and in times of crisis. From the late 1870s its half-yearly

* The Bank's administration, its investment and deposit policies are discussed in more detail in the following sections.

meetings generally received some notice, if only brief and formal, and usually complimentary. By the late 1880s they regularly earned separate, detailed and invariably flattering reports, and sometimes even an editorial. Commenting on the six months ending February 1888 an *Examiner* editorial of 9 March complimented the Bank on its 'very gratifying report', which provided such 'valuable testimony to the thrifty and provident habits of the community'. Eighteen months later on 7 September 1889 another *Examiner* editorial, commenting similarly that the Bank for Savings' accounts told 'a very gratifying tale' made the further interesting suggestion that the Bank was now clearly providing the means for people to purchase 'the long-desired allotments on which to start a home'. In splendid Victorian tone it opined that

> the possession of a home imparts a feeling of manly independence which should have an elevating intellectual and moral, as well as physical influence on the generation that is growing up amid such favourable environments.

Leaders and officers

The organization and administration of the Bank for Savings during the 1870s and 1880s followed essentially the pattern which had evolved in the 1860s. Dominant in the affairs of the Bank was the Executive Committee, composed initially of seven members, subsequently increased to nine, and drawn almost exclusively from the Launceston business community. Normally meeting once a week, the Executive Committee effectively determined the general policy of the Bank and made many detailed decisions, particularly about individual loans. Except that its members were unpaid, the Executive Committee closely resembled a board of directors, and by the 1880s had generally become known as 'the Board'. Nominally it was responsible to the Managers of the Bank, but in practice the function of the latter was to endorse Executive Committee decisions and provide a reservoir of personnel from which the Executive Committee replenished its numbers. To administer the decisions of the Executive Committee, and conduct day-to-day business, the Bank had a full-time staff, initially the actuary and his assistant, but enlarged by degrees to a total of five officers by the 1890s.

While membership of the Executive Committee remained the preserve of Launceston's business community, there was a considerable turnover in personnel and important changes in the type of businessman represented on the Committee. Most obvious was the loss, through death or retirement, of many of 'those early navigators who guided the destinies of the Bank through the perilous financial seas of the '60s'. Among them were W. S. Button, the Committee's chairman from 1862 until his retirement in 1872; Thomas Corbett, who had been associated with the Bank since

1843 and frequently stood in as actuary for both Dowling and Pullen until his retirement in 1875; and James Aikenhead, who retired in 1886 after twenty-four continuous years on the Committee. And in 1885 Henry Dowling died. Dominant figure in the Bank for over thirty years, Dowling after his retirement had served actively on the Executive Committee, and after Corbett's retirement stood in for Pullen on many occasions.

New members of the Committee were generally less eminent, in both public and philanthropic affairs, than the men they replaced; to some extent this was inevitable since, with the town's growing maturity and prosperity, there were no longer the great political and social issues of former years. Without exception, however, new members of the Committee were established and respected businessmen, well qualified to direct the Bank's affairs. Some still were of the early pioneer generation—'grand old colonists' as they were invariably called in their obituaries. Landon Fairthorne, for example, who served on the Committee from 1881, had come to Australia in 1839, established himself as a druggist and chemist in Launceston during the 1840s and by the 1880s had a big and thriving business. In 1884 he built the large and elegant building which still graces St John Street, and in 1887 had the honour to be president of the Pharmaceutical Society of Australasia. More commonly, newcomers to the Committee were of a younger or second generation, particularly evident in a spate of new appointments towards the end of the 1880s that included men such as Frederick Lewis Fysh, younger brother of the politician Philip Oakley Fysh, Richard Green junior, William Johnstone junior, and Hardwicke Weedon, son of the auctioneer C. J. Weedon. All were appointed when in their forties and were successful businessmen in their own right but, except for Hardwicke Weedon,* were never notable public figures.

A capable, if in some respects less-distinguished Executive Committee received strong support from a competent and dedicated actuary. In George Pullen, who continued as actuary until ill-health forced his retirement in 1887, the Bank had a man well worth the modest £350 per annum he was paid at the start, and the still fairly modest £450 he received from 1877. Pullen was highly experienced, completely devoted to the welfare of the Bank, and displayed great ability in the many tasks he had to perform. He showed a meticulous attention to detail, a conscientious if somewhat paternal interest in the welfare of depositors, and considerable tact and discretion in handling prospective and actual borrowers, and also on occasions his superiors.

Pullen's only real failing was that his zeal and personal identification with the Bank were sometimes carried to excess. His aggressively indignant

* Some of Weedon's many public activities and his professional career with the Bank for Savings are discussed at greater length in the following chapter.

reply to the Colonial Secretary's circular of 1880 could hardly have improved relations with the Tasmanian government, whose debentures the Bank eagerly sought, and this was not the only time he acted undiplomatically. As the years passed Pullen seems to have become increasingly obsessed with his personal record. Rather sadly, his farewell speech was little more than an exercise in self-praise. He expressed 'his gratification, on severing his connection with the Bank, at leaving it in a sounder, more solid, and substantial position than it had ever occupied before', and boasted that his thirty-four years' service with the Bank was five years longer than that of his predecessor, and more than twice as long as that of any other paid officer of the Bank. To make sure that later generations at the Bank remembered the fact, before finally leaving Pullen re-opened the old Minute Book which recorded the Managers' thanks to Dowling on 4 September 1868 for his thirty-three years of service, to pencil in the margin 'From this 33 years did not about 4 years in England & one year Mr Sherwin was Actuary 1843 to 1844, G.P.'

Pullen's successor was John Cathcart, previously cashier at the Commercial Bank of Tasmania. In some respects Cathcart was very different from Pullen. Extrovert, well-known and popular in the community, Cathcart had keen sporting and outdoor interests. Once a rower of some distinction, Cathcart had also built boats, served as an officer in the Launceston Artillery and was still a keen hunter and fisherman. Perhaps reflecting his character and interests, Cathcart tended to be a little more confident and dynamic in his new job than Pullen. Otherwise, in his professional capacity he had much in common with his predecessor. At the age of forty-seven he had already some thirty-three years of banking experience in Launceston and proved thoroughly competent and conscientious as the new actuary, while again, like Pullen, remaining very much subordinate to his socially and economically powerful Executive Committee. Also like Pullen, he engaged in no political or other commercial activities, though this may not have been through his own choice, since the Executive Committee insisted on this as a condition of his appointment.

Until 1880 the actuary had only one assistant at the Bank. His job mainly was to keep the ledgers, but also on occasions to relieve the actuary at the counter. When Pullen became actuary in 1868, the Executive Committee appointed James Sherwin, Isaac Sherwin's son, as his assistant. In the following year James Sherwin resigned and was replaced by John Dickens, previously a clerk with the Customs Department and, at the age of fifty-six, some five years older than Pullen. With the revival and expansion of Bank business Dickens' work increased considerably, and in recognition of this his salary rose from £150 per annum when he was first appointed, to £275 by 1880.

In 1880 the Executive Committee decided to appoint a third officer and selected Alfred Barrett Biggs, Pullen's brother-in-law. Aged fifty-five and a schoolteacher by profession, Biggs was to be ledger-keeper at a salary of £150 per annum. He remained in that position until 1900 when he was retired with a pension.* Despite his undistinguished career, Biggs was a remarkably talented man, with an amazing variety of intellectual pursuits, which perhaps explain why he made little headway professionally. Biggs conducted choirs and composed a considerable amount of church music. He was a prolific writer of letters to newspapers on political and other issues. He was an enthusiastic microscopist, and was reputed to have installed the first telephone in the southern hemisphere. Above all, he was a highly distinguished astronomer and seismologist. For his work in these fields he was elected a Fellow of the Royal Society in 1885. Biggs also found time to raise a family of five daughters and one son.

With the appointment of Biggs as ledger-keeper, Dickens acted mainly as the Bank's teller, formally designated cashier in 1882. However, he was not to survive long in that position. Now close to seventy years of age, Dickens seems to have become increasingly insubordinate and irresponsible. After exceeding his holiday leave without permission in 1883, he was required to resign. Of twenty-three applicants for his position the Committee finally chose Ambrose Dowling, Henry Dowling's cousin and earlier employed by the Bank until he became the victim of economy measures in 1866. Very little is known about Ambrose Dowling, but he also was clearly not a young man at the time of his appointment. His overall record and the occasional letters he wrote suggest that he was conscientious but rather limited. Retired officers of the Bank remember him principally for his mild and gentle disposition.

Despite the smallness of the staff and their close personal ties, the Bank's administration acquired an important degree of formal organization in the 1880s. Already in 1881 the Executive Committee had clarified the position of the two subordinate officers by making them formally responsible to the actuary, rescinding the curious and rather unorthodox ruling of 1861 which had made each officer responsible directly to the Executive Committee. In 1883 the Committee went a stage further, to formally delineate the division between cashier and ledger-keeper, fixing maximum salaries and annual increments. In 1887, shortly after Cathcart became actuary, the Executive Committee appointed a junior clerk, and in 1890 a second junior clerk; with these appointments, which brought the total staff to five, the Bank was beginning to acquire the appearance of a normal small business hierarchy. However, the decision to appoint two junior clerks, virtu-

* During his twenty years with the Bank, Biggs was also its 'caretaker', living in the residence above the Bank premises.

ally as personal assistants to Dowling and Biggs respectively, was, one may suspect, not just a straightforward sign of an expanding business, but a judicious piece of diplomacy: both Dowling and Biggs had been unsuccessful applicants for the actuary's position when Pullen retired.

Investment policy

Undoubtedly the sphere in which the Executive Committee and the actuary could best display their ability and judgement was in the Bank's investments. Broadly, the aim was to earn the maximum return compatible with the safety demanded by the purpose of the institution; and safety meant both ample security on investments and sufficient liquidity to meet any major withdrawals.

Until 1874 there were two basic objectives: to get rid of the unprofitable mortgage loans and foreclosed properties with minimum loss; and to invest as far as possible in government securities. By 1874 the first of these objectives had at last been achieved, and the second partially. In August 1874 the Bank held nearly £28,000 worth of government stock, compared with some £37,000 of mortgage loans. Most of the government stock consisted of local water-works debentures.* There was also a sum of £10,000 invested in Treasury Bills, converted early in 1875 to debentures maturing in 1878 and 1880.

From 1874 the importance of government securities in the Bank's investments declined markedly, but not at the wish of the Executive Committee. Government stock was still keenly sought. In applying for the £10,000 of debentures at the end of 1874, for example, the Executive Committee had not hesitated to use the aims of the Bank to support its claim for the debentures: 'I am further instructed', Pullen had written to the Colonial Treasurer, 'respectfully to represent to you the importance of supporting institutions like the present, which have for their objects the encouragement of provident habits among the working classes.' Priority to government securities was the Bank's established policy, regularly endorsed at half-yearly general meetings, and every effort was made to enlarge the Bank's holdings of government stock. Efforts failed, however, because there was no stock available, or none available at a reasonable rate of return. After the initial issue of water-works debentures at the end of the 1850s Launceston's Council made no further issues until the 1890s. Meanwhile the Tasmanian government, although it borrowed extensively and increasingly in the 1870s and 1880s, now borrowed on the London market where it could raise funds at or around four per cent—too low a rate to be economic for the Bank. The net result was that firstly, as the 1875 debentures matured, the Bank's holdings of government stock fell to less than £20,000

* A considerable portion of these the Bank had recently bought from Henry Dowling.

by 1880, then consisting almost entirely of the water-works debentures; when these matured in 1887, holdings of government stock were almost negligible, and by 1888 were non-existent.

The main development of the 1870s and 1880s was investment in fixed deposits of commercial banks. Late in 1874 the Executive Committee made the first moves in this direction, placing £3,000 with each of the three local banks in six-month deposits yielding four per cent. In the following year it sensibly decided to transfer the funds to twelve-month deposits which returned a higher rate of five per cent. In 1877 investment in fixed deposits became a declared policy of the Bank when the Managers resolved that first priority now should be given to government stock *or* fixed deposits. By 1878 holdings of fixed deposits had risen to £30,000. In 1880 they were placed with the Australasia and Union Banks, as well as the three local banks, and by 1882 amounted to £68,000, or more than half the Bank's total assets. After that they declined somewhat, but, fluctuating around £60,000, remained the Bank's largest single asset until 1886.

The main problem about holding such a large proportion of its assets in fixed deposits was that the Bank for Savings had of necessity to pay its own depositors a lower rate of interest. Savings-bank depositors therefore had an obvious inducement to invest directly in fixed deposits. Undoubtedly this had been why the Executive Committee had not considered fixed deposits in the critical years of the 1860s. However, conditions were now different in that with a rapidly growing business and virtually no non-paying assets, the Bank for Savings could operate on a much finer margin. Whereas in the 1860s the Bank had been struggling to pay four per cent to depositors while at the same time charging seven per cent to most borrowers, by the late 1870s it could pay four per cent while itself earning only five per cent on fixed deposits and still have enough left over to add to reserves. Although both rates fluctuated in the 1880s, five per cent on its fixed deposits and four per cent to its own depositors mostly prevailed. In practice, therefore, the advantage to small investors of a fixed deposit was only slight, and against this had to be set the disadvantages of locking up funds for twelve months, when in the Bank for Savings they could be virtually withdrawn at call.

To the Executive Committee fixed deposits had a special attraction, since for the Bank, if not the individual, they were virtually a liquid asset.* On 5 January 1877, when renewing deposits with the three local banks, Pullen wrote to each of their managers:

> This deposit is made, as in former cases, on the arrangement hitherto tacitly, or verbally, understood, that in the event of a necessity arising for with-

* As before, the Bank for Savings retained a minimum cash balance in the 1870s and 1880s, normally below £5,000.

drawal of same, or any portion thereof, interest shall be allowed "*pro rata*" up to the time of withdrawal.

When the necessity did arise, the actual procedure seems to have been a slightly different one: fixed deposits were used as security for a temporary overdraft.

While acquiring a large holding of fixed deposits, the Executive Committee by no means neglected its mortgage business. Mortgage loans, although more troublesome than fixed deposits, had the advantages of a slightly higher rate of return and long-term stability; while technically terminable at six months' notice by either side, they mostly ran on for years, sometimes decades. Mortgage loans and fixed deposits complemented each other, and while priority was given to the latter, mortgage loans were not only maintained but in the long run increased. Between August 1874 and August 1886 total outstanding loans on mortgage rose from £37,000 to £59,000.

The Executive Committee's business sense and acumen were most evident in its mortgage business. Remembering the lessons of the 1860s the overall policy was one of prudence. The general rule was not to lend more than fifty per cent of the value of the security, this being determined professionally, and wherever applicable, insurance cover was required. It reflects to the credit of the Executive Committee that no major default occurred in the period, although inevitably some interest payments were late. In the type of property on which it lent, the Executive Committee spread its risks judicially between three main groups of borrowers: the large established landowners of the northern plains; small farmers in various parts of northern Tasmania; and local residents of Launceston, who mostly borrowed only small sums. The Executive Committee also used a range of interest rates, from the minimum fixed at half-yearly general meetings to half of one per cent and one per cent above that minimum, the latter normally asked of small borrowers because of the greater administrative cost relative to the size of the loan.

In terms of the total value of mortgage loans, though not the number of borrowers, the large landowners of the northern plains were dominant. Among the securities they offered were some of the great estates of the north, of which today at least the houses and outbuildings still survive in their splendour. The Honourable Thomas Reibey, for example, once Premier of the colony, borrowed extensively on his two properties, 'The Oaks' and 'Entally'. The Gatenby family borrowed on a string of properties, including 'View Point'. Several members of the Archer family raised loans from the Bank, most notably Robert J. Archer of 'Saundridge' and Thomas Cathcart Archer of 'Woolmers'. Some of these loans were for very large amounts. In 1880, for example, R. J. Archer received a record individual loan of £13,500, then worth nearly one-quarter of all the Bank's mortgage loans. Six years later this record was broken when the trustees to the Gatenby estates borrowed £15,000.

There is no doubt that the Executive Committee preferred lending to the landed upper classes. Per pound lent, they involved negligible expense and trouble, and for that reason almost invariably paid the minimum rate of interest; they were, or certainly appeared to be the safest prospects; and generally speaking they were much longer term loans than those to small farmers or urban dwellers, who were inclined to pay back fairly quickly. Often the Executive Committee was prepared to bend its rules if it meant capturing or retaining a large borrower. Although the legal length of a loan was only six months, exceptions were made for the large borrowers. In April 1874, for example, Mrs Edward Archer was informed that the Managers,

> taking into consideration the undeniable nature of the security held by them —the promptness of the payment of interest etc are willing to make an exception in this case, and to extend the term for *four* years longer, from 31 July next.

On a slightly more informal level Pullen wrote to Basil Archer, borrowing £7,000 in May 1887, that 'In your case, the Mortgage would remain practically as long as you pleased.' Similarly, while the general rule was that a borrower repaid in full and never in instalments and this was confirmed as a strict point of policy in April 1879, nevertheless R. J. Archer, when borrowing his £13,500 in the following year, was given permission to repay in £1,000 instalments. Occasionally the rate of interest allowed was below the minimum specified. When, for example, in October 1887 the Gatenby trustees informed the Bank that they could get £15,000 elsewhere at only five per cent, the Executive Committee accepted a reduction to five per cent, even though the Managers had recently resolved on a minimum of five and a half per cent. All this was good business, and there is no suggestion that the Managers or anyone else disapproved of the Executive Committee's discreet flexibility.

On occasions, however, the social pretensions of large borrowers clearly caused problems for the Bank. One such instance occurred when a large landowner was negotiating a loan for £6,000. At the start he was anxious not to have the mortgage formally registered, but when he was told that was impossible, and when the Bank compromised by dispensing with the formal valuation requirement, he apparently acquiesced. However, when he received a package through the post with 'Mortgage Deeds' written on the envelope, declaring to the whole world, or at least his servants and the postman, that he was borrowing money, his wrath was aroused. Exactly what he said to the Bank is unfortunately not known, but in reply Cathcart had to point out carefully and in suitably apologetic language that those offending words were written to comply with the Post Office Act. Cathcart also had to request, in equally humble terms, the return of the deeds upon which the client was sitting tight. In the end the deeds must have been returned, for the loan was made.

Investment in mortgage loans received a great boost when, late in 1886, an Act to regulate the investment of savings-bank funds in fixed deposits came into force. There is little record of the debates over the Bill, although apparently it aroused some controversy. As finally passed, however, it clearly had a dual purpose. The first is indicated by its title, An Act *to enable* the Funds of Savings Banks to be placed out at Interest in other Banks (my italics). The 1848 Act had made no specific provisions for such a form of investment, and the Act was clearly intended formally to legalize a practice established for some years. The second purpose is indicated in the clause which limited this form of investment to thirty per cent of total funds. From the little reported of the parliamentary debates, it appears that there was some concern about the wisdom of investing large amounts in fixed deposits.

When the law came into operation, fixed deposits held by the Launceston Bank for Savings greatly exceeded the thirty per cent limit and this was quickly pointed out at an Executive Committee meeting on 16 December 1886. In practice, however, plenty of time seems to have been given for savings banks to adjust their investments. There was no further mention of the law in the Minutes, although technically the Bank continued to break the law for some time, and there is little evidence that a great effort was made to reduce the level of fixed deposits. Essentially, it seems, the Bank aimed to conform with the law by building up its mortgage business rather than by reducing its fixed deposits. At first, even this seems to have been half-hearted. Although more than twice as many mortgage loans were made in 1887 as in 1886, still more could easily have been made. As time passed, however, with only slow progress being made towards the legal requirement, efforts intensified. By March 1888 the minimum mortgage rate had been reduced to five per cent, and in the following September the Managers resolved for the first time to give equal priority to mortgage loans, government securities and fixed deposits. By then, as a result of a big increase in mortgage loans, the distribution of funds was just about legal.

Having met the legal requirement the Bank now, almost perversely, began for the first time to run its fixed deposits down at a rapid rate, investing the proceeds in further mortgage loans. Between August 1889 and August 1891 total fixed deposits fell from £56,000 to £20,000, while mortgage loans rose from £104,000 to £136,000. There is no obvious explanation for this sudden major switch. Certainly it was not required by law, there is not even a hint of a planned change in policy, and there was no sudden reduction in the rate of interest on fixed deposits; the rate was unchanged at five per cent, which was also the minimum rate for mortgage loans.

Two developments might possibly help to explain this sudden change. One is that from 1889, as commercial banks and other lending institutions greatly tightened their credit policies, more would-be borrowers turned to the Bank for Savings. This considerably enhanced the attractions of mortgage business in comparison with fixed deposits, since on the one hand the Bank could be more selective in choosing its borrowers and make safer loans than previously, and on the other hand it could in practice charge a rate of interest higher than the nominal minimum of five per cent. The first point is difficult to prove, but the latter is certainly true: in 1890 every new loan was charged at six per cent, irrespective of its size; in 1891 only three loans were made at below six per cent, and all at five and a half per cent rather than the minimum of five per cent.

A second possible explanation is that as the speculative boom of the 1880s came to an end and doubts were being expressed about at least some of Australia's financial institutions, the Executive Committee foresaw something of the banking disasters that were eventually to cripple the Australian economy. On three previous occasions the Committee had shown a keen awareness of the weaknesses of banks in which it held fixed deposits. It may be, although there is no direct evidence, that from late 1889 it was deliberately playing safe. In particular it may not have been entirely coincidental that its fixed deposits reached their low point at almost exactly the same time as the Bank of Van Diemen's Land suspended payment. Foresight is impossible to prove, but it certainly cannot be discounted.

The depositors

Trends in deposits during the 1870s and 1880s were subject to a very different set of influences than in earlier years. On the one hand, the growth of deposits was strongly encouraged by a growing population, especially of Launceston itself, by rising incomes, and at least from the late 1870s by almost uninterrupted prosperity. On the other hand, operating against that expansion was an increasing range of alternative investment outlets. In the event, the former set of influences proved the stronger. Over the two decades total deposits in the Bank more than doubled, from around £70,000 to over £150,000; and the number of depositors trebled, from around 3,000 to around 9,000.

This expansion had two main characteristics. One was a rapid rise in the number of large accounts. Depositors with accounts worth more than £100 increased from about 150 to nearly 500 between 1870 and 1890. At each date they represented only about five per cent of all depositors but probably accounted for more than a third of the Bank's total funds. Although the expansion of these large accounts was about in line with the overall rate of growth, given alternative investment outlets one might have expected a much less than proportionate rise, since large depositors were more likely to look elsewhere to invest their funds. That they did not do so was largely to the credit of the Bank for Savings. In general, through its highly successful investment activities it was able to pay a rate of return normally only one per cent below that on twelve-month deposits in commercial banks, and by the end of the 1880s only half of one per cent below the fixed deposit rates. More particularly, the Executive Committee and the actuary, fully appreciating the value of large accounts, did their utmost to cultivate them. They quite legally circumvented the maximum deposit rule of £150 by allowing and even encouraging the opening of second, third or more accounts by one person; this became particularly important towards the end of the 1880s. To some extent they also allowed depositors to operate what were in effect cheque accounts by leaving their pass-books at the Bank and using withdrawal forms virtually as cheques. This privileged method of operation was traditionally available only to charitable organizations, but was now extended to other depositors, particularly country depositors, though it is impossible even to guess at how widespread was the practice.

The other major characteristic of the growth of deposits was the very large rise in the number of small accounts. Between 1870 and 1890 the number of depositors with accounts of less than £10 increased from less than 2,000 to around 7,000, a more rapid increase than in any other group of depositors. Allowing for the inroads made into country deposits by post-office savings banks, this probably meant that the proportion of Launceston's population with Bank for Savings accounts doubled over the period. By 1890 about one in three Launcestonians had Bank for Savings accounts, though most held small sums. Essentially this great expansion would seem to reflect the growing prosperity of the area and the development of the saving habit by a whole new range of people. Unlike the rise in large deposits, it cannot be attributed to any great extent to Bank policy, since in general the Executive Committee was rather conservative in seeking new depositors. Rarely did it advertise in the press or elsewhere, and only once, as far as is known, did it go out of its way to chase ordinary business; that was in 1885 when there was a large influx of workers to build a railway line to St Marys and the Bank distributed placards and notices along the line, advertising its facilities.

Changes in saving behaviour in the 1870s and 1880s were consistent with the improved economic conditions. A 'complete history' sample of seventy-five accounts opened in 1874–5 shows a much higher rate of survival than at any time previously; nearly half of these seventy-five accounts remained open for more than three years, and about a quarter were still open after ten years. The sample also shows a much stronger tendency for accounts to accumulate funds, although the ideal saver was still a rare being; about half of the sampled accounts more than doubled in size over the years and eleven of the seventy-five showed more than a tenfold increase. There was also a much greater tendency for accounts to be actively operated, both for depositing and withdrawing, although only one of the sample clearly approximated to a current account, and still over half the accounts were essentially idle.*

In general, new depositors in the 1870s and 1880s resembled those of earlier decades; they were predominantly working class, with a high proportion of dependants and others with no formal occupations. However, there were two distinct though not dramatic differences. One was an increasing proportion of depositors with formally stated occupations. Whereas in the 1860s, and indeed to the early 1870s, a clear majority of depositors were formally non-occupational, now most new depositors had occupations, reflecting clearly a healthy economy, as well as a more healthy population structure with fewer young men departing for the mainland. The other change was a tendency towards more diversity among new depositors with stated occupations. Professional and other non-manual workers came to form quite a significant group, similarly farmers, miners, and other self-employed or independent workers. However, with the establishment of post-office savings banks in 1882, at least one of these important new groups, the farmers, declined sharply in importance.

Undoubtedly the greatest change in the period was in the geographic distribution of new depositors, reflecting mainly the impact of the post-office savings banks. For some years prior to their establishment most new depositors were from outside Launceston, including many from relatively remote areas who used the generous postal concessions of the 1862 Act. After 1882, however, post-office savings banks captured a large proportion of new savers in country areas, though probably few established savers. The proportion of new depositors at the Launceston Bank for Savings from country areas fell sharply to a quarter or less of the total. Once more Launceston came to supply three-quarters of new accounts. Although to some extent this reflected the growing importance of Launceston itself, the primary factor was post-office savings banking. The post office accounts strongly support this view. In 1890, of the £22,000 deposited in post-office savings accounts in northern Tasmania, over £16,000 was deposited in country centres. The Launceston Post Office, at a disadvantage compared with the Launceston Bank for Savings, held less than £6,000 of deposits.

* All these characteristics are similarly shown in a cross-section sample of all accounts open in the period 1877–8.

CHAPTER NINE

Proud Prosperity 1890–1910

Tasmania and Launceston in the 1890s

During the 1890s Australia suffered one of the worst depressions on record—certainly more severe than any previously experienced—and in some respects more severe than the more infamous depression of the 1930s. Already by the end of the 1880s ominous signs were appearing, particularly in Victoria where the precarious financial superstructure built on the land boom was beginning to crumble. From 1890 export prices showed a general and severe decline. British capital became scarce and in 1891 the first great wave of financial disasters occurred, principally among the land and building finance companies and building societies in Victoria. In 1892 investment collapsed generally and the Australian economy plunged into depression. The spectacular failure of most Australian banks during the following year brought financial paralysis until reconstruction schemes were devised, and in the longer run resulted in a further deterioration of economic conditions. In 1895, at the worst point of the depression, estimated living standards had fallen on average at least twenty-five per cent and in Victoria, the worst-hit colony, probably much more than that. Recovery was long, slow, and intermittent, retarded by a lack of confidence reminiscent of Tasmania in the 1860s, and the worst mainland drought ever recorded. In terms of living standards full recovery was not achieved until about 1910.

Inevitably, Tasmania experienced some of the difficulties which crippled the larger neighbouring colonies. Indeed the first major bank failure of the 1890s in Australia occurred in Tasmania, when in August 1891 the Bank of Van Diemen's Land suspended payments. Established in 1823, the Bank of Van Diemen's Land was the oldest and one of the most respected in Tasmania, but in a fit of aberration was apparently led astray by the example of more adventurous institutions on the mainland. Lending heavily to dubious mining interests and running down its liquid assets to dangerously low levels, in July 1891 it produced a totally misleading report, accompanied by an increased dividend, then, following a withdrawal of British deposits, was forced to suspend operations on 3 August 1891. The bank's failure came as a complete surprise. According to the *Launceston Examiner* of the day following, 'not the faintest intimation was given to the local directors, or to the managers or any of the country branches that such a step was imminent or even contemplated'. Countless reconstruction schemes followed, including proposals for amalgamation with the National Bank of Tasmania which nearly succeeded, but in the end the bank liquidated.

Tasmania also suffered, like the rest of Australia, from falling export prices and a drying up of overseas capital. The sharp contraction of government capital expenditure was a particularly serious blow and for a time unemployment was a major problem. During 1894 a parliamentary Select Committee investigated the situation at great length, but its recommendations were, to say the least, of doubtful value. In the main, the Committee advocated increased government expenditure, which was impracticable at the time. Apart from this, it suggested that the government might assist in reopening mines, legislate to make the erection of rabbit-proof fencing compulsory, thus creating employment, and help the timber industry develop an export trade in paving-blocks for London streets. There is little evidence that the government took much notice of the Select Committee's recommendations.

Although Tasmania was certainly hit by depression in the 1890s, the crisis was much less severe and prolonged than in any other colony, except Western Australia. Perhaps the most certain indication of this is that in every year during the decade there was still net migration to the island. Indeed, from 1896 to 1899 the excess of arrivals over departures averaged more than 4,000 per annum, a record intake, reflecting boom conditions which by then undoubtedly generally prevailed. With the exception of the Bank of Van Diemen's Land, banking institutions came through unscathed, in striking contrast with banks in other colonies. In part, this may be attributed to the absence in Tasmania of the fever of land speculation which had gripped Melbourne and to a lesser extent other urban centres in the 1880s. In part, it was also a matter of good fortune that the only non-Tasmanian banks operating on a large scale in Tasmania were the Australasia and the Union, perhaps the safest banks in Australia, which were never in danger of default.

More important, perhaps, among the forces which saved Tasmania from great disaster, were certain opportunities for expansion which were lacking or less strong in most Australian colonies. On the north-west coast there was still great scope for agricultural expansion, in the traditional products and also now in dairying, because of the development of new techniques, particularly the introduction of the butter factory. During the 1890s dairying developed rapidly in the north-west and a string of butter factories was established, though at this stage they supplied only the Tasmanian market. For the Huon valley, Tamar valley and other areas suited to fruit growing the development of refrigerated shipping now opened up the prospect of an overseas export trade in apples; in 1891, the year the Bank of Van Diemen's Land fell, the first shipments were made to Britain in a trade which was to earn Tasmania the name of 'the apple isle'.

Above all there was a further spectacular expansion of mining. In this Tasmania was not alone. Generally the 1890s was a period of mining revival, resulting to a large extent from depression which encouraged mining development in various ways.* However, except for Western Australia, no Australian colony experienced such expansion as occurred in Tasmania. The exploitation of the Zeehan silver field from the start of the decade and of the Mount Lyell copper field from about 1893 were among the most sensational and spectacular developments in Australian mining history. By 1900 Zeehan silver and Lyell copper, along with the established minerals, tin and gold, were exported to the value of more than £1.6 million; by then Tasmania's total exports amounted to £2.6 million, compared with only £1.5 million ten years earlier.

Broadly, Launceston's fortunes reflected those of Tasmania generally. In the early 1890s economic conditions certainly deteriorated, but without such financial disasters as crippled Melbourne, with employment offering on the booming mineral fields, and with the many indirect benefits which the mines brought to the city, depression was neither severe nor prolonged. From contemporary accounts it would seem that by the end of 1894 it was already over. Indeed, while Launceston's population increased only slightly on balance, the 1890s as a whole saw major progress, at least in the public affairs of the city. Not only, it seems, was depression quickly shaken off, but it was succeeded by bounding confidence and optimism. As early as 1893 construction work began for the Launceston City Council on a small hydro-electric power-station some two miles upstream on the South Esk River. When the power-station, together with a connecting tunnel, was completed in December 1895 at a cost of around £50,000, Launceston, it was claimed, became the first city in the world to be lit by hydro-electric power. In the following year work commenced on a new and larger Tamar Street bridge, eventually completed in 1899. During 1897 two hospital buildings were started and before the end of the decade the Corporation

* The connection has recently been expounded convincingly by G. N. Blainey in 'A Theory of Mineral Discovery: Australia in the Nineteenth Century', *Economic History Review*, August 1970.

Baths were opened in Paterson Street, complete, so the advertisement stated, with a large swimming basin, hot and cold water plunges, and the most modern Turkish bathing facilities.

Perhaps the most significant event of the decade was the promotion of the Cataract Gorge as a major recreational and tourist attraction. From the time Launceston was first settled the Gorge was the subject of more ecstatic description than perhaps any other natural feature in northern Tasmania. Henry Button had innumerable precedents when he later wrote of the Gorge as:

> a spot of unsurpassed beauty. A huge chasm cut by the South Esk through the hill to a depth of over three hundred feet, exposes immense masses of columnar diorite piled up from bottom to top. Add to this the river foaming and forcing its resistless course through its rocky bed, into which detached blocks have fallen and been rolled in wildest confusion, with an endless variety of indigenous and exotic plants boldly claiming the right of existence wherever there is sufficient soil for a seed to strike, and you have a picture grandly delightful—indeed almost awe-inspiring. This charming scenery is not more than three-quarters of a mile from the Post-office, but how little until recent years was it appreciated by local residents; so true is it that 'familiarity breeds contempt'.

It was not until the end of the 1880s, when the tourist trade was developing rapidly, that anything was done to promote the Gorge. In 1889 the Launceston City and Suburbs Improvement Association was established and immediately acquired rights over the area. With slim finances it could only achieve its objective piecemeal as funds by public subscription slowly rolled in. In the end, however, the works consisted of a path winding around the northern precipitous slopes of the South Esk, solidly railed and equipped with 'rustic seats and shelter arbours . . . at convenient intervals'; the planting of innumerable trees, shrubs and ferns; the construction of a complex of buildings where the South Esk widened out to form the so-called First Basin; and a little upstream a delightfully flimsy suspension bridge which visitors could cross to return by the so-called Zig Zag over the hill to the south of the Gorge. By 1897 the over-enthusiastic association was in serious debt, but was rescued the following year when the whole area was taken over by the city council. Today the Cataract Gorge, with all its quaint and rustic improvements of the 1890s, remains one of Launceston's tourist attractions.

The Bank in the 1890s

The Launceston Bank for Savings emerged from the depression of the 1890s almost completely unscathed. Never was there any suggestion of a large-scale withdrawal of deposits or widespread default among borrowers,

Mount Bischoff mine, Waratah

Inveresk under flood, 1929

The Gorge, Launceston, *c.* 1900

as had happened in the 1860s. One reason for this, of course, was that Launceston, and Tasmania generally, experienced only a mild depression. Though Hobart was harder hit, a similar situation prevailed: for a few years deposits in the Hobart Savings Bank declined, but only gradually, and the fall caused little embarrassment to the bank's managers. By contrast, in the financial crisis of 1893 the governments of both Victoria and New South Wales were forced to intervene on behalf of their savings banks to prevent panic withdrawals by guaranteeing that all depositors would be paid in full if the banks closed.

The Launceston Bank for Savings' easy passage through the 1890s, however, also owed much to its management. Over the years the Executive Committee had built up a strong investment portfolio, distributing its risks, and with ample security. What is perhaps just as important is that the general public knew this. Commenting on the Bank's half-yearly general meeting in September 1891, only weeks after the Bank of Van Diemen's Land failure, the *Launceston Examiner* remarked that 'In these days of financial unrest it is gratifying to find that the affairs of the Launceston Savings Bank . . . are in such a satisfactory condition.' It went on to stress that the total value of the Bank's mortgage loans, some £135,530, amounted to barely one-quarter of their security as valued by the government assessor. In similar vein the *Daily Telegraph** on 8 March 1893 declared the Bank was an institution to be proud of, and in particular commented that its investments of the 1880s clearly showed the Bank had learned the lesson of the 1860s.

Furthermore, at the very end of the 1880s boom such investments had been made very largely at the expense of holdings of fixed deposits. Whether it was deliberate or not, this switch certainly stood the Bank in good stead when the Bank of Van Diemen's Land failed in August 1891. At that time the Bank's fixed deposits amounted to little more than one-third of their value two years earlier. The ultimate loss it sustained through the failure of the Bank of Van Diemen's Land was therefore much less than it might have been.

Partly also, the Bank's successful record in the 1890s reflected the skill of the Executive Committee and the actuary, their willingness to adapt and improvise in order to consolidate and improve the Bank's position. As in many earlier times of difficulty, the Bank was lucky in its leaders. It had a strong Executive Committee of established and successful businessmen, now perhaps further strengthened by the appointment of a formal chairman. Initially this position was held by the rich and capable merchant, Richard Green junior, but for most of the decade by Hardwicke Weedon.

* Established in 1881 in the premises of the *Cornwall Chronicle* shortly after the latter's take-over by the *Examiner*.

In conjunction with their experienced and opportunist actuary, John Cathcart, the Executive Committee employed a variety of devices to protect the Bank in these crisis years of Australian finance.

Principal among these was a new method of paying interest to depositors. Since the early 1850s the Bank had announced in advance the rate of interest it would pay only for those accounts closed during the next six-month period. Interest to be paid on accounts still open at the end of the six months was not decided until the results of the period were known. Generally this rate was substantially above that paid on accounts closed—usually around one per cent. In 1892 this differential was deliberately turned to advantage by announcing both rates in advance and widening the margin between them. For each of the six-month periods beginning March and September 1892 the Managers declared in advance a rate of interest on accounts that remained open of five per cent,* but only three and a half per cent on those closed during the half year. This formally stated differential continued so long as Australian financial affairs remained so unsettled.

Among other policies of the period, the Bank further carefully added to its reserves, more than proportionately to the increase in deposits, and in every year from 1893 by the maximum allowed under the 1848 Act. Further, it also added quietly to the profit and loss account to meet the eventual losses on its fixed deposits held at the Bank of Van Diemen's Land, without disturbing the more formal and publicized official reserves.† On the other side of the balance-sheet, in the 1890s the Bank also in practice abandoned its rather inflexible policy towards mortgage borrowers of allowing only full repayment, in favour of partial repayments, though it did not adopt the formal instalment system then coming into vogue in other parts of Australia. The ability to repay a loan bit by bit both enhanced the popularity of such loans, and made mortgage lending on balance safer for the Bank, since the initial security for a loan was generally retained as the loan was repaid, providing a progressively greater margin of cover.

The Bank's strength and success in the 1890s proved in the circumstances to be self-reinforcing. Because the Bank was so highly regarded, many people, particularly wealthier people, switched funds to the relatively safe institution. During the 1890s numerous new accounts were opened for £150, many of them multiple accounts. During 1892, for example, one

* This was the highest rate paid since the 1840s, and one made possible because a very large proportion of the Bank's mortgage borrowers now paid six per cent.

† In 1898, with the final settlement of the affairs of the Bank of Van Diemen's Land, the Bank for Savings incurred a loss on its fixed deposits of £2,200. This amount was written off against the profit and loss account which then had ample cover of nearly £5,000 to its credit.

married woman opened four accounts in her own name, three of them for £150; another married woman, already with three accounts, opened two more, while a farmer and his wife opened in their joint names six such accounts. The practice was not only condoned by the Bank but encouraged, since it was not breaking the law, though perhaps it circumvented its intention. On more than one occasion during 1893 and 1894 Cathcart, on his own initiative, opened second accounts for depositors whose funds came to exceed £150.

In 1894 the tendency for wealthier people to open savings-bank accounts was greatly strengthened when the rate on twelve-month fixed deposits paid by commercial banks was cut sharply from five per cent to three per cent. With the Bank for Savings still paying four and a half per cent, this made a savings-bank account a relatively profitable investment, as well as a safe one. During 1894 two depositors each opened no less than eight large accounts. By 1896 interest on Bank for Savings' deposits had fallen to three per cent, but in that year the rate on twelve-month fixed deposits was also reduced to two and a half per cent, still leaving half a per cent margin in favour of the Bank for Savings. These rates remained the same to 1900.

Through a combination of astute policies and relatively favourable outside circumstances the Launceston Bank for Savings encountered remarkably few problems during the early 1890s, and over the decade as a whole greatly expanded its business. Between 1890 and 1900 total deposits nearly doubled, from around £150,000 to around £275,000, a rate of expansion greater than at any time since the 1850s. Boosted by the deposits of wealthier investors, the average size of the Bank's accounts rose from about £16 in 1890 to £20 in 1900; by then accounts of more than £100 probably supplied nearly half of the Bank's total funds. Most of the Bank's extra funds were invested, as before, in mortgage loans. However, there was some considerable revival in holdings of fixed deposits and, more significantly in the long run, government securities reappeared among its investments; the first of these, acquired in 1897, were local debentures issued for the city's power-station and lighting.

The Bank's record in the 1890s compared very favourably with that of its southern counterpart. Already in the previous twenty years the northern bank had been gradually catching up, with deposits only a little over one-third those of the Hobart bank in 1870 but over one-half by 1890. During the 1890s the trend accelerated, with deposits at the Launceston Bank for Savings reaching three-quarters of the level of those in the Hobart bank by 1900.

The success of the Bank for Savings was particularly significant in view of the great expansion of the post-office savings bank during the decade.

Of little importance in 1890, the post-office savings bank first showed a large growth of deposits in 1891. Probably this was a reaction to the failure of the Bank of Van Diemen's Land, which turned many investors to the ultimate in safe securities, those of the government. Deposits then continued to grow for the next three years but not very rapidly. The real transition came in 1895 and 1896 when in line with market forces the trustee savings banks' rate of interest was reduced from four and a half per cent to three per cent, while the post-office savings bank rate remained at three and a half per cent. The post-office savings bank seems to have been as oblivious to market forces in the 1890s as it had been in the 1880s. But whereas in the 1880s this had been to its disadvantage, now it was to its decided advantage. Offering a rate of return higher than the trustee savings banks, and indeed higher than the rate at which the government could have raised debenture funds directly, the post-office savings bank nearly trebled its deposits between the end of 1894 and the end of 1900. Yet over the same period the Launceston Bank for Savings also was able to expand rapidly, and in 1900 still held a much greater share of savings bank deposits in northern Tasmania than did its government rival.

With some justification the reports of the Executive Committee displayed considerable self-satisfaction.* Also, as in the late 1880s, the Bank received consistently good publicity in Launceston's two newspapers, with favourable reports on the half-yearly meetings, and occasionally editorials which elaborated on its virtues. For example, in an editorial for 4 September 1896 the *Launceston Examiner* began in customary vein: 'The Launceston Savings Bank continues to pursue the even tenor of its way, increasing its business steadily year by year'. It then complimented Launcestonians on their thrift, and the good use to which their funds were put. However, the editorial tone was now much less patronizing and paternal than in earlier years. Foreshadowing perhaps the end of the Victorian era and the development of more egalitarian values, the writer added:

> Some individuals with their modest £10 or £20 which represents their stand-by against a rainy day, may be disposed to envy the seemingly wealthy landowner who passes them by in the street. But if the truth could be ascertained, who knows but that he is their debtor, and that part of the profit of his broad acres has to be set aside to provide their few shillings of interest each year.

If the function of the Bank for Savings was essentially unaltered, the moral atmosphere in which it operated was changing.

The expanding business of the Bank for Savings in the late 1890s

* It may be indicative of the Bank's basic strength in the 1890s that the number of meetings of the Executive Committee, averaging about one a month, was smaller than in any other decade since the Bank registered under the 1848 Act.

created at least one major problem, a growing shortage of office space. Particularly after the appointment of another junior clerk in February 1898 the facilities in Paterson Street were becoming increasingly cramped and inadequate. In 1899 the St John Street premises of the Bank of Van Diemen's Land, vacated some time since, came on to the market. A large, dignified building, erected at the height of the mining boom in 1881, it immediately attracted the interest of the Executive Committee. At the September half-yearly general meeting the Bank's Managers agreed that the Executive Committee should make further enquiries, and at the following meeting in March 1900 authorized it to negotiate for a price to £6,500. After considerable haggling the Committee found that it was unable to buy for less than £6,500, and accepted the price. On 23 June 1900 Cathcart and his staff moved into the new building that, although greatly extended and altered, today still remains the Bank's headquarters.

Tasmania and the Bank after 1900

The opening years of the twentieth century saw a continuation of the prosperity which had become evident in Tasmania during the late 1890s. As always, the key lay in the island's ability to export, and in this two factors were of critical importance. One was the continued success of Tasmanian mining. Although the prolific Mount Lyell field passed its peak in 1900, the production of copper continued at a high level. In addition, both silver and tin exports increased in the early part of the decade. When metal prices generally rose in 1906 and 1907, exports of minerals rose to a record value in excess of £2 million in 1907. The other factor, and in the long run more important, was that Tasmanian primary producers had new, freer access to mainland markets, the result of Federation and the elimination of tariff barriers within Australia. Exports of farm produce rose greatly in a wide range of items, most notably potatoes and fruit, including processed fruit, particularly jam, but also hops, oats, peas, beans, butter, and, in some years, hay and chaff. Although exports of individual items fluctuated greatly from year to year, according to seasonal conditions, exports of farm produce as a whole roughly doubled in value from around £0.5 million per annum in the late 1890s to £1 million by the early 1900s. At a more modest level, the elimination of internal barriers to trade also resulted in a considerable expansion of timber exports to the mainland. Overall, from an already high level of £2.6 million in 1900, Tasmania's exports rose to a peak of £4.1 million in 1907. In addition, tourism, after a considerable setback in the 1890s depression, was once more a major and rapidly increasing source of profit to Tasmania.

Launceston of the 1900s, although achieving, as in the 1890s, only a modest increase in population, was undoubtedly wealthy and progressive.

Most notable evidence of this was perhaps the major revival of its port, reflecting both the growth of exports and the revived tourist trade. By 1910 shipping had increased to such an extent that a Harbour League was formed to press for major port and river improvement. Throughout the decade, it would seem, the building trade was very active, but now in a very different garb. The stuccoed ornateness of the Victorian era was discarded for the simpler chunkier Edwardian style of predominantly exposed brick and bold cream bands, though towards the end of the decade with the additional element of Art Nouveau decoration, now more evident in Launceston than almost any other Australian city. Meanwhile the Launceston City Council continued its good works of the 1890s. Among its various achievements of the 1900s were extensions and improvements to the power-station, waterworks and sewerage, duplication of the South Esk bridge, additions to the Cataract Gorge facilities, and provision of separate bathing facilities for ladies at the Corporation Baths. Most progressive of all was the laying down of the first electric tramway in the city; initially proposed in 1906, some seven miles of tramway were in operation by 1911. The official *Handbook of Tasmania* was able to comment with some truth that 'Launceston is pardonably proud of its City Council'.

Again, Launceston's prosperity was reflected in the performance of its savings bank. During the 1900s deposits in the Launceston Bank for Savings rose from £276,000 to £451,000, a greater absolute increase than in either of the two previous boom decades.* This growth in deposits is particularly significant since depositors were still, as they had been since the early 1880s, predominantly from the city itself, yet the population of the city increased very little during the decade—including suburbs, by less than ten per cent. Two main factors were involved. Firstly, many more people, who were apparently dependants, opened accounts at the Bank; by the 1900s they considerably outnumbered those with formally stated occupations among new depositors. To some extent this may reflect an increasing number of working housewives, who did not actually state their occupations. More fundamentally it probably resulted from the greater affluence of the decade which encouraged working families to open more than one account, and frequently several. By 1910 there were probably at least two Bank for Savings accounts for every three members of the wage-earning classes. Secondly, and again largely reflecting the affluence of the times, was the increasing proportion of new accounts which stayed open, a higher percentage than ever before, and the increasing proportion of accounts

* With this increase, the margin between Launceston and Hobart narrowed still further. By 1910 the Launceston Bank for Savings had deposits equal to about four-fifths of those of the Hobart Savings Bank, although Launceston and suburbs had a population well under two-thirds that of the capital.

which on balance accumulated funds during the decade. Out of a sample of sixty new accounts opened between April 1900 and January 1901 more than half remained open for more than three years and a third for more than ten years; most of these were greatly added to during the decade, though, as before, in a very irregular manner. Overall, the average size of all deposits rose from about £20 in 1900 to nearly £23 by 1910.

The increased funds of the Bank were invested in the traditional outlets of mortgage loans, fixed deposits and government securities. Fixed deposits, though an essential part of the Bank's portfolio, since they were virtually liquid assets and the Bank held very little in cash, were only a little more rewarding than in the 1890s, generally for two-year terms paying only the same as the Bank paid its own depositors; they rose only slightly on balance from £69,000 to £79,000. Mortgage loans continued as easily the largest single form of investment, rising in value from £175,000 to £301,000. Until 1905 the minimum rate of mortgage loans was a comfortable one per cent above the rate paid to depositors; from 1905 no minimum was specified, but roughly the same differential seems to have continued. Initially least important, but rapidly growing during the 1900s, were holdings of government securities, particularly Local Inscribed Stock of the Tasmanian government. From the late 1890s, with the general fall in private interest rates relative to those on government stock, the latter again became a viable investment; not quite so profitable as mortgage loans, but safer and less troublesome. By 1910 the Bank for Savings' holdings of government securities had increased to £98,000.

The Launceston Bank for Savings undoubtedly reached a peak of popularity and prestige during the 1900s. Not only had it a rapidly growing volume of business, but with the opening of the new building in 1900, its business was conducted in 'one of the most handsome and convenient banking rooms in the city'. The two facts were not wholly unrelated. In its first report after the new building opened, the Executive Committee commented that the record number of new accounts recently opened demonstrated the public's appreciation of the new building. The Bank seems to have been anxious to preserve its new and profitable image, installing telephone equipment in the following year and four years later purchasing a novel piece of office machinery—a typewriter.

In the same year that the Bank moved into its new building its prestige was bolstered in another and very different way, with the appointment as actuary of Hardwicke Weedon. In October John Cathcart was forced to resign because of serious ill-health; he died shortly afterwards. Although a highly competent professional banker with a fine record cut short at a relatively early age, Cathcart had been, like Pullen before him, essentially a paid officer with little standing outside the Bank. Weedon was a man of very different mould. While perhaps lacking the professional expertise of his predecessor, he was, because of his family background and his own achievements, one of Launceston's outstanding public figures at the time of his appointment. In his generation Weedon was probably as eminent in the affairs of Launceston as Henry Dowling had been in earlier years.

Hardwicke Weedon was the eldest son of C. J. Weedon, one of Launceston's pioneer settlers and for a long time a leading auctioneer. Born in 1845, educated at the Launceston Church Grammar School, and throughout his long life a devout Anglican, Hardwicke Weedon worked as a partner in his father's business for some years, eventually leaving to become manager of the Derwent and Tamar Assurance Company. Weedon's real interest, however, lay in serving the community of Launceston rather than making money out of it. This probably is the explanation for his willingness and indeed eagerness to become actuary of the Bank. Although offering a modest salary, it was a secure job in which he could serve the public and have plenty of time for outside activities. At the time of his appointment Weedon held innumerable official positions of importance in the city: the *Cyclopedia of Tasmania* recorded that he was the chairman of the Executive Committee of the Bank for Savings, the Fire Brigade, Underwriters Association and Launceston District Nursing Association; president of the Horticultural Society, Poultry Society and Kennel Club; director of the Launceston Gas Company and local director of the National Life Assurance Company; a member of the Fisheries Board, Launceston Hospital Board, and the Licensing Bench; magistrate for the territory, visiting justice of the peace at the gaol, and a commissioner of the Supreme Court of Tasmania. The *Cyclopedia of Tasmania* added 'etc. etc.; besides other offices'. Previously Weedon had gained great distinction as one of the leaders of the movement to improve the Cataract Gorge, now officially taken over by the city council. The only major omission among Weedon's formidable range of activities seems to have been a lack of interest in (or time for) politics.

Weedon's appointment resulted in a major shift in the 'balance of power' within the Bank. As a member of the Executive Committee since 1885 and its formally appointed chairman since 1893, not to mention his standing outside the Bank, Weedon was clearly senior in every respect to any member of the Executive Committee at the time of his appointment. As actuary he had to formally resign from the Committee, and indeed now became technically an employee of the Committee, but there can be little doubt that he played a major part in shaping the decisions of the Committee, although by the nature of the records direct evidence for this is lacking. The new authority of the actuary was, at least in the 1900s, enhanced by the existence of an Executive Committee lacking strong leadership or personalities. Significantly, no member was apparently willing or able to act as chairman for any length of time; between 1900 and 1910 there were five different chairmen. Furthermore, committee members of the 1900s were almost entirely of two types: men such as Richard Green or Frank Hart, old hands on the Committee but also well advanced in years; or younger men, such as George Edward Harrap and P. O. Fysh junior, later to serve the Committee with distinction, but at this time newly appointed and very much novices in the growing complexities of the Bank's affairs.

While Weedon came to exercise a major influence in the decisions of the Executive Committee, in the day-to-day affairs of the Bank he was undisputed ruler. To his staff Weedon was an aristocratic figure, in appearance and in manner. Dressed immaculately, with winged collars and carefully cultivated moustache, he had a loud and commanding voice, stern manner and fiery temper. Set apart in his well-furnished private office, he was undoubtedly the master, and his staff the servants. Yet if a stern master, he was by no means a harsh one. Those who served under him remember Weedon as essentially fair to his staff, with a bark much worse than his bite, and willing to retract a hasty or ill-tempered decision. One retired officer of the Bank recalls how as a junior clerk he was unable to read a draft letter written by Weedon—Weedon's handwriting was difficult to read at the best of times. The master administered a sound rebuke, then picked up the letter, found that even he could not read it, and apologized gracefully. Weedon is remembered as much as the 'real gentleman' as the aristocrat.

Furthermore, if the gulf between actuary and staff widened and the degree of subservience increased under Weedon, the change was not all of his own making. To some extent it reflected the qualities of the staff themselves. Even before Weedon took office, one of the two senior members of the staff, Alfred Biggs, had been retired on account of his age and physical disability. The other senior member, Ambrose Dowling, was kept on as second-in-command, but more, one feels, out of motives of kindness than for his ability. Dowling in the 1900s seems to have been a rather sad old figure, twice defeated for the post of actuary, lingering on until forced to retire because of his advanced years and failing eyesight. Next in line below Dowling was the cashier, Alfred Littler, quiet, conscientious, and barely thirty when Weedon came to the Bank. Younger still than Littler, at twenty-six and nineteen respectively were the Harrison brothers, Ernest and Raymond, who were nephews of the new actuary. At the bottom of the hierarchy was the newly appointed clerk, Alfred Harris. Weedon's staff were not likely to dispute his authority.

Signs of complacency

Hardwicke Weedon brought prestige to the Launceston Bank for Savings, but little in the way of new ideas. Perhaps his creative energies were too fully concentrated in other channels, or perhaps he felt that the Bank was already fulfilling its role. Certainly there is little evidence of an attempt to enlarge, extend, or improve the business he inherited from Cathcart in 1900. Equally, there is little evidence that the Executive Committee had any ideas in this direction. In fact, the nature of the Bank's business became so settled and predictable that from 1908 the Executive Committee began to use printed forms for its half-yearly reports, with blank spaces for changing amounts.

By the 1900s, perhaps for the first time in the history of the Bank, its leaders were displaying a degree of conservatism and complacency that was not wholly warranted. The strong position of the Bank and settled economic conditions made it an ideal time to experiment and innovate, but there is not even a suggestion of change. There is no evidence, for example, that the Executive Committee or the actuary discussed the possibility of establishing branches, or operating loans with regular instalment repayments. In neighbouring Victoria both were proving a great success. Perhaps they would not have succeeded to the same extent in Tasmania, but at least they might have been considered.

On the contrary, rather than consider ways of improving or extending savings habits, the Bank's tendency in Weedon's early years was to impose increasing restrictions on depositors. Large accounts were discouraged, even from such worthy institutions as the University of Tasmania or the local Union Jack Gymnasium. Similarly, either on his own initiative or informally instructed by the Executive Committee,* Weedon progressively clamped down on multiple deposits, initially restricting any depositor to two, but by the end of 1903 banning them almost completely. Above all, Weedon became increasingly severe with depositors whose accounts hinted at being current accounts. At the outset he made it clear in correspondence with depositors that such current accounts were restricted to charitable institutions; otherwise one or two withdrawals per month was the maximum he would allow, and anyone wishing to exceed this number was advised to go to a commercial bank. In 1902 he applied the same rules to charitable institutions. By 1907 he was advising all new depositors and those who transgressed his rules that three or four withdrawals per year was the maximum that would be tolerated.

The increasing restrictions imposed on depositors are not wholly inexplicable. With a secure and rising volume of business the Bank could

* There is no record of any formal resolution passed to this effect.

afford to be more fussy—to seek to avoid the inconvenience of sudden large withdrawals, or the extra labour imposed by over-active accounts. Again, as Weedon pointed out to one depositor, the Bank's staff was so hard worked that it could not cope with extra business—though why the Bank chose not to appoint more staff is something of a mystery. Or it may be quite simply that Weedon believed in the old-style savings bank in which there was no place for large, multiple or over-active accounts.

Weedon, the Executive Committee and the Managers alike seem to have had the utmost confidence in the security and future prospects of the Bank, a not unreasonable belief in the light of past performances. However, not all was as sound as it seemed. Certainly by the end of the decade two problems should have started to become apparent. Whether they were noticed, and whether anything could have been done about them at the time, are open questions.

One was the ominously successful record of the Post Office Savings Bank, renamed the Tasmanian State Savings Bank when the federal government took over the post offices in 1902 but allowed their savings facilities to continue. Between 1900 and 1910 deposits in the State Savings Bank more than doubled and by 1910 greatly exceeded those of either the Launceston Bank for Savings or the Hobart Savings Bank, even though the rate of interest paid to depositors was now the same as that of the trustee savings banks. The State Savings Bank had the advantage of a virtual monopoly of savings business in the rapidly growing areas outside Hobart and Launceston. From 1902 it also had the advantage of a maximum deposit size of £250, compared with £150 for the trustee savings banks, and provision for fixed deposits, also with a limit of £250 per person. A rapid increase in the average size of deposits at the State Savings Bank in the 1900s suggests that these were very considerable advantages.

Quite apart from the problem of a progressively larger share of savings business going to the state, the State Savings Bank posed other threats. For a brief period in 1902, while the Post Office Savings Bank was being reorganized into the State Savings Bank, the postal concessions on savings-bank business were withdrawn; without them the trustee savings banks would have lost virtually the whole of their country business, and after considerable outcry the concessions were restored. More persistent was the danger of forced amalgamation of the trustee savings banks with the State Savings Bank. The danger first appeared in 1902 when the State Savings Bank was being established; again in 1904 when the Premier, W. B. Propsting, advocated amalgamation; once more in 1907 when the general manager of the Victorian State Savings Bank, Alexander Cooch, reporting on the method of operation of the Tasmanian State Savings Bank, recommended among other measures amalgamation with the trustee savings banks, providing some very persuasive arguments in favour of it; and yet again in 1910 when a new State Savings Bank Bill was being discussed in Parliament. The reaction of the Launceston Bank for Savings seems to have been surprisingly apathetic, even slightly contemptuous.

The second problem which should have become apparent by 1910 was that Tasmania's long spell of vigorous expansion, upon which the success of the Launceston Bank for Savings had been largely based, was coming to an end. Already by the mid-1900s farmers were failing to make further headway in their exports to the mainland. More seriously, Tasmanian mining, lucrative for so long, was clearly on the decline after 1907 as prices fell and ore reserves dwindled, though few at the time were prepared to believe it. Between 1907 and 1910 Tasmanian exports as a whole failed to advance. Meanwhile the great hopes held out for an efficient Tasmanian manufacturing industry, using cheap hydro-electricity and supplying an Australia-wide market had not yet materialized. Rather, for the time being the reverse applied. Many small-scale, comparatively inefficient Tasmanian industrial enterprises suffered from increased competition by mainland manufacturers. Overall, the census of 1911 records fewer industrial workers in Tasmania than ten years earlier. The creation of a tariff-free market even meant that some agricultural products suffered, particularly wheat, which in earlier decades had been one of the island's chief exports but was now imported in increasing quantities.

In retrospect at least, the most certain sign of Tasmania's changing fortunes is once again provided by figures for arrivals to and departures from the island. From 1900 to 1903 Tasmania had a substantial excess of arrivals over departures, though not so great as in the closing years of the 1890s. From 1904 to 1907 there was on balance a very slight net immigration. From 1908 departures began to exceed arrivals. The old problem of the drain to the mainland had reappeared, though few realized at the time that it was to be the prevailing trend for the next twenty years.

CHAPTER TEN

'To Serve a City or a Region?' New Challenges 1910–1920

Tasmania and the Bank around 1910

When Ambrose Dowling resigned in 1907 the Launceston Bank for Savings lost its last personal link with the bad times of earlier years. By then, none of the Managers, members of the Executive Committee or paid staff had been associated with any but a successful and expanding institution. Since the early 1870s the Bank had enjoyed almost uninterrupted progress and freedom from the major crises which had been so characteristic of its formation years. In part this reflected the careful, but alert and flexible policies of the Executive Committee and the actuary, in part the sustained boom conditions of the Tasmanian economy; since 1877 Tasmania's rate of population growth had almost matched the rate of growth on the mainland, and its initially low standard of living had almost caught up with that of the rest of Australia. By the 1900s the Bank's success had been so great that it could afford to adopt a more restrictive and conservative policy towards depositors, something unknown since the early 1850s.

In the late 1900s Tasmania's long-sustained boom was coming to an end, but the transition to less prosperous times was a fairly gentle one. Contemporary opinion remained optimistic, though more cautious and qualified than before. The annual reviews, for example, by the *Launceston Examiner* and Launceston's Chamber of Commerce recognized the weaknesses and dangers, especially of the island's mainstay, its mining industry, but overall considered conditions satisfactory and the future still fairly bright. And their assessments were not wholly without justification. Exports, which had stagnated in value between 1907 and 1910, showed a substantial increase in the next three years, with better prices generally and buoyant export trades in fruit and timber in particular overshadowing a stagnating mining industry. Meanwhile tourism, stimulated by prosperity and the proliferation of tourist organizations, was booming. In such conditions the renewed drift to the mainland was not yet of alarming proportions and for a brief period just before World War I stopped almost completely. It was not until the 1920s that stagnation and depression were to become really serious.

Broadly, the Launceston Bank for Savings' performance in the immediate pre-war years reflected these conditions. Between 1907 and 1910 deposits increased at a markedly slower rate than before, but from then until the early part of 1913 increased quite briskly with the apparent revival of economic conditions. Almost all of these additional funds were invested in Local Inscribed Stock of the Tasmanian government. Borrowing freely at an increasing rate of interest and offering a return only slightly below that on mortgage loans, the Tasmanian government provided an easy and profitable outlet for the investment of the Bank's funds. Government securities were now the Bank's prime objective in seeking investments and indeed continued to be so until late in the 1920s. During that period, mortgage loans, traditionally the major outlet for the Bank's funds, became a minor part of the Bank's business.

Part of the Bank's success in the pre-war years can undoubtedly be attributed to its increasingly efficient and economical administration. For some fifteen years from 1898 no additions were made to the number of paid officers, yet over that period the number of depositors nearly doubled and the value of their transactions more than doubled. This was a remarkable achievement, reflecting a combination of increased ability, proficiency through experience, and teamwork on the part of Weedon's young staff. Leading the team in 1913 was Alfred Littler, accountant since 1907, perhaps a little slow and already hampered by asthma which was to trouble him more and more as time passed, but after twenty-six years' experience with the Bank, highly competent, reliable, and popular with his juniors. Two years younger than Littler was the cashier or paying teller, Ernest Harrison, twenty-three years with the Bank and thoroughly expert at his job, though with some of the brusque mannerisms of his uncle, Weedon. Raymond Harrison, his thirty-one-year-old brother, appointed in 1898, now kept the ledgers very efficiently. The two most junior officials, both to have long and distinguished careers with the Bank, were Keith Westbrook, appointed in 1905, now at the age of twenty-five the receiving teller, and Ronald Tyson, appointed in 1907, twenty-one years old and acting as general clerk.

Weedon's youthful but nevertheless experienced and competent staff achieved an unusual degree of camaraderie in the pre-war years, because of its small size, because of the long-established association of its members, and because of their common interests. Outstanding among these was their devotion to sport. Littler, in his earlier years a skilled oarsman, was now a keen yachtsman and motor-boat enthusiast. The rest of the staff spread their energies widely over many sports, with cricket perhaps as their special strength. Ernest Harrison would have played for Australia in a Test series against New Zealand in the summer of 1909–10, if the Bank had allowed him the six weeks' leave he sought for the tour. For a time he captained northern Tasmania in its annual Christmas match against the south. Westbrook was also a regular member of that team, and in the 1912 match Tyson was twelfth man; he might have been in the eleven but for the fact that the Bank, which was open on the last day's play, was precariously short-staffed.

The Commonwealth Savings Bank

On 1 November 1911 the Labor Prime Minister, Andrew Fisher, introduced into Federal Parliament legislation to establish a Commonwealth Bank. One of the major provisions of the Bill was the creation of savings-bank facilities. Operating on a uniform Australia-wide basis, and enjoying great economies of scale, Fisher envisaged that this department of the Commonwealth Bank would ultimately acquire a monopoly of savings-bank business in Australia. Clearly with this in mind, the federal government had earlier in the year abolished the privilege of registered penny postage for savings-bank packages. At the time the legislation was introduced it was made clear that the post offices, through which state savings banks were then chiefly conducted, would be available only to the new Commonwealth Bank savings department. And once established, the Commonwealth Bank formally offered to take over the savings banks of the various state governments.

The Commonwealth Bank proposals, and those relating to savings banking in particular, aroused fierce opposition inside, and even more so outside Parliament. Some opposition was of a simple party political nature and suggested that Labor sought savings-bank funds to finance extravagant government schemes. Most criticism, however, focussed on the claim that the Commonwealth would be usurping state funds. Indeed, it was a Labor Premier, J. S. T. McGowen of New South Wales, who took the initiative, calling a conference of Premiers early in November and before the end of the month sending a telegram on their behalf to the Prime Minister. Regarding it as 'a matter of paramount urgency to let you know our views', McGowen voiced the Premiers' condemnation of proposals which 'will act inimically upon the depositors in savings banks and most seriously affect the financial interests of the governments of the several states'. Meanwhile the press condemned the scheme in still stronger language. The *Sydney Morning Herald* of 17 November 1911, for example, judged it as 'little better than a species of wholesale confiscation, and it should be resisted to the last ditch.' Later, from a distinctively Tasmanian viewpoint the *Launceston Examiner* commented bitterly that 'there is every prospect that such funds will be applied to building railways on the mainland or be sunk in the bush capital.'

The Commonwealth Bank Bill eventually became law, and between the middle of 1912 and early 1913 government savings banks state by state relinquished their post-office facilities. In an attempt to establish the Commonwealth Bank as the sole savings bank, the federal government conducted prolonged negotiations with the various state governments, promising that seventy-five per cent of deposits would be retained for use in each state. No agreement was reached, however, and the various mainland government banks prepared to meet the new challenge, some in a fiercely aggressive mood. In Victoria, for example, the State Savings Bank, first to relinquish the post-office facilities in the winter of 1912, had within a month established thirty-four new branches and 319 new agencies. Before the end of the year it had increased the rate of interest to depositors, raised the maximum deposit size to £350 (as against the Commonwealth Bank's maximum of £300), and established for the first time safe custody facilities, provisions for fixed deposits, and school banks.

The Tasmanian State Savings Bank differed in two important respects from its mainland counterparts. Firstly, it operated solely through the post-office system, having no independent branches of its own, as were common in other states. Secondly, it already faced strong competition from the trustee savings banks in the two major centres of population: in 1912 the deposits of the Hobart Savings Bank and the Launceston Bank for Savings together still exceeded those of the State Savings Bank. Being in a much weaker position than the mainland banks, the Tasmanian State Savings Bank was much more vulnerable to the challenge posed by the new Commonwealth Bank. Indeed it has been suggested that the Tasmanian government wanted to get rid of its savings bank. The evidence, however, points to the contrary. In November 1911 the Premier, N. E. Lewis, although unable to attend the conference of Premiers, gave McGowen his unqualified support. In the same month, when contacted by George Harrap (on behalf of the Launceston Chamber of Commerce), Lewis reaffirmed his views, though expressing pessimism about the strong competition ahead.

In June 1912 Lewis was succeeded as Premier by A. E. Solomon, a man who not only opposed the Commonwealth Bank proposals, but took active steps to meet the challenge. In an attempt to save the State Savings Bank, Solomon proposed amalgamation with the two trustee savings banks. Both banks, however, were against the scheme. At a special meeting of the Executive Committee of the Launceston Bank for Savings on 20 August, the proposals were unanimously rejected. After a joint delegation from

Launceston Bank for Savings, St John Street, Launceston

Office of the Launceston Bank
vings, St John Street, showing
-day facade

John Duncan

Ronald S. Tyson

B. Leslie Hooper

Sinclair J. Thyne

the two banks had conferred with the Premier in September, the latter dropped his proposals, while intimating that a new scheme would be prepared. Solomon apparently abandoned further efforts, however, and accepted the take-over offer of the Commonwealth Bank.

In November 1912 Denison Miller, Governor of the Commonwealth Bank, visited Tasmania to complete the deal, and at the same time took the opportunity to approach the two trustee savings banks, but without success. Early in December the Tasmanian government passed legislation to transfer the State Savings Bank business to the Commonwealth Bank, and after prolonged haggling over detailed terms the take-over formally went through in June 1913. This was the Commonwealth Bank's first success, and its only success with the savings banks for many years.

When Miller had met the Executive Committee of the Launceston Bank for Savings in November 1912 and found his proposals rejected, he had declared with perhaps ominous ambiguity that:

> if the Bank was not disposed to join the Commonwealth Bank there the matter would end as far as he was concerned as he was not out to fight or try to obtain our business but was going to conduct the Commonwealth Savings Bank on thorough business lines.

Clearly the Commonwealth Savings Bank posed a much greater threat to the Launceston Bank for Savings than its state-run predecessor. Already the Bank's hold on country depositors had been weakened by the abolition of the postal concessions. Now it faced the prospect of a nation-wide savings bank, offering great advantages to interstate travellers, with a maximum legal-deposit size twice that of its own, and obviously determined to gain much more business than the old State Savings Bank. Among the many little things it did to attract business, the Commonwealth Savings Bank issued free blotters with its pass-books, remained open on certain evenings at many post offices, and publicized all its facilities in a colour folder, freely available at every post office. More seriously for the trustee savings banks, complete savings-banking facilities became available in both Hobart and Launceston at an early date with the establishment by the Commonwealth Bank of its own branches, quite separate from the post offices.

In its first years the Commonwealth Bank at least partially achieved its objective, gaining a greater share of Tasmanian savings banking. Yet at the same time the business of both trustee savings banks increased, which in the circumstances was no mean achievement. The Launceston Bank for Savings met the new challenge with a variety of counter-measures. The loss of its postal privileges was in part offset by the device of holding pass-books at the Bank and conducting business with country depositors by means of cheque or postal notes, which could be safely transmitted at the standard cost of one penny. Apparently the Executive Committee also considered, but decided against the opening of country branches. The advantage of nation-wide facilities offered by the Commonwealth Savings Bank was countered by a reciprocity agreement with mainland savings banks, initially suggested to the Bank for Savings by the State Savings Bank of Victoria in January 1913, and eagerly accepted in the same month. At every opportunity the Bank advertised perhaps its one major trump card, that it paid a higher rate of interest than the Commonwealth Savings Bank. And in general it adopted a more competitive attitude towards attracting or retaining depositors.

Unfortunately, no depositors' letter-books exist for the period from 1909 to the end of 1913, but there is no doubt that attitudes and policies changed radically. Early in 1914, for example, Littler was trying valiantly to persuade a lady from Victoria now living in Ulverstone not to transfer her savings account to the Commonwealth Savings Bank. A few months later Weedon was doing the same with a potential depositor in Devonport claiming, with a smart dig at the Commonwealth Savings Bank, that 'We pride ourselves that we do not observe red-tape rules in this Bank, and we offer our depositors all facilities for depositing or withdrawing.' In the search for business most of Weedon's restrictive measures of the 1900s were abandoned. Once more, large accounts were actively encouraged, multiple accounts no longer disallowed, and there was a noticeable absence of the warning letters about over-active accounts, so common in earlier years.

World War I

With the outbreak of World War I in August 1914 the Launceston Bank for Savings faced new problems. Most immediate was the loss of deposits in a minor financial panic that affected most of Australia's banking institutions. Between 3 and 12 August the Bank for Savings lost £10,000 of deposits, and with the threat of further withdrawals a special meeting of the Executive Committee was convened on 13 August. Members decided, however, that there was no real cause for alarm. The Bank had ample cash in hand, and could borrow against its fixed deposits at the commercial banks. To allay the fears of depositors the usual notice for withdrawal of large sums was waived, and before the end of the month conditions were back to normal, though from that time the Bank held a significantly higher proportion of its assets as cash in hand or in current accounts at the commercial banks.

Like most similar institutions, the Bank encountered staffing problems during the war as members left to join the Australian armed forces. First to leave was Ernest Harrison in March 1915, followed by his brother Raymond in December of the same year; at least one other member of the staff would have joined up but was declared medically unfit. The positions of the Harrison brothers were kept open for their return, and while serving in the forces they received half-pay from the Bank. For a time their absence meant added work for the remaining staff until replacements were found, and the slightly unsettling effect of temporary promotion for other staff pending their return. Raymond Harrison died in May 1916 after being seriously wounded. Ernest Harrison eventually returned to his former position as paying teller.

The greatest problem encountered by the Bank was the new competition for funds from the Commonwealth government. Again it was a problem which affected all savings institutions to a greater or lesser degree. During the war the Commonwealth government attracted funds, first through direct subscriptions to various war loans and later through the issue of war-savings certificates designed specifically for the small saver. Although the latter in particular posed a major threat to savings-bank deposits, savings banks, as a matter of national duty, acted as agents for the disposal of such certificates, receiving a small commission for their services. The diversion of funds to the war effort clearly limited the level of savings-bank business, although it has been claimed that in the long run the war was beneficial in widening the saving habit.

Overall, the affairs of the Launceston Bank for Savings, if disturbed and restricted by the war, were never seriously undermined. Indeed in one respect the Bank gained, through the availability of a new and profitable source of investment, the Commonwealth war loans. First taken up in August 1915, the Bank's holdings of war-loan stock exceeded £100,000 by the end of the war. Yielding four and a half per cent, and with interest rates generally at a higher level* the Bank for Savings was now able to pay a return to depositors of four per cent. This rate was higher than at any time since the early 1890s. It was also only half of one per cent below that paid on war-savings certificates; and the latter, while possessing certain patriotic appeal, had a currency of three years, compared with savings-bank deposits which were virtually at call. Perhaps because of its good rate of return to depositors, the Bank for Savings managed to increase deposits during World War I, despite the pressures exerted on the public to channel savings directly into the war effort.

Towards the end of the war the position of Tasmania's two trustee savings banks was greatly strengthened by new legislation. After extensive groundwork by the two banks, in 1917 the Tasmanian Parliament approved the most important Savings Bank Act since the original Act of 1848.

* The state government paid five per cent on some of its issues.

Among other provisions it gave the Hobart and Launceston banks corporate status, thus dispensing with the need for formal trustees, which had often proved troublesome in the past; following tradition, however, the two banks continued to be known as trustee savings banks. The 1917 Act also made changes in official titles: now the actuary was renamed manager, and the Managers became the General Committee. Most importantly, the Act increased the maximum size of individual accounts to £300, in line with the Commonwealth Savings Bank and closer to the mainland institutions. Although frequently the maximum deposit size had been circumvented unofficially by multiple accounts, this device had only partially solved the problem. Perhaps because of this new legal maximum the rate of growth of deposits, fairly sluggish for most of the war, now accelerated; by February 1919 deposits exceeded three-quarters of a million pounds, compared with something under £600,000 at the start of the war.

To serve a city or a region?

At the end of World War I the Launceston Bank for Savings was from every point of view in a sound position. It had basically succeeded in meeting the challenge of the Commonwealth Savings Bank, although in relative terms losing a certain amount of ground to the latter. It had met the problem of war conditions without much difficulty, especially maintaining the expansion, if overall slower expansion, of its deposits. With close to half of its funds in government stock of one kind or another, nearly another fifteen per cent in fixed deposits, and approaching ten per cent in cash, leaving less than a third in mortgage loans, its asset position was virtually unassailable. And now with the new legislation there was every promise of a more rapid growth of business.

While free of any obvious problems, at the end of the war the Bank faced a fundamental issue, the response to which would determine in large part its future development. Was the Bank for Savings to remain a savings bank for a city or become genuinely the savings bank for a whole region? The issue had confronted the Bank almost since its establishment and certainly from the 1850s, but now more than ever before. In three important respects circumstances had changed, making a clear decision a matter of immediate importance.

In the first place, by the end of the war the Bank for Savings had become the savings bank of a city, more completely than at any time in its history. After 1911 its already fairly light contingent of country depositors had been reduced first by the abolition of the postal privileges, then by the more progressive policies and greater prestige of the Commonwealth Savings Bank. During 1918 no less than four-fifths of the Bank's new depositors lived in Launceston itself; most of the remainder lived within a fifteen to twenty miles' radius of the city. If the Bank still claimed the image of a bank serving the whole of northern Tasmania, it was very much a hollow image.

In the second place, while the Bank's depositors became increasingly concentrated in the city and immediate environs, the population of northern Tasmania was becoming increasingly located in regions relatively distant from Launceston. One of these regions was that of Scottsdale, to the north-east. Originally occupied by tin miners, following the completion of the railway to Scottsdale in 1889 the region had been invaded by the timber-cutters and farmers. After 1900, with the opening of the mainland market, saw-milling and farming had both expanded rapidly, receiving further boosts with railway extensions to the east in 1911 and again in 1919. By the end of the war a closely settled district around and to the east of Scottsdale supported a population of about 7,500 and Scottsdale itself was rapidly developing as an important urban centre. Not long afterwards a local resident wrote of the town:

> Twenty years ago it was a scattered group of dirty red cottages, the ruddy tint being lent by the collection of clouds of chocolate soil dust. Today . . . [there are] beautiful homes well kept and intelligently designed . . . Scottsdale is a picture, and wherever the eye turns it lights on a newly-improved property.

On the north-west coast the Scottsdale success story was repeated in a similar manner but on a much larger scale. Endowed with an extremely rich soil, proximity to mainland markets and an ever-extending railway system, several closely settled farming districts, each focussing on a substantial port, had developed into major centres of population by the end of World War I. At the 1921 census five municipalities alone, Circular Head, Table Cape, Emu Bay, Leven and Devonport, each boasted a population in excess of 5,000. The largest, that of Devonport, had well over 6,000, of which 4,500 lived in the port itself. Overall in the thirty years to 1921 the population of the north-west had almost doubled, and by then it was nearly twice the size of the city of Launceston. The importance and continued growth of the north-west coast, where the Commonwealth Savings Bank had a virtual monopoly of savings-bank business, must have been very apparent to the Executive Committee of the Bank for Savings, isolated in its one city.

The third factor which made the city-versus-region issue more relevant was that in southern Tasmania the Hobart Savings Bank, managed by its energetic new actuary, Robert John Murdoch,* had now established branches outside Hobart. In February 1913 the first of these branches opened at New Norfolk, a well-populated district of more than 6,000

* He, it would seem, was largely instrumental in pushing through the new legislation of 1917.

inhabitants. From the start the New Norfolk branch proved a great success, and more branches may have been opened but for the war. Not long after the war ended, a second branch, to which were attached two sub-branches, was opened at Huonville.

With its own business increasingly confined to the city, with the rapid growth of closely settled districts in the north-east and north-west, and with the example before it of the Hobart Savings Bank, the Executive Committee must have been well aware at the end of the war that the time had never been so right for the creation of branches. In fact the issue had been raised formally in March 1917 by the chairman of the Executive Committee, W. H. Ferrall. All members took part in the discussion, but decided that the time was not opportune. How often between then and the end of 1919 the issue was discussed is not known; there is no formal record of any such discussion in the Minutes. Certainly, whether by formal resolution, or tacit agreement, the decision was to take no action.

The reasoning behind this decision is difficult to assess, particularly since the opportunities for the Launceston Bank for Savings in northern Tasmania were far greater than those of the Hobart Savings Bank in the south; at the 1921 census, for example, the Huon district with only just over 4,000 people was less populous than at least six northern districts. The immediate answer would seem to be simple inertia. The Bank, if not progressing at a spectacular rate, was performing quite satisfactorily. Deposits were increasing as the city expanded and more people came to take advantage of the increased maximum-deposit size. And if the Executive Committee observed the increasing dominance of the Commonwealth Savings Bank in other areas with some regret, there was no danger of any serious encroachment in the city of Launceston itself; there the Bank could provide superior service, a higher rate of interest, and had a considerable amount of local loyalty.

Yet this hardly provides a complete explanation. In particular there is a striking contrast with the Hobart Savings Bank. The latter had less scope for branch banking in the south, and it had less incentive to extend beyond the confines of Hobart, since by comparison with Launceston the capital was now going ahead by leaps and bounds. With the completion of the Great Lake hydro-electric power scheme in 1916, Hobart had attracted major new industries, particularly the Risdon refinery of the Electrolytic Zinc Company, and also large carbide works. As a result, the population of Hobart and its suburbs rose from 38,000 to 53,000 between 1911 and 1921, compared with a rise in Launceston from only 23,000 to 26,000. Despite scope for expansion within the Hobart area, the Hobart Savings Bank still established branches when and where the opportunity arose.

Clearly this was one occasion when the Bank for Savings seriously lacked initiative, and in this an important contributing factor may well have been the advanced age of its decision makers. At the time, the Bank had the oldest Executive Committee it has ever had. Since 1909 only two changes had taken place in its composition, both in 1913; one of the new members was aged sixty-five and the other seventy-three. By 1919 only two of the seven members of the Committee were under seventy, and the average age was seventy-two. The manager, Weedon, was himself seventy-four years of age. Advanced age did not imply incompetence or even an inability to act quickly. But it was certainly not conducive to new ways of thinking, particularly to what would have amounted to radical redirection of the Bank into a very different role from the one it had played, with considerable success, for several decades.

Branch banking

At one of the normal fortnightly meetings of the Executive Committee on 20 November 1919 the last item on the agenda concerned a letter from Murdoch, the manager of the Hobart Savings Bank. Without a full attendance, the matter was deferred for a special meeting to be held four days later. At that meeting on 24 November it was revealed that the Hobart Savings Bank proposed to extend its branch network to the north-west coast. This may not have come as a complete surprise to Weedon, since he had already been asked by Murdoch if the Launceston Bank for Savings had any plans for opening branches on the north-west coast. Certainly it was a complete surprise to the Executive Committee, and now, shaken out of its complacency by this intrusion from the south, it reacted with great vigour and speed. Weedon was instructed to write a strongly-worded letter to Murdoch, expressing the Committee's great surprise, since the Launceston Bank for Savings had never said definitely that it would not open branches in the north-west. He was also instructed to say that 'the Board would look upon the action of the Hobart Savings Bank as an unfriendly one, in that they were contemplating opening in what is essentially a Northern territory'. It was decided to advertise immediately in the local press that the Launceston Bank for Savings intended opening branches at Devonport and Burnie; Ulverstone was also kept in mind for another possible branch. Ernest Harrison, recently returned from the war, and Alfred Littler took the first train west out of Launceston to make appropriate arrangements. Meanwhile Harrap and Ferrall headed south to try to persuade Murdoch to change his mind. A conference was held on 28 November, but the Hobart Savings Bank stood firm.

Harrison and Littler performed their tasks efficiently. At Devonport, Littler purchased a weatherboard cottage to provide temporary quarters;

at Burnie, Harrison leased suitable premises; a similar arrangement was made at Ulverstone. Three young local men, ex-servicemen with banking experience, were quickly recruited as branch managers, each to be assisted for a time by a junior clerk. The Devonport and Burnie branches opened on 8 December, just two weeks after the Executive Committee had first discussed the matter, and the Ulverstone branch on 22 December. Meanwhile the Hobart Savings Bank, perhaps a little taken aback by the Launceston Bank for Savings' new lease of life, contented itself for the time being with just the one branch at Burnie. In the half-yearly report of the Bank for Savings' Executive Committee which announced these new developments, no reference was made to the Hobart Savings Bank. Either the Committee was not anxious to admit its own early inactivity, or was unwilling to publicize the fact that the Hobart Savings Bank, for so many years a strong ally, had now become an untrustworthy competitor. In explaining its actions the Executive Committee simply referred to the number of depositors on the north-west coast, the Bank's many investments there, and the growing importance of the area.

Only days after the Devonport and Burnie branches opened, the Executive Committee was considering establishing a fourth branch, at Wynyard, twelve miles west of Burnie. Probably because of the town's smaller size and its proximity to Burnie, the matter was deferred. During January the Committee was still toying with the idea, in particular considering whether it should establish a full branch or just an agency of the neighbouring Burnie branch, but again no decision was reached. Eventually, however, on 26 February 1920 the Devonport manager was deputed to make arrangements for a branch at Wynyard, almost certainly in response to information received that the Hobart Savings Bank had plans for that town. Both banks were playing it secretly, but now each knew of the other's intentions the Hobart Savings Bank came into the open in an attempt to forestall its competitor. At 1 p.m. on Saturday, 28 February Weedon received a telegram from the Hobart Savings Bank:

> Cannot understand your action opening Wynyard. We have purchased premises & are opening Monday. Your action likely to make trouble for both Institutions. Cannot something be done.

A special meeting was convened two hours later and the Executive Committee not surprisingly took a firm stand. Weedon replied:

> Telegram received re Wynyard, my Board have made all arrangements to open there, and other Tasmanian centres, too late to alter position now, writing.

The Bank for Savings was learning the competitive game fast; there were no plans at the time to open in other Tasmanian centres. The Devonport manager opened the Wynyard branch on Monday, 1 March, the same day as the Hobart Savings Bank branch opened, and shortly afterwards recruited an officer from the Commercial Bank of Australia as permanent manager.*

Having fully committed itself to branch banking the Executive Committee now turned its attention to the other area in the north with obvious potential—the Scottsdale district. This time there is no evidence that the Committee was prompted by fear of competition from the Hobart Savings Bank. On the other hand it has been suggested that the Scottsdale branch was largely instigated by Albert Biggs, a local businessman and son of the Bank's former ledger-keeper. The Minutes throw no light on the exact circumstances, only that the decision to establish a branch at Scottsdale was made on 30 March 1920, and that one month later it opened in premises rented from Biggs, with Biggs as the manager.

The early record of the Bank for Savings' branches was very satisfactory. No major establishment problems appear to have been encountered. The five branch managers were well chosen and quickly settled down into their new jobs; already by June 1920 the Executive Committee was confident enough to dispense with the services of the junior clerks at Devonport, Burnie and Ulverstone. Above all, local depositors were recruited at a very pleasing rate, given the competition from the established Commonwealth Savings Bank and, in two centres, also from the Hobart Savings Bank. Part of this success reflects fortunate timing, for with the return of ex-servicemen, rising prices and incomes, and temporarily at least, buoyant economic conditions, savings-bank business was booming generally; in the two years from February 1919 to February 1921 the Launceston Bank for Savings' total deposits rose from a little over £0.75 million to nearly £1 million; deposits at the Hobart Savings Bank rose even more rapidly. These years were particularly notable for the sharp rise in the volume of transactions, much greater even than the rise in deposits. It would suggest that with the now larger maximum-deposit size many perhaps more affluent people were opening what were at least semi-current accounts. It may be no coincidence that for the first time in some years Weedon was again writing letters to people whose accounts he considered over-active.

Branch banking quickly became accepted as part of the Bank's business. Already by 1922 the Bank had a well-developed system for their effective

* During March 1920 the Hobart Savings Bank also opened a branch at Queenstown, which aroused little opposition since this was not regarded as northern territory. More surprisingly, in the previous month it had opened a branch at Deloraine, without much reaction from the Launceston Bank for Savings. Possibly the Bank considered its rival's Deloraine branch would not be successful because the area it served was too scattered and because it was too close to Launceston itself.

operation involving regular inspection, the submission of half-yearly branch reports, and relieving managers. Shortly afterwards it made the first moves to establish permanent quarters at the various centres, although in this it tended to lag behind the Hobart Savings Bank. In April 1922 a building sub-committee was formally established to handle the construction of branch buildings as well as alterations to the Head Office in Launceston. It immediately made plans for Devonport, acquired land, called for tenders and saw the completion of its first permanent branch building there in 1923, at a cost of more than £5,000. In that year it also started construction work on land already acquired at Ulverstone; this second new branch building opened in 1924 at a cost of nearly £7,000.

Following the initial success of its first branches the Launceston Bank for Savings established two more branches in the early 1920s. Perhaps still apprehensive about potential competition from the Hobart Savings Bank the Executive Committee in March 1921 investigated the possibilities at Smithton in the far north-west. Although not a large town compared with others where branches were established, Smithton was the centre of quite a large agricultural district and could also expect to gain some business from the port of Stanley; the municipality of Circular Head, which included both towns, then had a population of more than 5,000. In May 1921 the Bank for Savings opened a branch at Smithton, with the Wynyard manager transferred to manage it. Meanwhile, Keith Westbrook was dispatched from Launceston to manage Wynyard. This was the first of many, and not always welcome, transfers of personnel from Head Office to the branches.

The other new branch was at St Marys in the South Esk valley. In some respects this was the least promising centre for a branch to that date. The population of the district was very scattered, numbered little more than 3,000 and was largely composed of miners from the various collieries, whose political leanings made them more than unusually loyal supporters of the government bank. Weedon and Ferrall visited St Marys in May 1923 and although their report was by no means favourable, in September 1923 the Executive Committee felt confident enough to go ahead. The St Marys branch opened in February 1924 with another officer transferred from Head Office as its first manager.

CHAPTER ELEVEN

'Poverty and Hard Times'
The Inter-war Years

Tasmania's economic troubles of the 1920s

For Tasmania, as for the rest of Australia, the end of World War I brought difficult times, with widespread strikes, serious shipping and other shortages, rapid inflation and the problem of soldier resettlement. Yet for a while they were fairly prosperous times as state and federal governments spent freely, and as a world-wide re-stocking boom brought rich returns to local producers. Tasmanian overseas exports, which in 1918–19 were already double their pre-war level, doubled again in 1919–20 to exceed £2 million. With the returned soldiers came migrants from overseas, the first in nearly two decades. But the boom was short-lived, for in 1921 world commodity markets collapsed. On the mainland this caused only a temporary set-back; rapid manufacturing development and heavy public-works expenditure brought a quick return to prosperity. For Tasmania, however, 1921 marked the beginning of another major period of depression.

The most pressing problem was the lack of profitable outlets for farm produce. Earlier good returns had induced a large expansion of Tasmanian orchards, but now neither Britain nor the mainland would take Tasmanian apples at a paying price. Apple growing was not the kind of process which could be reversed when times were less favourable; growers waited helplessly and in increasing poverty for apple prices to increase. In any event, there was little to which they could have turned, since most other commercial crops were in similar difficulties. Dairying alone among small-scale farming activities remained reasonably rewarding. Some farmers were able to switch to dairying, but many, like the apple-growers, sank into an impoverished, semi-subsistence existence. Wool growing, the most rewarding rural activity of the early 1920s, was impracticable for the small farmer and remained, as before, the preserve of the large estates.

More important in the long run was the decline of Tasmanian mining, for decades the mainstay of the Tasmanian economy. Not since the opening of the Mount Lyell field had any major finds been recorded, and existing fields were approaching exhaustion. Already the famous 'Tasmania' gold mine at Beaconsfield had closed. Mount Lyell seemed on the verge of closure in the early 1920s and Mount Bischoff was now a minor producer. By the following year mining provided employment for only about 2,500 men, compared with 7,000 at the start of the century; and most of these 2,500, working in tributing parties at the larger mines, or in small groups, or alone at the old alluvial fields, were barely making enough to buy food for themselves.

Adding to the problems of an impoverished farm community and an exhausted mining industry was a sharp decline in Tasmania's tourist trade in the early 1920s, disrupted first by the war, then hampered by inflated shipping costs. One authoritative report claimed a drop of thirty per cent in the number of tourists who came to Tasmania in the first half of the 1920s, compared with before the war.

First evident in 1921, the slump had already reached serious proportions by the following year. On 22 July 1922 the *Launceston Examiner* reported heavy demands on the local soup kitchen, particularly from returned soldiers and their families. For that year Tasmania recorded far more departures than arrivals, and the exodus to the mainland continued; in 1926 Tasmania lost on balance some 6,000 people. The population then was less than it had been five years earlier. Yet in spite of the drain to the mainland, unemployment mounted, and in 1926 reached fourteen per cent.

In October 1923 a new government was formed in Tasmania by the Labor Party, headed by the forceful Joseph Lyons, later Prime Minister of Australia. With a boundless faith in state intervention, Lyons and his colleagues made herculean efforts to bring prosperity back to Tasmania. Barely a month after the government was formed, a lengthy and carefully documented claim for special financial consideration was submitted to the federal government. This was the first of many such submissions, culminating in 1925 with the report of a specially appointed committee of important politicians and economists, including the later highly eminent J. B. Brigden and L. F. Giblin; Roland Wilson was the committee's secretary. Tasmania's case was strong, but it had to be admitted, nevertheless, that the state gave less than it received from the federal government, and little relief came from that direction. Meanwhile Lyons was pushing through a spate of self-help legislation. At the end of 1923 the State Development Board was established and in the next three years Bills were introduced to encourage the establishment of a pulp and paper industry, fish canning, rubber manufacturing, even wallaby and opossum fur farming, but with few results.

Two great hopes for recovery lay in the exploitation of Tasmania's vast forest resources for pulp and paper, and in the development of extensive shale-oil deposits in the Latrobe-Railton region to supply a booming demand for petroleum products. By 1923 it had been established that hardwoods were technically and economically feasible as raw material for the manufacture of paper. In that year a scheme for a paper factory at Burnie was propounded by mainland mining interests, but the plan fell through despite government encouragement. Later another group of promoters established a small pilot plant at Geeveston in southern Tasmania; it never developed beyond that stage. In the north several independent attempts were made to exploit the shale-oil deposits, again with every encouragement from the state government, and the offer of a bounty from the federal government, but these also were unsuccessful. Their history resembles closely that of attempts to develop the Tamar iron-ore deposits half a century before. Three major companies, two based in Victoria, all managed to produce oil products for a time, but in the end technical problems and high costs of production proved too great. Large sums of money were lost, and efforts were finally abandoned in the 1930s.

The only major success of the 1920s was the establishment and development of new large-scale manufacturing industry in Tasmania's two 'capitals', encouraged by the promise of cheap hydro-electric power. In 1916 the government had opened its first Great Lake hydro-electric plant. Shortly afterwards a Melbourne company established a calcium carbide works near Hobart, and the Electrolytic Zinc Company its zinc refinery at Risdon, north-east of Hobart across the Derwent; by the middle of the 1920s Risdon was producing refined zinc worth over £1.5 million each year. The Hobart industrial complex had received a further boost with the construction of a large factory in 1921 by the British company, Cadbury. At Launceston the early 1920s saw the establishment of two big woollen-textile factories also for British companies: in 1923 Kelsall and Kemp opened their Invermay factory, producing mainly flannels; and in the following year Patons and Baldwins opened their Glen Dhu plant to manufacture knitting wools. Reputed to have 'the finest installation one could find in the world', Patons and Baldwins employed over 1,000 workers by 1928 and were then exporting extensively to all parts of Australia. During the 1920s Launceston also formally became the railway-engineering centre of Tasmania. These several developments meant that Hobart and Launceston were relatively lightly hit by the depression of the 1920s compared with the rest of Tasmania, and between them they accounted for by far the greater part of Tasmania's population growth during the decade.

At the half-yearly general meeting of the Launceston Bank for Savings in September 1926 the chairman of the Executive Committee, Walter

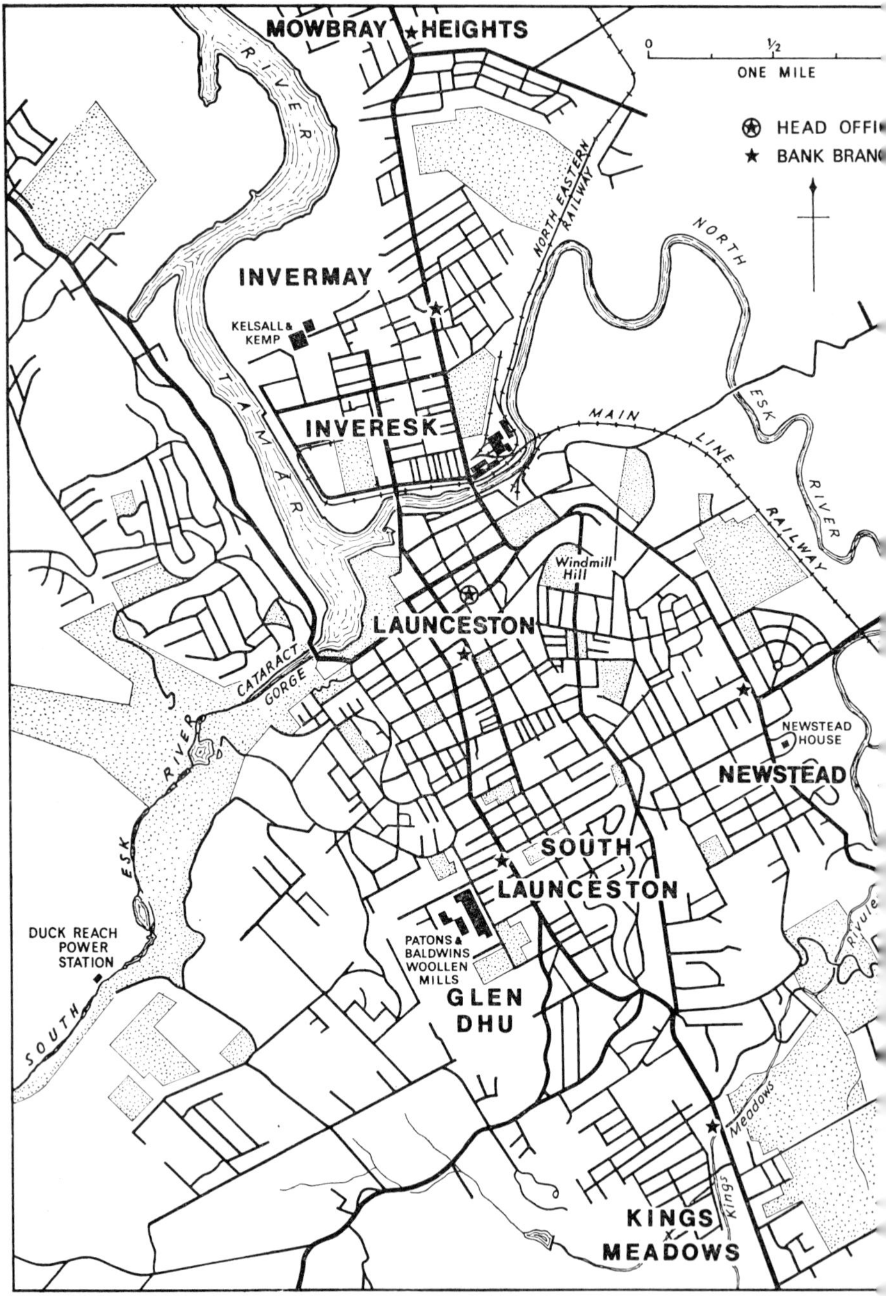

Launceston and suburbs

Henry Ferrall, predicted a much brighter economic future for Tasmania. His prediction was broadly fulfilled, though revival was neither very strong nor lasting. During 1927 and 1928 the agricultural situation improved, particularly for the apple-growers who, obtaining better prices, exported extensively and at a profit both to Britain and the mainland of Australia. By then the booming manufacturing industries of Hobart and Launceston were bringing certain secondary and indirect benefits to the rest of the island. There was also a notable revival in the tourist trade, the result of lower fares and a concerted effort by Tasmania's various tourist organizations who, for once combining their energies, conducted a major 'Come to Tasmania' campaign aimed particularly at potential off-season visitors. Again perhaps the ratio of arrivals to departures provides the best guide to general recovery; the record departure level of some 6,000 people in 1926 dropped sharply to only 2,000 in 1927 and 1928, and in 1929 arrivals matched departures.

General economic recovery and its own relatively successful record in the second half of the 1920s brought a new wave of civic pride to Launceston, involving not a little competition with Hobart which, including its suburbs, was still about twice the size of Launceston. In these years a 50,000 League was established, named after the population level which was its goal; it may not be coincidental that the population of Hobart was currently about 50,000. Under the auspices of the League, J. S. Gill brought out a glossy volume entitled *Launceston. The Northern Capital of Tasmania and Why*, which taken at face value must have left readers wondering why Launceston was not the capital of all Tasmania. To some extent deeds accompanied words and ambitions. Launceston apparently out-did Hobart in the lavishness of its preparations for the visit by the Duke and Duchess of York in April 1927. It had the pleasure in July of the same year of seeing a local girl crowned Miss Australia. And barely two months later, at a cost of some £5,000, Launceston's Queen Victoria Museum filched the celebrated Beattie collection of Tasmaniana from under the nose of Hobart's Tasmania Museum.

The Bank's performance 1919–1929

In broad terms, the fortunes of the Launceston Bank for Savings reflected those of the area it served, now virtually the whole of the northern Tasmania. Boosted by the post-war re-stocking boom, and the existence of branches in the north-west and north-east, for a while deposits in the Bank rose at a more rapid rate than at any time since the gold rushes of the 1850s. In its accounts for the six months ending August 1921 the Executive Committee could proudly display total deposits for the first time exceeding £1 million. The £0.25 million received since the war ended had been invested mainly in Local Inscribed Stock of the Tasmanian government and Commonwealth Loans, including the large Peace Loan of 1919. Mortgage loans rose only slightly and fixed deposits actually fell. Holdings of cash by 1921 had more than doubled to nearly thirteen per cent of depositors—a clear indication that the rise in deposits was so rapid that the rate of investment could not keep pace.

Over the next four years deposits in the Bank for Savings rose far more slowly. Despite a large rise in the number of depositors from 28,000 to 35,000, which reflected energetic recruiting by the various branches, and despite an increased rate of return to depositors from four per cent to four and a half per cent by 1923, the total value of deposits rose by little more than £150,000. That is, only a fifteen per cent increase for the four years.

In explaining its relatively poor performance from 1921, the Bank rather curiously emphasized investments offering to potential depositors. In 1921 it blamed the alternative attraction of Local Inscribed Stock, in 1922 a large issue of Launceston City Council debentures, and in 1925 a major Commonwealth Loan. Clearly, however, the basic explanation lay in the generally depressed conditions, which meant that many accounts were run down and many fewer than before were added to. Another important, though incalculable factor was the drain of population to the mainland. As in earlier years many of those who fled were the more enterprising, with more funds, a large part of which had been held in the Bank for Savings and was now withdrawn. Typical was the Ulverstone depositor with a fat account at the local branch, who moved to Melbourne late in 1921 taking most of his savings with him. Finding even this insufficient, he wrote from Melbourne to the Ulverstone branch manager on 2 January 1922: 'Money flies here faster than an aeroplane!—In consequence I must draw the balance of my credit with you, and close the account for the present.' The Bank's branch correspondence and Head Office letter-books record many similar instances. From the early 1920s the Launceston Bank for Savings also faced increased competition from the Commonwealth Savings Bank, now with full branches at Burnie and Devonport, as well as Launceston.

From August 1925 to August 1929 the Bank for Savings overall fared much better, and much better than might have been expected in view of the mildness and brevity of the general economic recovery. As before, the number of depositors increased largely, from 35,000 to 42,000, but the value of deposits increased even more rapidly. Total deposits over these years rose by nearly forty per cent, to more than £1.6 million by August 1929. To some extent the explanation for this rapid increase may lie in the boom conditions which prevailed in Launceston itself, which still supplied most of the Bank's business. Perhaps, also, the branches were improving their performance as they became more established, a question considered later at greater length.

The large additional funds of the late 1920s were invested mainly in state and federal government stock, according to the Bank's now established practice, but there were also significant increases in other forms of investment. Local municipal council loans, though still very small, nearly doubled in size, and from 1927 when the Bank lent to the municipality of Emu Bay, councils other than Launceston shared in the Bank's investments, a change which reflects the Bank's widened geographic interest. Over the same period fixed deposits held also showed a large rise, a result mainly of the narrowing differential between rates of interest on fixed deposits and on government stock, but perhaps also a reflection of greater awareness on the part of the Bank of the need for friendly relations with the commercial banks at a local level. Again in this period the Bank broke new ground by holding many of its fixed deposits at branches of commercial banks where the Bank for Savings also had branches. Finally, there was also a rise in mortgage loans. Although not spectacular, it was notable as the first major increase in mortgage loans since 1910. From 1927 to 1929 mortgage lending was particularly active, mainly as before on large landed estates, although these were now located chiefly in the north-west and north-east, rather than on the northern plains. Similarly, urban borrowers now included a much higher proportion in towns other than Launceston. In both respects, again the changes largely reflect the Bank's widened sphere of activity brought about by branch banking.

The 1930s depression

In the closing months of 1929 Tasmania's brief period of recovery and mild prosperity came to a rapid end. The cause was simple but devastating —the whole western world was heading towards the greatest slump it had ever known. Directly, through the collapse of overseas markets which Tasmania supplied, and indirectly, through the collapse of its markets on the Australian mainland, the island's economy was once again undermined. On the whole, Tasmania probably suffered less than the mainland. It escaped the collapse of an overseas-financed investment boom, since there had not been much investment in Tasmania in the 1920s. Also its exporters were not so hard hit as those elsewhere in Australia, since they exported chiefly to the mainland rather than overseas, and while mainland prices and markets slumped, the fall was less than in overseas markets. Nevertheless, Tasmania was hard hit, and it was little consolation that neighbouring states were harder hit.

For Launceston the depression was a particularly severe blow, since only months before it began the city had been shattered by the most severe flood on record. Early in April 1929 torrential rains had turned the South Esk and its tributaries into raging flood-waters. Devastating much of the northern plains, they converged to pour madly down the Cataract Gorge, destroy the power-station and burst out into Launceston's harbour to overwhelm the low-lying suburbs of Inveresk and Invermay. About a thousand houses were destroyed or damaged and the commerce of the whole city was disrupted by extensive damage to the wharves. One of the many casualties was the factory of the Rapson Tyre Company, which had made a shaky start in the manufacture of rubber tyres the year before. The company may have failed, anyway, but its fate was certainly sealed by the flood damage, and was a serious blow to the city.

Already shaken by the flood disasters, Launceston was particularly vulnerable to the world slump and during 1930 depression became clearly evident in the city. Almost exactly one year after the flood the first of many mass meetings of unemployed was held. Shortly afterwards a special delegation to the city council pressed for an additional rate to finance public relief works. Although for a time in the second half of 1930 the construction of a new road to the Cliff Grounds in the Gorge provided employment, the city council was virtually powerless. So, too, was the Tasmanian government which lacked the means to assist Launceston or any other part of the island. As the world depression deepened, poverty and unemployment increased and by 1932 many people were being evicted from their homes. One of the first of numerous much-publicized evictions occurred in January 1932 when the evicted tenant, a Communist, led a solemn procession of one thousand supporters to the Launceston Town Hall. There, piling pieces of his furniture in front of the noble edifice, they held an impressive demonstration. Wisely, the police stood quietly on the sidelines.

Within Tasmania the degree of depression varied considerably from region to region, something characteristic of most depressions, but one usually neglected for the overall view. The half-yearly reports of the Bank for Savings' branch managers provide a clear, continuing and sometimes vivid account of how the depression affected various parts of the north. While a gloomy tone predominated, one is struck by the very considerable differences in the fortunes of different areas. Whereas, for example, St Marys suffered immense hardships, with a severe slump in coal mining, and coal miners worked only two to three days a week, Scottsdale to the north, with a reviving tin-mining industry and sound dairy industry catering for local demands, was relatively unscathed. On the north-west coast the developing centre of Smithton in the far west, and at the eastern end, Devonport, with major sewerage works in progress and an expanding export trade in peas and beans, appear to have escaped relatively lightly. On the other hand, Ulverstone, Burnie and Wynyard suffered greatly from the collapse of the mainland potato and overseas butter markets. As late as February 1934 the Burnie branch manager could quote in his half-yearly report the comments of the Van Diemen's Land Company:

> the position of the North West Coast farmers could hardly be worse. Four successive seasons have proved so unprofitable to the average farmer that the majority have for some time been living on such capital as they imagined they possessed . . . The low price of 6½d paid by the dairy companies for butter fat is merely a starvation price. The position of the coastal farmer is so appalling that it can hardly be exaggerated.

The year 1932 undoubtedly marked the low point of the depression for Tasmania, as for the rest of Australia. In that year Tasmania registered both its lowest birth rate and its highest unemployment rate on record; on average during 1932 more than one in four registered trade unionists were on the dole. From the latter part of 1932 there were clear signs of improvement, but for at least two more years the rate of revival was agonizingly slow; the branch managers' reports amply bear out this point. As late as July 1935 a Rotary Club investigation could still reveal with dismay that a startlingly large number of 'half-starved, half-naked children' were attending Launceston schools. But by then, at last, recovery was gathering pace. World markets and internal Australian markets were showing marked advances, and Tasmania's vital export trades once more were beginning to prosper and expand. These improvements in turn induced in the latter part of the 1930s a major boom in the building trades, long held back by adverse conditions, but now encouraged by general recovery and low interest rates.

Tasmania's export sector acquired two notable additions in the 1930s. One was the development of an export trade to Britain in frozen lamb. Initially attempted from Hobart in 1931 and conducted there spasmodically for some years, it received a great boost from the opening of large freezing works at Somerset on the north-west coast in 1938. Second, and more important was the establishment of the long-hoped-for pulp and paper industry at Burnie. For years the pulp and paper 'ghost' mill had earned the derision of all but Burnie optimists. Weedon is reported to have dismissed it scornfully in the late 1920s with the comment 'Pulp be damned! Burnie will bust.' His successor, John Duncan, was equally scathing, commenting in 1933 that 'Unfortunately the people at Burnie will not realise that the world of imagination in which they lived for so long has vanished'. The ever-optimistic residents of Burnie had the last laugh when in 1936 the Broken Hill mining group launched the Australian Pulp and Paper Mills Company. Announcing the detailed plans on 9 April 1936, the *Launceston Examiner* predicted that some 600 to 800 men would be employed in the construction of the plant. When the factory eventually opened in 1938 A.P.P.M. had a direct payroll of 250 employees, and many hundreds of others were employed in the cutting and carrying of timber, its raw material. By the outbreak of World War II, Burnie, with A.P.P.M. shipping its products to every part of Australia, was the boom town of a state where boom conditions generally prevailed.

The Bank in depression and recovery

During the 1930s depression the Launceston Bank for Savings experienced the first significant fall in its deposits for seventy years. Between August 1929 and February 1932 total deposits fell by some thirteen per cent. In highly depressed conditions, a fall in deposits was hardly surprising; the same thing happened in savings banks throughout Australia, and indeed the world generally. Within Tasmania both other savings institutions saw their deposits decline, the Commonwealth Savings Bank's by a somewhat greater amount, the Hobart Savings Bank's somewhat less than those of the Launceston Bank for Savings.

The more surprising fact, perhaps, is that deposits did not fall more or over a longer period. The 'rainy day' withdrawal was still a fundamental tenet of savings-bank philosophy, and many accounts, one may suppose, were intended for use in emergencies. Given the severity of the depression, a drop of thirteen per cent in deposits was perhaps less than might have been expected. There is no simple explanation, as there is for the 1890s when a new class of depositors switched funds on a large scale to a safer form of investment; evidence for this in the 1930s is very slight.* To some extent in the 1930s, as at all times, there was an inbuilt upward bias in the trend in deposits, created by idle, semi-dormant or wholly dormant accounts which simply continued to accumulate compound interest, and by the continuing growth of population which resulted in a modest but definite rise in the number of the Bank's depositors from 42,000 to 44,000 over these two and a half years. More fundamentally, however, the relatively good performance of the Bank in the 1930s probably reflects two other factors: the nature of the depression, and the nature of the Bank's depositors.

While unemployment was undoubtedly high and the unemployed suffered severely, those who remained in employment were, because general prices fell more than their salaries or wages, clearly better off than before. For savings banks this meant that heavy withdrawals by the unemployed were in large part offset by increasing deposits from those fortunate enough to remain employed. It also meant that the 'net withdrawal' phase was

* As in the early 1920s, the Bank's half-yearly reports are comparatively unenlightening about the trends in its deposit business.

relatively short; whereas the accounts of the unemployed were quickly exhausted, accounts of those in work continued to build up over a longer period. The actual trend in deposits of the Launceston Bank for Savings strongly supports this interpretation, with a rapid reduction in the first eighteen months, then a much slower decline over the next twelve months to the low point of the depression, from which time deposits again began to rise strongly.

With respect to the nature of depositors, it is clear that by the 1930s the Bank for Savings held a large proportion of accounts, and a much larger proportion of total deposits, which were not true 'rainy day' savings. These were the investments of retired or otherwise non-employed people unaffected by the depression, or the investments of wealthier people who were comparatively unaffected, or who had no need to draw on their savings accounts since these were probably one of many investments, in the 1930s depression undoubtedly the safest and last to be touched.

Despite these compensating factors, there is no lack of evidence of the adverse effects of the depression on depositors—of the forced withdrawals, the inability to open new accounts or to add to existing accounts. The Bank's branch correspondence particularly provides innumerable examples. Among the more graphic stories was that of a potato-farmer's wife at Moorleah, near Wynyard. Having struggled to build up her family account to nearly £50 before the depression, she had run it down to only five shillings and twopence by the end of 1931. It remained at that level until she heard of the impending transfer to Head Office of the Wynyard manager, C. Henri, in August 1933. She then wrote to him:

> I hear you are going away & am very sorry to here same I would like you to just drop me a line to let me know if there is any money left in [my husband's] account or mine as times have been to bad to bank of late & also Mr Henri if you or Mrs Henri had any things that is no more use to you there are some very poor people up hear you could leave them with the Don store they would bring them up for me & I wont forget you after you get to town.

Added in the margin was the promise 'I will send you some potatoes.' Mr Henri must have informed her that there was still five shillings and twopence to her name, since by the end of the month the account had been reduced to the minimum allowable of one shilling. In the same month that the Moorleah farmer's wife was 'negotiating' with the Wynyard manager, an equally distressed woman depositor near Smithton was writing humbly and apologetically to her own manager:

> I am most exceedingly sorry to know I have been unable to carry out my promise to you when I started that Banking account, I promised you that I would try and put a pound in by the end of the year, but to tell you the real

trouth, poverty and hard times, I realy cant get anything to put in as my income is only £2/10 shillings a year, and that is getting desidelly less a year, and my husband only gets about 1 pound a week and sometimes not that, thank God better times are coming I hope dear Sir I am sending you the book in again for you to draw that poor little amount and send it to me, when it is most convenient for you to do so

Undoubtedly the most poignant story, if in retrospect slightly amusing, was that of the depositor who, presumably having exhausted his account and sold off whatever possessions he could afford to lose, early in 1932 sent to the Burnie manager his dental plates which contained a considerable amount of gold, suggesting they might be melted down at the Mint. The Burnie manager rather hastily sent them on to Head Office where Weedon found that an assay would cost sixteen shillings, commented sarcastically about 'this so-called bullion', and sent the plates back to Burnie. The Burnie manager sold them locally for £3 15s 0. Whether they were melted down, or used by some other person is not recorded.

While officers of the Bank for Savings were undoubtedly much distressed by the plight of their depositors and showed much understanding and sympathy, the fall in deposits as such posed no serious problems to the Bank's finances. Whether by chance or by design, the Bank was in an extremely liquid position at the onset of the depression; the August 1929 accounts showed a record £232,000 held in cash, and almost that amount in fixed deposits, against which the Bank could draw if necessary. Only after eighteen months of heavy withdrawals, by which time most of the Bank's cash was exhausted, did the Executive Committee show any concern. In February 1931 it finally decided to introduce its own system of fixed deposits, as the Hobart Savings Bank had done some years earlier. On these twelve-month deposits the Bank for Savings paid five per cent, half a per cent more than on ordinary accounts. Later in May of the same year the Bank formally confirmed with the commercial banks that, if necessary, overdrafts would be allowed against the fixed deposits which it held. In the event, neither precaution was needed. No overdrafts were arranged, and less than two months after its own fixed-deposit system had been set up, Weedon was informing branch managers that at present the Bank was not anxious to accept such deposits. By then the fall in ordinary deposits had almost petered out, although to restore the Bank's liquidity the Executive Committee reduced its investments as the opportunity arose. Some holdings of government and municipal stock and, to a lesser extent, fixed deposits in commercial banks, were realized to restore cash in hand to a comfortable level.

During the 1930s depression the Executive Committee seemed much less worried by the fall in deposits than it was by the activities of the federal government. One major point of conflict had first arisen at the end of 1928 when the federal government attempted to subject the Bank's earnings to federal income tax. Since government savings banks were exempt from the tax, the Bank for Savings naturally reacted strongly, initially refused to pay, then, with the Hobart Savings Bank, took the matter to court. Proceedings extended into 1930 when, to the chagrin of the banks, the decision went against them. The Launceston Bank for Savings harboured its grievance for a long time, repeatedly condemning the unjust tax at its half-yearly general meetings. As late as March 1932, for example, the chairman's prepared speech referred to the federal government's 'iniquitous demands' and to 'opportunism and injustice', although these phrases were omitted when the speech was actually delivered at the half-yearly general meeting. In 1933 the federal government finally bowed before the persistent barrage of criticism and amended the legislation to exempt trustee savings banks from the tax.

In the meantime, another point of friction with the federal government had arisen as a result of the Premiers' Plan, introduced in mid-1931. Fundamental to the Plan was the concept of 'equality of sacrifice' which among other things involved a general reduction of rates of interest, including those on mortgages. On 5 August 1931 the Mortgage Interest Reduction Act forcibly reduced interest on all mortgages by twenty-two and a half per cent. The Act swept aside the basic principle of six months' notice of termination on which the Bank had operated for nearly ninety years, and aroused fierce opposition. Speaking at the half-yearly general meeting in September 1931 John Duncan, then chairman, could hardly contain his anger:

> However ingenious and plausible the statements may be as to the causes assigned for our financial troubles, the fact remains that had our Parliament and Government, both past and present, possessed a proper outlook and control of affairs, instead of blind optimism and incompetence Australia's position would not have been discredited as it is today.
>
> Contracts hitherto looked upon as inviolable have been broken by Parliament and default, hitherto looked upon as the most serious thing, not only advocated but given effect to.

Perhaps the most serious problem the Bank for Savings encountered in the 1930s was in the early stages of recovery, when deposit business was reviving rapidly but there was virtually no outlet for investment. At the time government borrowing was negligible, the demands from private borrowers very small, and rate of return on commercial-bank fixed deposits too low to be profitable. Other forms of investment were precluded by the Trustee Act under which the Bank for Savings operated. Even before the end of 1932 the problem was becoming evident; in July of that year branch managers had been informed that the Bank was not anxious to take fixed deposits and were given specific instructions to remove all display placards about this facility. As deposits continued to mount, the lack of investment outlets caused increasing embarrassment; by August 1933 cash in hand exceeded £200,000, and by 1935 the Bank had nearly £300,000 idle. The only significant outlet for investment to that time was in local municipal stock, but that was still very small. Financial institutions in general had similar problems, and it is an indication of this that interest rates at the time were very low. From 1933, for example, the Tasmanian trustee savings banks paid only two and three-quarter per cent to depositors, the lowest rate then on record and a striking contrast to the four and a half per cent they had paid in the 1920s.

From 1935 the problem receded as recovery gathered pace and both public and private borrowing resumed on a large scale. Central government borrowing* increased markedly to 1939, but the Bank was less interested now in this form of investment than it had been from 1910 to the 1930s depression. By 1939 holdings of government stock had declined to around forty-five per cent of all income-paying assets of the Bank, compared with nearly sixty per cent ten years earlier. All other forms of investment by the Bank increased strongly in the late 1930s. Fixed deposits more than doubled, though much of this was in effect a substitute for cash as such; over the same period actual cash on hand was cut back to less than £100,000, or less than five per cent of deposits. Holdings of municipal stock rose very rapidly, although in absolute terms they remained the smallest of the Bank's paying assets. Mortgage loans also showed a marked expansion.

The revival of mortgage lending in the late 1930s, though hardly spectacular, has particular significance both as the first major revival of this type of lending since the 1900s, and because borrowers were now of a very different type. These years saw the real beginnings of the small-scale lending for house-building or buying which was to become one of the most important departments of the Bank's business in the post-war period. Samples of loans made in the late 1930s show that the overwhelming majority of borrowers were house-builders or buyers, and probably most of the funds lent out went to such people; one cannot be completely sure on the latter point because there was still a fair number of large loans on landed estates. With the rise of housing loans, terms of repayment became more formalized. Previously the Bank had only specified the minimum instalment repayment a borrower might make if he wished. Now it required a repayment of four per cent of the principal annually—an

* In 1929 the federal government had, through the mechanism of the Loan Council, formally taken over all state debts and subsequent loan-raising.

easy rate of repayment which in effect gave a housing loan twenty-five years' duration.

The Bank's achievement 1919–1939

In an overall evaluation of the Launceston Bank for Savings during the inter-war years it is apparent that by the most basic criterion of total deposits the Bank was highly successful. And in explaining its success, clearly the critical factor was the new and fundamentally different system of branch banking adopted in 1919. Directly, the branches of the Bank for Savings accounted for almost half of the increase in deposits over the twenty years. Indirectly they boosted the Bank's deposit record by making intra-state transfers easy and by arranging profitable mortgage and municipal loans in their own areas. Furthermore, as the size of the Bank's business increased, largely because of the branches, it was able to increase efficiency through economies of scale and division of labour. In various ways the branches helped to increase deposits in Launceston, as well as in their own areas.

The institution of branch banking by the Hobart Savings Bank and by the Launceston Bank for Savings was the primary reason for the striking performance of savings banks in Tasmania as compared with Australia as a whole in the inter-war period. There is no evidence that between 1919 and 1939 Tasmania's standard of living increased relative to that on the mainland; if anything, taking account particularly of the very depressed years of the 1920s, Tasmania may have fallen behind. Yet, whereas in 1919 Tasmania was well behind Australia as a whole in savings banking, with only £17 of savings deposits per head of population, compared with £25 for all Australia, by 1939 the difference had been completely eliminated; then, both in Tasmania and Australia as a whole, savings-bank deposits per head of population averaged some £35, and among the different states only Victoria and South Australia had a higher average than Tasmania.

Even more obviously, branch banking was the primary factor in the highly successful performance of the Hobart Savings Bank and Launceston Bank for Savings within Tasmania, as compared with the Commonwealth Savings Bank. Once the two trustee savings banks had decided to establish branches, the relative decline of the Commonwealth Savings Bank was almost a foregone conclusion. In the centres where the trustee savings banks competed with the Commonwealth Savings Bank the latter had only one competitive advantage, a higher maximum deposit—from 1920 some £1,300 as against £300 for the other two banks. Since the £300 maximum was frequently circumvented, however, it was not a great advantage. On the other hand the Commonwealth Savings Bank had two serious disadvantages. Firstly, in all but four centres, Hobart, Launceston, Burnie and Devonport, it was a mere adjunct of the post offices and could not provide the same high standard of service to customers as the specialist full-time branches. Secondly, through almost the whole period it paid a lower rate of interest to depositors than the trustee savings banks. During the 1920s its rate of interest, at three and a half per cent, was one per cent below that paid by the trustee banks. The difference narrowed in the depression and briefly in 1932 was eliminated altogether, but reappeared shortly afterwards and by 1937 the rate paid by the Commonwealth Savings Bank was again one per cent below that of the Hobart Savings Bank and Launceston Bank for Savings. Given these major disadvantages it is not surprising that the Commonwealth Savings Bank lost ground. Whereas in 1919 it was the largest of the three banks, with about forty per cent of all savings-bank deposits in Tasmania, in 1939 it was the smallest of the three, with its share reduced to only about twenty-five per cent.

Perhaps the most interesting aspect of the inter-war period was the comparative position of the Launceston Bank for Savings and the Hobart Savings Bank. In terms of total deposits their relative position was almost exactly the same in 1939 as in 1919. At both times the Hobart Savings Bank had approximately forty per cent more deposit funds than the Launceston Bank for Savings, and each bank increased its business about two and a half fold in the twenty years. However, when certain allowances are made, the fact that the Launceston Bank for Savings maintained its relative position can be regarded as a considerable achievement. From the start the Hobart Savings Bank was the more ambitious of the two in its branch banking. With branches on the north-west coast, at Deloraine, at the west-coast mining centres, as well as in southern Tasmania, the Hobart Savings Bank became active in a far greater area than the Launceston Bank for Savings, which operated only in northern Tasmania, excluding the west coast. Again, because it was the larger of the two banks, in principle the Hobart Savings Bank should have been the more efficient and effective in accumulating deposits. Further, since three of the Commonwealth Savings Bank's four full branches were located in northern Tasmania, the Launceston Bank for Savings could justifiably claim to have faced stronger competition from that source than its southern rival. Above all, in marked contrast with the previously long-established pattern, southern Tasmania in the inter-war period was growing more rapidly than northern Tasmania. Most of the population increase between the wars occurred in what was essentially southern territory where the only competition for the Hobart Savings Bank came from the Commonwealth Savings Bank.

Against these competitive disadvantages the Launceston Bank for Savings had only one possible advantage. In the north, which still accounted for most of Tasmania's population, local sentiment generally favoured it. Just how significant this may have been is impossible to calculate, but certainly it would be easy to overrate. In the one area where the banks openly competed, in the north-west, ties with Launceston were much less strong than in, say, Deloraine or Scottsdale. For many years the region had been developing its own identity, was proud of its growth and achievements, and neither socially nor economically was it a satellite area of Launceston. If residents of the north-west had a preference for Launceston over Hobart it can not have been a very strong one.

In the context of the Launceston Bank for Savings' ability to hold its own, despite considerable disadvantages, it is interesting that in July 1936 the Hobart Savings Bank proposed amalgamation. The Bank for Savings' Executive Committee had no objection to at least discussing the matter. It invited representatives from Hobart to Launceston, and planned to entertain them well with a lavish dinner at the Brisbane Hotel, until it had second thoughts because of the suspicions and speculation that might result. Talks were held in private, terms were discussed, and the Hobart delegation left the Launceston Bank for Savings still considering the matter. Probably the Executive Committee never had any serious intention of amalgamation, since few advantages would accrue to the northern institution. It was holding its own well enough, and amalgamation, given the relative size of the two institutions, really meant a take-over by the Hobart Savings Bank. The Bank for Savings eventually replied rejecting the scheme. In justifying its decision it diplomatically avoided potentially offensive points, putting emphasis on a desire to retain its own identity, adding almost apologetically that it was largely a question of sentiment. No doubt there was truth in the claim, but it was certainly not the whole explanation. Much more basic was the fact that the Launceston Bank for Savings was competing successfully, and getting along extremely well on its own. The explanation for its success requires a closer examination of the Bank itself in these years, its leaders and personnel, its policies and practices.

CHAPTER TWELVE

'Zeal, Activity and Diligence'
A Competitive Bank

The leaders

Although conditions were radically different after World War I, the organization of the Launceston Bank for Savings remained essentially as it had evolved in the nineteenth century. As before, the manager had direct and complete control over his paid staff, now much more numerous and geographically dispersed. On the other hand, all policy and other major decisions, including decisions about individual investments, remained formally in the hands of the unpaid Executive Committee, to which the manager was directly responsible. In turn, the Executive Committee was responsible to the General Committee, the ultimate authority, but one which in fact played a fairly passive role, generally endorsing the decisions of the Executive Committee and serving as a reserve of personnel for replacements on the Executive Committee.*

While the organization remained the same, in practice decision-making in the period became much more concentrated in the hands of a small group of dominant and powerful individuals. Between 1919 and 1939 there were three different managers, each in his own way strong, efficient and influential, not only in the day-to-day administration, but in shaping overall policy. All three managers appear to have acted in close conjunction with one or two key members of the Executive Committee, usually including the chairman, to form the real policy-making body. Generally other members of the Executive Committee seem to have been content to follow the lead of the inner group.

Until July 1932 Hardwicke Weedon continued as manager. Although aged seventy-four when branches were first established in 1919 and eighty-

* Additions to the General Committee, necessary from time to time, were made by the Court of Quarter Sessions on the advice of the Bank. Normally the Court's agreement was a mere formality. Once, however, in 1934, the Court rejected four of the Bank's nominations in favour of four of its own. The reason is not clear, but the action prompted a vigorous move by the Bank to amend the existing legislation.

seven when he finally retired, there was never any suggestion that his advanced years seriously hampered his conduct of affairs. Weedon appears to have taken in his stride the changed conditions of the 1920s with the speed and ease of a much younger man. He continued to exercise a firm and efficient control over a greatly enlarged staff at Head Office, though ably assisted by his second-in-command, Alfred Littler. More significantly, with his experience and administrative ability, he had little trouble in handling the new branch system and all the problems it entailed: in his voluminous correspondence with branch managers Weedon displayed clarity of thought, conciseness, flexibility and simple good sense. At the same time he acted in close liaison with his Executive Committee and clearly played a large part in its decisions. And despite his age and more demanding duties at the Bank, Weedon continued to be active in the public affairs of Launceston, indeed in some respects still more active. In 1922, for example, he was elected to the important position of chairman of the Launceston Hospital Board.

The only suggestion of waning powers or energies came right at the end of his long term of office at the Bank, when in December 1931 he expressed his wish to retire. The Executive Committee accepted his resignation, since, it was recorded: 'Mr Weedon's advanced age was against his undertaking the responsibility connected with any necessary changes [in methods of administration]'. The changes the Executive Committee had in mind had been recommended by the Chief Inspector of the State Savings Bank of Victoria, J. Thornton Jones, who at its request had investigated the Bank's administration earlier in the year. Weedon, it appears, was now just too old to handle the proposed changes. Otherwise his advanced years were betrayed only in occasionally old-fashioned views, or in harmless eccentricities. Born, brought up and having lived for most of his life in an age when a woman's place was in the home, he took a very dim view of the employment of female staff. During the 1920s, for example, the very capable daughter of the Scottsdale branch manager occasionally helped out at the Bank, sometimes taking charge when her father was away. Weedon was most unhappy about such arrangements, insisting that she never be left alone at the branch, though normally justifying his opposition on the rather slender grounds that she was not officially a member of the Bank staff. Similarly, Weedon was most disturbed when the first woman joined the staff at Head Office shortly before his retirement. Most obvious among his eccentric habits was his fetish of going home for lunch at the same time on the same tram, whatever the circumstances. With the increasing pressure of work, he became increasingly unpunctual, although the obliging tram driver would usually wait until the little old man dashed from his office, brushing customers aside to perform his daily ritual.

By the time he reached his late eighties and was still going strong, Weedon had understandably become something of a legend in the city. In November 1930 when the new road to the Cataract Gorge was opened he was singled out as the one person still surviving from the 1890s group which had first begun to develop the facilities of the Gorge; Weedon, of course, was present at the ceremony and made a suitable speech in response to the praise of the younger generation. On his retirement from the Bank in July 1932 he received one of the finest compliments a man could be paid. The *Launceston Examiner* wrote:

> It is safe to say that no Tasmanian citizen, probably none in Australia, has given unbroken service over such long periods as Mr Weedon has done. . . . The biography of Mr Weedon would be a history of Launceston for the last two generations, and there are many who hope that he will occupy some of his leisure hours in setting down some of his reminiscences of the city and its development.

Perhaps true to form, Hardwicke Weedon never had time to write his reminiscences, for he continued to occupy himself with his many beloved causes until his death in 1937.

Until 1930 Weedon had acted in close conjunction with the chairman of the Executive Committee, W. H. Ferrall. Only three years younger than Weedon, Ferrall also displayed great vitality in Bank and other matters. He had had rather an unusual career. In 1868 he established himself as a butcher. The business prospered and some of the proceeds were invested in Mount Bischoff shares which had prospered even more; in 1891, at the age of forty-six, Ferrall simply retired to live on his fortune and devote the rest of his life to public causes which interested him. Initially active in local politics, Ferrall was mayor of Launceston in 1894, but after that turned his attention increasingly to a variety of interests, his church, the Benevolent Society, sporting and agricultural associations, but perhaps above all, in his later years to the Bank for Savings. Initially elected to the Executive Committee in 1913, Ferrall became the chairman in the following year and held the position for sixteen years. With his experience, and with ample time to devote to the affairs of the Bank, Ferrall gave invaluable service to the institution. He remained on the Executive Committee after relinquishing the chair, but died shortly afterwards in 1932.

The other figure who stands out in the 1920s, and indeed for most of the 1930s, is George Harrap, son of Alfred Harrap who had built up a large auctioneering, wool-broking and stock-and-station business in the city. Like Weedon and Ferrall, Harrap had unlimited energy, a wide range of interests, and lived to a great old age. Apart from the family business, of which he was now joint manager, Harrap was active in other business ventures, in the Chamber of Commerce, agricultural and pastoral associations, amateur theatricals, but above all in local military affairs, particularly the Launceston Artillery, in which he achieved the rank of colonel. Harrap would have served in World War I but for bad eyesight; instead he was made head of the local censorship organization.

From 1900 Harrap was a member of the Executive Committee of the Bank for Savings, and from an early date was notable for his strong views and clear creative mind. However, it was not until the 1920s, by which time he was well into his sixties, that he took a continuously active role in the Bank's affairs. In 1923 Harrap became vice-chairman of the Executive Committee. From then he devoted a tremendous amount of time to the institution, and with his powerful intellect became a dominating force. From 1923 until his death in 1937 he served on almost every major subcommittee, on many was clearly the leading figure, and was the sponsor of numerous innovations; it was he, for example, who had the bright idea in 1926 to keep relieving managers at branch banks for a few days longer than necessary, to allow the regular manager to get out among the people and canvass the district. When the Bank decided to supply its branch managers with revolvers for protection, it was Harrap to whom the Executive Committee turned for advice. And when the Executive Committee received the half-yearly reports from the branches, almost invariably it was Harrap who read, criticized and offered suggestions for ways in which the reports could be improved.

When Ferrall retired as chairman of the Executive Committee in 1930, his place was taken by John Duncan, then sixty years of age. By profession a wholesale grocer and produce merchant, Duncan had joined the Committee in 1921, and in the 1920s was active chiefly on the building sub-committee, to which he was able to contribute some expertise from his long-standing interest in architecture; as a teenager Duncan had submitted the prize-winning designs for both Launceston's Queen Victoria Museum and Albert Hall. A tall, upright figure, with a stern countenance, Duncan, on his appointment as chairman, immediately lived up to his appearance with some strong speeches, directed chiefly at the federal government. When Weedon announced his retirement, and it had become clear that ill-health precluded Littler from the position,* Duncan himself applied for the manager's position. The exact circumstances are unknown. Perhaps he preferred modest security to the uncertain returns of a large business now in the throes of severe depression. Or perhaps like Weedon before him, as chairman of the Committee Duncan had become so devoted to the welfare of the institution as such, he wished to further his interest

* Littler died only a few months later in November 1932.

full-time. Duncan was appointed manager in 1932. Although he died just four years later, his brief term of office coincided with a particularly difficult period for the Bank and Duncan had qualities perhaps well-suited to the times. His stern and highly economy-minded outlook, though making him unpopular with many of his staff, and his ability to act forcibly and closely with his Executive Committee made for powerful leadership at a time when it was much needed.

When Duncan became manager in 1932, Harrap filled in as chairman of the Executive Committee until the appointment of Albert William Monds in 1933. Monds had been on the Executive Committee since 1926 and then served as chairman of the Committee until shortly before his death in 1945. Monds was a member of the wealthy flour-milling family, three times mayor of the city, and had many important public interests. His public standing brought considerable prestige to the institution, and although by no means its most outstanding chairman, on many occasions he certainly did good work on the Bank's behalf. As a practised and fluent public speaker, Monds was particularly useful on ceremonial occasions, as when the Bank celebrated its centenary in 1935, or when it opened new branches or new branch buildings.

The third of the Bank's managers in the inter-war period, Ronald Tyson, came to office following Duncan's sudden death in 1936. Tyson had a very different background from his two predecessors. Weedon and Duncan were both eminent 'outsiders'; Tyson came up through the ranks of the Bank itself. First appointed as junior clerk in 1907, he early became noted for two of the specialist skills of a successful savings banker: a phenomenal memory for account numbers, and slick arithmetic; he was one of few able to add columns of pounds, shillings and pence in one operation and on many occasions had officers from other banks watch him with admiration. More importantly, when it came to the higher level of administration, Tyson was a tremendously hard worker and a great organizer. Until he became manager of the Bank for Savings these qualities had been displayed chiefly in administrative work for the many sporting organizations to which he belonged.

Tyson had a somewhat chequered early career with the Bank for Savings. During World War I he had become acting cashier, but was demoted on Ernest Harrison's return. He again became cashier in 1923 when Harrison retired, and with Littler being groomed for manager when Weedon retired, had the prospect of becoming accountant at a fairly early date. Weedon, however, continued for nine more years. By that time Littler was seriously ill, and Tyson might have become manager in 1932 but for Duncan's own application. After Littler's death a few months later, Tyson became accountant. Technically he was Duncan's second-in-command,

Launceston Bank for Savings Executive Committee 1971-2; (*left to right, standing*) Gilbert C. McKinlay, R. John Simmons, Raymond A. Ferrall, B. Leslie Hooper, general manager; (*seated*) John Gunn, William O. Layh, vice-president, Sinclair J. Thyne, president, and Robert J. Bain.

Launceston Bank for Savings, Kings Meadow branch

Launceston Bank for Savings, South Launceston branch

but little love was lost between them. Indeed, Tyson all but ended his career with the Bank under Duncan when it became known early in 1935 that he was conducting some of his sporting organization business in banking hours. Even though it seems this happened only when his own bank work was finished for the day, frequently by mid-afternoon, Tyson came close to losing his job. A special sub-committee reported that Tyson had 'so belittled his position as to surreptitiously carry on private work within the Bank during official working hours', an example of 'flagrant disobedience', and it recommended the severest of reprimands. It was certainly a tribute to Tyson's abilities that little more than a year later he was unanimously elected manager.

Like his predecessor, Tyson was unpopular with some of his staff, to whom his particular brand of administrative efficiency appeared ruthless and at times vindictive. Yet from the viewpoint of the Bank as a whole, he was an outstanding manager. Combining a dynamic outlook, technical expertise, organizational ability and a remarkable capacity for sheer hard work, Tyson was perhaps more dominant in the conduct of the Bank's affairs than any manager since Henry Dowling. For some time the Launceston Bank for Savings was known by many as 'Ronnie Tyson's Bank'.

Attracting depositors

After the initial round of hostilities and heated exchanges of 1919 and 1920, relations between the Launceston Bank for Savings and the Hobart Savings Bank quickly became more cordial. While they were now open competitors, ever-watchful for new moves by the other party, it was a battle fought within limits. From the start there was no competition through interest rates; a common rate was negotiated by the two banks, though when opinions differed negotiations could be prolonged and heated. As time passed, it became convention to inform each other in advance of a proposed new development; in 1926, for example, the Hobart Savings Bank, having decided to extend its facilities to include fixed deposits, informed the Launceston Bank for Savings well before it was done. In the towns where the banks competed, the respective managers would canvass the uncommitted, but rarely attempted to poach each other's customers, and in general their relations were very friendly. In its relations with the Commonwealth Savings Bank, the Launceston Bank for Savings similarly retained a spirit of friendly competition. Weedon summed up the position well when he wrote to the Ulverstone manager on 7 February 1923:

> Our relations with [the Commonwealth Savings Bank] here are very friendly and you must be careful not to do anything that will disturb these relations. You will of course not refuse any business that is brought to you but do nothing to entice any of their depositors to come to us. There is no objection

to your letting probable depositors know what our rate of Interest is and what facilities we can offer them.

In the search for deposit business, certainly the uncommitted were actively canvassed, and to bolster such efforts the Launceston Bank for Savings conducted an extensive advertising campaign through the press and later on radio. But in large part it relied for success on well-tried methods, now adapted to new circumstances. The 'facilities' of which Weedon spoke included the long-established practices of accepting multiple accounts and in many instances allowing pass-books to be held at the Bank; the main difference was that now branch managers and others made every effort to make these special facilities known. Emphasis was given, as before, to conducting Bank business in convenient pleasant surroundings, and in dealing with depositors quickly and courteously. In 1936, for example, a Head Office Circular instructed that at all times customers must be treated with the utmost civility, that they should be made to feel that doing business with the Bank was a pleasure; and rather more specifically that:

> Officers are forbidden to enter into any dispute or altercation with depositors and are to return Pass Books to them in an agreeable and courteous manner, always seeing that the Pass Book is closed so that the entries will not be revealed to a bystander.

From an early date the manager and Executive Committee were particularly conscious of the advantage of the best physical facilities—a well-situated building with an imposing exterior and a pleasant, convenient banking chamber; in the branch towns there was the further advantage that a new expensive building created business for builders and others, which might be returned in due course. Although not so quick off the mark as the Hobart Savings Bank, the Launceston Bank for Savings had built substantial, well-located branch buildings at Devonport by 1923 and Ulverstone by 1924. Three years later it was planning a new imposing building at its third large branch, Burnie. Perhaps because this was the first centre in which it built where there was also competition from the Hobart Savings Bank, both the building and opening ceremony received special attention from Head Office. Eight days before the opening on 25 September 1928 Weedon sent detailed instructions to the branch manager, Keith Westbrook:

> you will arrange with the Bay View people to supply half a dozen bottles of Minchinberry in quart or larger bottles, a supply of soft drinks, such as dry ginger ale, lemonade, etc. and good cigarettes, also, of course, some edibles in the way of sandwiches, cakes etc and the necessary glass and crockery, etc. We want everything to be nice and presentable.

Three days later Weedon was writing again, increasingly anxious as the opening approached, expressing fears that too many people had been invited; and adding whisky to the list of beverages to be available. The opening ceremony was apparently a great success, and the building itself was described as 'a notable addition to the architectural beauties of the town'. More new buildings might have followed but for the onset of the depression. However, in the late 1930s the Bank embarked on a spate of new building, at Latrobe,* Scottsdale, Wynyard, and the new suburban branch of Invermay. By 1939 only the two weakest branches, Smithton and St Marys, still operated in rented premises.

Among the facilities provided by the Bank one that was particularly favoured in the new competitive world was the provision for pass-books to be held by the Bank if the customer wished. By this device depositors distant from a branch of the Bank could use withdrawal forms from time to time to pay bills or make other remittances to third parties, since the forms could easily be cashed at the bank which held the pass-book, or even cashed indirectly through the commercial banks. Thus withdrawal forms virtually became cheques. In this practice the Launceston Bank for Savings was unique, and the point was stressed in the search for business. Clearly the practice was highly valued, for it was persisted with even though it created endless problems. In 1924, for example, the state government threatened to impose stamp duty upon such 'cheques' and it required great effort and ingenuity on Weedon's part to avert the threat. On countless occasions the practice ran foul of the commercial banks which received the withdrawal slips as cheques. Sometimes they imposed a special collection fee, but mostly the Bank for Savings compromised by promising to be more restrictive. On one occasion Weedon had to resort to the seemingly plausible but rather dubious argument that the facility in fact benefited the commercial banks, because it was so similar to commercial banking that it would encourage savings-bank depositors to open accounts at the commercial banks.

One practice which might have given the Bank a competitive advantage, but which Weedon in particular opposed, was the use of Bank for Savings' accounts as, in effect, active current or trading accounts. On innumerable occasions since he had become manager, Weedon had clamped down on suspected trading accounts and could truthfully write to the State Treasurer at the time of the stamp-duty crisis in 1924 that 'We do not permit depositors to keep trading accounts in the Bank, and in several cases where it has been suspected that such has been the case, steps have been taken and the accounts closed.' There would seem to have been two main reasons why such a firm stand was taken on this issue. Firstly,

* The Bank had a sub-branch there from 1927. See p. 161.

if trading accounts were permitted it would certainly antagonize the commercial banks. The Bank for Savings could not risk such antagonism, because it relied on the co-operation of the commercial banks for the success of its withdrawal-slip-cheque system, because it depended on the commercial banks for overdraft facilities in an emergency, and because it would have led to retaliation; commercial banks could easily have tried to persuade savings-bank depositors to switch to commercial-bank fixed deposits. Secondly, Weedon, at least, had a deep and genuine belief that a savings bank should stick to legitimate savings-bank business, a point he made on countless occasions and which went back to the original savings-bank philosophy. To Weedon the ideal savings-bank depositor was still the working-class man or dependant who deposited money regularly each week and withdrew it only in emergencies, or for very special reasons. And as long as Weedon remained manager this was a basic aim of the Bank. As late as 1931 the Bank's full-page advertisement in the *Post Office Directory* emphasized that:

> The doors of the Bank are wide open to the man or woman who saves a little each week . . . The habit of laying aside regularly a small amount from the weekly wage is one of the most valuable habits a young man or woman can acquire. The amount is not missed, the sum rapidly increases, interest accumulates . . .

It appears slightly paradoxical that while the Bank clung to this ideal, which so few depositors had ever attained, other policies and practices facilitated and encouraged still further movement away from the original savings-bank concept—particularly in the type of depositor. As time passed, the manual worker and his family were becoming less important. Among Head Office depositors there was a continued trend towards white-collar salaried workers, small businessmen, professional people, and others in the broad category of 'middle class'. Increasing diversity of occupations and the dissolving of class distinctions in the twentieth century makes precise calculations impossible. In the most approximate terms, however, samples from Head Office records suggest that by the 1930s new depositors from the traditional working classes were at least equalled in number by other occupational groups, and easily surpassed by the latter in the value of deposits. Though less is known directly of branch depositors, it is clear from correspondence that a large percentage of them were either of the type becoming so important at Head Office, or, and these were very important, from the small-farmer community.

Innovations

In the search for deposit business in the new competitive world, the

Launceston Bank for Savings not only stepped up or adapted well-tried methods, but greatly extended its facilities. This involved both a geographic expansion of such facilities and the devising of new methods of attracting business, although in practice the two are not clearly separable.

At first glance, it is surprising that after opening at St Marys in 1924 the Bank established no new full branches for another fourteen years. Essentially, it would seem, the Bank for Savings had no intention of extending beyond 'northern' territory, and that in the north there were now no more places that would clearly justify new branches. The Bank had branches in all the closely settled districts of the north-west, in the north-east, and in the not-so-closely settled valley of the South Esk. The only other heavily populated districts, particularly around Longford or Westbury on the northern plains, were not considered at the time, apparently because they were close enough to Head Office for depositors to use Head Office directly. However, the logic of this becomes less clear-cut with the opening in 1938 of the first suburban branch of the Bank at Invermay, just one mile north of Head Office, to cater for the large and growing population of the northern suburbs. Perhaps opinion was changing.

One interesting innovation of the period was the establishment of the Bank's only sub-branch, at Latrobe. In essence a sub-branch was just a geographical extension of the parent branch, a separate specialist office opened to receive deposits and allow withdrawals, but with all accounting done at the parent branch, in this case Devonport. Latrobe was ideal for such an arrangement, only a few miles from Devonport, with a fairly large population, but not large enough nor expanding enough to justify all the expense of a full branch. Latrobe had been considered by the Executive Committee as early as 1923, when the neighbouring shale-oil developments still appeared quite promising, but it was not until 1927, when there were rumours that the Hobart Savings Bank might establish there, that action was taken. In November 1927 a sub-branch was established in rented premises, to open on the two strategic days of the week: Monday, which was sale day, and Friday, which was pay day. The sub-branch was operated by the then recently appointed junior clerk at Devonport, B. Leslie Hooper, now general manager of the Bank for Savings. By 1933 the sub-branch was so successful that it was made full-time, and in 1937 removed to new premises, bought and renovated by the Bank.

A rather more important innovation was the establishment of agencies, operated, as in the 1850s, by local businessmen on commission, receiving deposits as at any branch, but with limited withdrawal facilities. Although the Hobart Savings Bank had shown the way in 1927, the Launceston Bank for Savings did not consider establishing agencies until 1929 when it investigated the possibilities at four northern towns. In the following year agencies were opened at Railton and Sheffield, attached, like the Latrobe sub-branch, to the Devonport branch. The first two agencies were apparently not strikingly successful, for several years elapsed before the system was extended. In 1937, however, with the commercial banks now willing to act as agents for the Launceston Bank for Savings, nine new agencies were opened. These included two in Hobart Savings Bank territory, at Oatlands in the south and Zeehan in the west; this may not be entirely coincidental, since only a few days before they opened, the Hobart Savings Bank had made another invasion into northern territory, at Smithton.

Certainly the most interesting, and perhaps most important development of the inter-war period was the inauguration of school savings banks. It was a system long since established on the mainland and elsewhere, and in essence resembled the penny savings bank system which had developed in Britain in the late 1850s and had extended to Tasmania by the 1860s, though apparently without much success. The basic idea of both was that an essentially charitable organization would receive regular deposits in much smaller amounts than were acceptable to a normal savings bank, usually one penny a week, as a preliminary step to the opening of a regular savings-bank account.

In Tasmania school savings banking was pioneered by the Scottsdale manager, Albert Walter Biggs, in co-operation with the headmaster of the local school, W. C. Morris. Biggs later recounted the origins of the scheme:

> Mr W. C. Morris BA (then Head Master of S'dale HS) and I, were talking of the advisability of training Young Australia to thrifty habits (early 1926) and this was the outcome. I drew up a set of Books, Pence-Cards, Withdrawals etc and he got them printed. At first the Director frowned on the idea—said children went to school to learn "their three Rs", but after argument & reasoning he accepted it as a good idea and on June 10 1926 the "District School Thrift A/c" and "Thrift A/c Expenses" were opened.

Meanwhile, Weedon had given his approval, though a rather qualified approval. Recognizing the intrinsic merit of the scheme and ultimate advantages that might accrue to the Bank, he agreed, provided that the school did the detailed accounting. There is no evidence that Weedon encouraged other branch managers to follow Biggs' example at the time, and Biggs may not have been far from the truth when he later claimed that the initial scheme had been opposed by both his and the headmaster's superiors.

In 1927 the Launceston Bank for Savings came to view the matter in a very different light when the Hobart Savings Bank followed Biggs' example. As with the initial opening of branches, the Bank for Savings had been slow to get off the mark, but once aroused, reacted quickly and vigorously. Curiously, perhaps, the first danger sign was ignored when the Hobart Savings Bank established facilities at the Upper Burnie State School on 21 June 1927. However, when the process was repeated at the Wynyard State School on 18 July 1927, Weedon the same day wrote to Biggs anxiously seeking details of his scheme. By October the Launceston Bank for Savings was operating school banks at all the branches. In the Burnie-Wynyard district, where the Hobart Savings Bank and the Launceston Bank for Savings openly competed, the local managers of the respective institutions battled vigorously to capture as many schools as possible. Overall, the Launceston Bank for Savings seems to have done well, for within twelve months there were more than fifty schools operating savings schemes with the Bank.

Opinion about the value of school banking was very mixed. In practice, the school banks provided little money for a very great deal of trouble. In the Burnie-Wynyard district, competition between the banks resulted in the payment of five per cent commission to teachers operating the scheme, which meant a direct financial loss. More generally, school banking created endless administrative problems. Frequently teachers did not keep proper accounts, or if they did, wrote them in pencil, to the horror of branch managers. Sometimes their errors were criticized in front of the children, arousing resentment among the teachers. During the depression of the 1930s many impoverished parents undermined the scheme by withdrawing their children's funds to ward off starvation. Above all, after an initial burst of enthusiasm, the schools themselves tended to become apathetic, and many teachers openly opposed all the extra work. It was a little ironical that after the departure of W. C. Morris, the Scottsdale school became one of the worst back-sliders of all. In 1935 Biggs reported to Head Office how business there was 'absolutely inert', and that the 'teachers consider this irksome and outside their regular routine'.

Yet to its credit the Launceston Bank for Savings persisted with the scheme. Certainly there was a strong argument that it was to the Bank's long-run advantage. Children taught to save at an early age and within the framework of the Launceston Bank for Savings would be, it was maintained, the Bank's depositors of the future. Yet it was not as simple as that; Keith Westbrook, one of the keenest believers in school banking among branch managers, believed that when children left school very many of them transferred their funds to the Commonwealth Savings Bank at the local post office. Long-run self-interest was not the whole explanation. Behind the Bank's persistence was a large measure of benevolent idealism, a firm belief that this was a public service, in the interests of the children and the community generally. Such a view was particularly evident among those who bore the brunt of the work involved—the branch managers. Some of these admirable men are described later.

Efficiency and economy

To be a successful competitor, it was important that the Launceston Bank for Savings should not only strive in every way to attract new customers, but that it should operate as efficiently and profitably as possible. Indeed competition placed a premium on profitability and efficiency, for unless the Bank could match the rate of interest paid to depositors by its competitor or competitors, it would lose business, even imperil its existence. Also, the ability to compete successfully depended on having ample funds, made available from profits, for 'advertising' expenditure. The Bank spent a considerable amount on direct advertising, much more on indirect advertising—expensive attractive buildings, school banking and agencies, unprofitable branches and extra personnel. All this depended on efficient and profitable operations overall.

In part, maximum efficiency involved obtaining the highest possible return from investments, within the limits imposed by safety and liquidity. Aspects of this have been discussed in the previous chapter. A much more difficult problem was to make certain that the Bank gained maximum value for money on its administrative outlays. With the institution of branch banking this was particularly important, for although overall branches may have been worth while, they considerably increased administrative outlays, particularly in the short run. For many years direct branch costs alone, salaries, rents and other expenses, were obviously high relative to branch deposits, although it was not until the 1930s that internal accounting procedures were devised to establish the profitability of individual branches. Furthermore, branch banking involved much additional work and expense at Head Office, in checking and incorporating branch accounts, making provision for relieving managers, regular inspections, and so on. Overall, between 1919 and 1925 the number of staff employed by the Bank rose from six to nineteen, and administrative costs by nearly three times, while the Bank's income less than doubled. The inflated ratio of expenses to income was only gradually reduced after that time.

Obtaining maximum value from a greatly enlarged administration involved many things. Reading the abundant records of the Bank for the inter-war years one is struck by the high degree of discipline maintained. This was particularly evident in the 1930s, when times were hard generally and the Bank was managed by two disciplinarians. When he came to office in 1932 Duncan instituted a system of Head Office Circulars which set out in no uncertain terms the standard of conduct he expected. Tyson con-

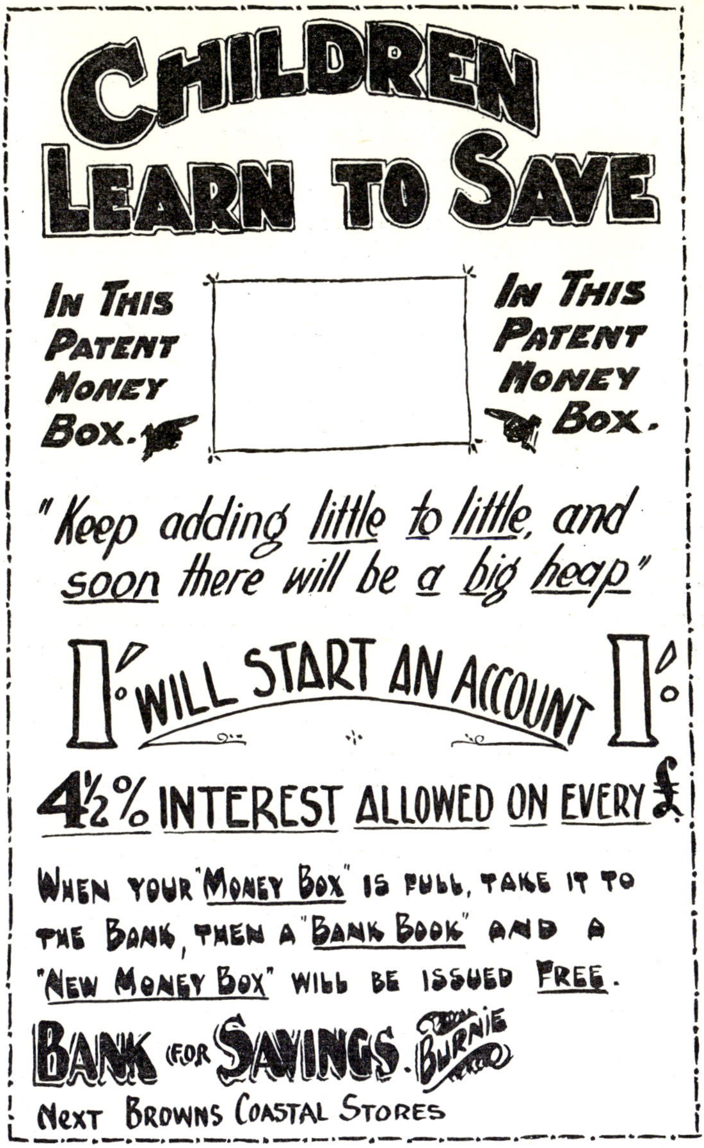

Hand-lettered advertisement to encourage Young Savers, *c.* 1920s, shortly before the introduction of school banking tinued the tight discipline of his predecessor. Head Office Circular No. 59 of July 1936, for example, specified that:

> It is required and expected of all the officers in the service of the Bank that they apply themselves with zeal, activity and diligence to the business and welfare of the Institution, and that they pay implicit obedience to the directions of their superior officers. A respectful demeanour towards their superiors is expected from all subordinates, and during office hours officers must use the prefix Mr, Mrs or Miss at all times when addressing another officer—no exception to be made in this respect.

Strict discipline applied to branch managers, as well as to Head Office staff, though supervision in their case was necessarily lacking. Branch managers were required always to answer correspondence from Head Office immediately, even if it was only a formal acknowledgment that was required; they had to get their regular financial returns in on time, or risk the severest censure, and where residences were attached to the bank building, they were required always to sleep there, except when on leave. At times the Bank's discipline had a distinctly moral element. Staff were forbidden to take part-time jobs with the totalisator or a bookmaker, and junior staff who were rather carefree about their health, or tended to patronize public houses too much, could expect stern criticism.

The Bank's records reveal also the frequently hard and difficult conditions under which the staff had to work. The early experiences of the Smithton manager in 1921, for example, were far removed from the normal view of banking as a sedate and comfortable profession. On arriving at Smithton the new manager found himself with a one-room unequipped 'bank'. Worse, he could find no suitable place to live; even at the Coffee Palace there was always a rough element, he reported, and no private board was available. There was no solution but to sleep in the bank. He bought a stretcher and sought permission to buy wash-basin, mirror, and a curtain to divide living from business quarters. He also asked for a revolver, for he had been warned that the town became 'very lively' at times. A little over a month after his arrival he wrote, with a considerable degree of understatement, that he had no wish to remain permanently at Smithton.

While the Smithton manager's experiences were rather exceptional, the typical branch manager lived a difficult life. The job was a lonely one: as late as 1939 only three of the eight managers had assistants. And except for those fortunate three, it was also very binding—six days a week in the office and seven nights a week sleeping on the premises all year round, except for the very limited holiday allowed. In 1935 it was formally provided that after five years' service an officer was entitled to fourteen working days holiday per annum, provided that it was practicable for the Bank to supply a relieving manager. Often it was not.

For most of the year the branch manager's working day admittedly was not a hard one, in fact it was often very leisurely. But at least twice a year, at balancing time, he was frantically busy, often working through the night calculating the half-yearly accounts. The balancing period was made particularly difficult, because with the accounts the manager had to send a comprehensive report

> regarding productivity, trade and all factors tending to the advancement or retardation of the District from a general and commercial point of view, supported where possible with statistical information and to express an opinion on the possibilities of expansion of Savings Bank business, also to review the progress of their branch.

Later the manager was also required to supply in these reports detailed information respecting values, sales and rentals of properties in his district. Again, while the normal working day may not have been too demanding, the branch manager was expected, as a matter of course, to spend a lot of time outside banking hours getting among the local residents, joining in their activities and subscribing to their societies and associations, with a view to increasing deposit business at the branch.

On top of all this, the branch manager frequently had to withstand severe censure from Head Office for apparent shortcomings. To one of his best branch managers, for example, even Weedon could write abruptly in 1927 that 'The impression I have is a slackness in your methods of doing the work in the office that cannot be allowed to continue.' Duncan appears to have been a particularly hard task-master. One manager, perhaps a little slower than most, was in almost continuous trouble. On 18 December 1934 he received the somewhat savage judgement that 'I fail to see any reason for the Branch being in arrears as you had it unless a large amount of time was wasted by local callers at the office exchanging gossip as is the case of patrons at a barber's shop'. For subsequent tardiness the unfortunate manager lost the holiday due to him at the end of 1935 and was frequently threatened with dismissal. During the difficult 1930s almost all managers were from time to time censured for not doing better. They may have been excused for regarding the improvement of internal accounting to provide a profit and loss statement for each branch as more of a whipping-post than a means of increasing efficiency. Sometimes the Head Office criticism was not only harsh but clearly unfair, as with the relieving manager who was first upbraided for arriving at the bank too early because it disturbed the regular manager's family, then for staying too late because it made the bank appear like a lighthouse.

Throughout almost the whole period economizing was a prevailing theme. It was as evident in small matters, such as use of electricity and stationery, travelling expenses, or donations to various causes, as on larger issues. Perhaps the most important, and undoubtedly the most controversial piece of economizing was the closure of the Smithton branch in 1933. Armed with the new tool of individual profit and loss accounts, a sub-committee carried out in May of that year a close investigation of the various branches and reported that Smithton was running at too great a loss. Despite fierce opposition from local residents and the local manager, who was told that his viewpoint was only explicable in the light of his being born in the district, the recommendation that the branch close was implemented. In theory, Smithton business was transferred to Wynyard to bolster another financially weak branch, and the official argument was that this was really in effect an amalgamation; that this applied in practice is dubious. On short-run financial grounds there is no doubt that the closure was completely justified, but from the long-run point of view the case seems much weaker. In September 1937 the Hobart Savings Bank took advantage of the Launceston Bank for Savings' withdrawal to open its own branch at Smithton. Predictably, the Bank for Savings immediately reopened its Smithton branch, but as a result of the earlier closure was now doubly worse-off: now it had competition which otherwise it probably would not have had; and it also had the long job of regaining the local support and goodwill which it had lost by closing in 1933.

Although the overall impression of the Bank for Savings between the wars is one of austerity and hard times, such features were tempered. While the standards set were exacting, and the work often hard, the Bank's leaders cared for and looked after their staff in many important ways. It is perhaps some indication of this that the Bank received a high degree of loyalty from its officers and that so many of them stayed with the Bank virtually from youth to retirement.

In times that were generally insecure the Bank gave a surprisingly high degree of security to its staff. Although never backward in criticism or discipline, the various managers very rarely took the ultimate step of dismissal. They seem to have been ever hopeful of reforming staff who failed to come up to standard, and certainly for a long time carried some whom other organizations may have sacked. In the whole twenty years only one officer was dismissed on account of inefficiency as such, although a few were dismissed on the more compelling grounds of fraud or malpractice.

Not only were the staff virtually assured of their positions over a period which included two major depressions, their salaries were also assured. Except for a rather extraordinary incident in 1920, when a Wages Board decision compelled the Bank to give large increases to certain members of staff which were rescinded when the decision no longer applied, no member of staff ever suffered a major cut in salary. Generally, even in the depressed conditions of the early 1920s, the trend was towards annual increases. The only major break occurred in the 1930s when for four years almost no increases were awarded. On the other hand, in these years, when most wages and salaries were being cut, the Bank made no reductions of any significance—a remarkable record, and one no doubt greatly appreciated by the staff.

Again, while in many respects economy-minded, the Bank gave rewards when they were due, and could be generous when the occasion was appropriate. Bonuses were one of its established practices, varied according to individual worth or general conditions; in 1931, for example, when staff worked considerable overtime to adjust interest rates in accordance with federal government policy, a special round of bonuses was awarded in recognition. Ailing or retiring members of staff received generous treatment after long service with the Bank. In 1923 Ernest Harrison, on account of deteriorating health, was first taken off counter work without reduction in salary, then granted three months' leave on half-pay, and finally, after his retirement, received a gratuity equivalent to twelve months' salary. The faithful and popular Littler in his declining years received perhaps even more considerate treatment; and after his death in 1932 his family was presented over a period of years with the equivalent of more than two years' salary. In 1929 a superannuation scheme was introduced to take care of future retirements or the misfortunes of long-service officers. On a lesser level, but still indicative of the Bank's sense of duty to its staff, was the invariable custom of giving five pounds or five guineas as a wedding present when a member of staff married; between the wars this was rather more than just a token gesture.

The branch managers

Whatever the policies and practices devised by the leaders of the Launceston Bank for Savings, their success was very much dependent on those who implemented them. Of particular importance were the branch managers, responsible for extending business in competition with the Commonwealth Savings Bank, and in some areas also the Hobart Savings Bank. It was they who sought out new depositors, encouraged and cultivated them by the various means available; they who operated the agencies and school banks, assisted Head Office greatly in its local investment decisions, and subsequently kept an eye on securities. The calibre of the branch managers inevitably varied, but overall was of a very high standard.

Of the fifteen men who at various times in the inter-war period managed branches, only one, the St Marys manager for the first ten years, was clearly not up to the job. Certainly he had one of the most difficult, if not the most difficult of the branches. The area it served had a smaller population than that of any other branch. It was also more spread out, extending thirty miles down the South Esk valley to Avoca, and over twenty miles north to St Helens. In the outer centres of population, therefore, it was particularly vulnerable to competition from the Commonwealth Savings Bank, operating through the local post offices. And the Commonwealth Savings Bank had a further advantage in that many of the people of this area were coal miners, particularly biased in favour of a government rather than private bank. Yet making full allowance for all these difficulties, the St Marys manager did not do well.

The St Marys branch initially opened on 18 February 1924. There was little business in the first day or two, and on 21 February Weedon was already writing sternly to the newly appointed manager that it was no use sitting in his office waiting for customers to turn up; he should get out among the people and actively canvass for business. By the end of the month, however, the branch had only twenty-four depositors, and by the end of May only seventy-two. After further altercations, in June Weedon threatened the local manager with dismissal. This must have shaken him up a little for he soon managed to get the Bank's circular into the pay-packets of miners at the neighbouring large mine at Cornwall. But still the branch had fewer than one hundred depositors at the end of June, and in the following month a more energetic manager temporarily took charge. Returning in November the St Marys manager continued to be in trouble during the rest of Weedon's term of office, as before for failing to acquire depositors, but now also for slipshod accounting, slowness in implementing school banking and in submitting returns to Head Office. Duncan took a sterner line than Weedon, and there was some improvement in the manager's work, but at a meeting in January 1934 it was noted that his services would expire at the end of February. In other words, he was dismissed. Evidently the manager, if not efficient, was at least popular in the district, and when his dismissal became known Head Office received a petition from residents of the district that he should be retained, but to no avail.

Two of the fifteen branch managers of the inter-war years ultimately revealed shortcomings of a rather different nature. They were the original managers at Devonport and Ulverstone, who for a long time performed their duties more than satisfactorily. From the extensive correspondence extant at the Ulverstone branch it is clear that the manager there was from the start a credit to the Bank. Aged twenty-six on his appointment, he had lost the sight of one eye during the war, but was reputed to be the best-dressed man in the town, was well known and popular. The Devonport manager, four years younger, was similarly much liked in the district, was excellent at training juniors, and his clerical work was so perfect that it was handed around the Bank as an example for all to follow. Unfortunately both managers had ideas grander than their positions. As early as 1921 the Ulverstone manager had sought special expenses because, as he wrote to Weedon:

> As you are doubtless aware I move amongst the progressive young men whom indulge in sport, such as Rowing, Football, Cricket, and such manly games, and the greater part of these are depositors in our Institution and it would be fatal to be parsimonious.

The Ulverstone manager was very class conscious, once reporting that the parents of a potential junior were 'only ordinary working-class people . . . but very respectable'. The Devonport manager may not have been so class conscious but certainly 'lived well', as people remember him. Both managers apparently found their salaries too small and the temptations of those fat accounts in the pass-books they held too great.

When the Ulverstone manager took his holiday in November 1930 Tyson, acting as relieving manager, discovered discrepancies in the accounts. His worst fears were confirmed, and on his return the manager was eventually persuaded to come clean, admitting that he had forged withdrawals since 1928 for an amount in excess of £1,600, nearly five times his annual salary. Although he was apparently most penitent, and although his father promised to do everything to refund the amount, Weedon would have none of the 'scheming scoundrel', as he described him, and put the matter in the hands of the police. The ex-manager received lenient treatment from the judge, who regarded the matter as one of 'absolute abnormality' which could be traced back to the war. The Bank honoured the depleted accounts and the matter seems to have been quickly put out of mind.

At the time of the Ulverstone manager's downfall the Devonport manager is reported to have told the wife of another Bank officer that he could not possibly understand a man like that doing such a thing. Only a little over three years later he did just such a thing himself, but on a rather larger scale, to the extent of over £4,000. The revelation, early in 1934, was an even greater shock than the earlier incident. One old lady, who had regularly given the manager a Christmas present of £5 and whose account had been doctored, simply refused to accept that such a nice man had become an embezzler. Again the Bank footed the bill, but now made more serious efforts to reduce holdings of pass-books at its various offices. Still, however, the practice was not completely eliminated, and early in 1936 a clerk at Head Office fleeced the accounts of two of his uncles for several hundred pounds, then fled the state. After that, the Executive Committee and the manager decided that no pass-books were now ever to remain at the Bank.

With the exception of the inefficient manager at St Marys and the two efficient ones who eventually went astray, the branch managers of the inter-war years were conscientious and reliable men, performing a difficult job very efficiently. Their record reflects to no small degree on the Bank's initial selection and suggests that its treatment of them, if in some respects hard, was overall to their satisfaction. Although judgement is to a degree arbitrary, three of these managers do seem to stand out for their excellent records.

One, William Claud Shaw, joined the Bank in 1923 at the age of twenty-six. A popular and genial figure, Shaw had a wide variety of interests, musical, sporting, and other. Surfing, for which he had plenty of scope on the north-west coast, and walking were among his particular recreations; on one occasion, presumably when manager at Burnie, he decided to walk back to town from Mount Bischoff instead of taking the train, covering the fifty miles in one day. Between 1926, when he was first appointed as a branch manager, and 1940 Shaw managed no less than five branches at different times. The principal reason why he was moved so much seems to be that he had a particular talent for reviving a flagging branch. It was Shaw who was appointed at Ulverstone after the defalcation, to restore some of the lost prestige of the Bank. At the end of 1931 he was able to report eagerly, if a little boastfully:

> Since I have taken charge of the Branch I have connected myself with all the Social, Sporting, and all movements pertaining to the welfare of the town, and have become very popular, which is a big factor in obtaining business in these country towns. So I am looking forward to a decided improvement in this office very shortly.

Apparently there was indeed a decided improvement, for after the Devonport defalcation Shaw was transferred there to perform a similar rescue operation. In 1940 Shaw was transferred to Head Office, but with his particular talent for rapid acceptance in a community, in the post-war branch boom he opened the new branches at Campbell Town, Railton and Stanley. Shaw retired in 1961 after more than thirty-eight years with the Bank.

Keith Westbrook had an even longer period of service with the Bank, nearly forty-seven years, from 1905 to 1952, then a record for any officer. For nearly all of the inter-war period he was a branch manager, first at Burnie in 1922, later at Ulverstone in 1934, and eventually at Invermay in 1938. Westbrook, regarded by many as a little eccentric, was a fitness fanatic with distinctive ideas about diet, in particular opposed to eating bread and meat, and a firm teetotaller who never stayed in hotels, always boarding-houses; it must have gone against the grain not a little when he

Burnie

Devonport, showing the Mersey River and a section of the town

Launceston

had to order all that champagne and whisky for the opening of the new branch building at Burnie in 1928. If a little eccentric, though, Westbrook was totally devoted to the cause of savings banking, inexhaustibly energetic, and overall highly successful. Westbrook, for example, was the man Weedon chose to smarten up the St Marys branch in 1924. Taking the bull by the horns, he immediately visited the Cornwall mine on pay day, addressing the miners as they queued up for their pay. Predictably, he received some unprintable comments, but also got some accounts. During his stay at St Marys he travelled far and wide, chopped firewood for farmers' wives to gain their custom, distributed money-boxes, enlisted the support of the Roman Catholic priest at Avoca, and by the time he left in November had increased the number of accounts from eighty-nine at the end of June to 271.

Westbrook was an ardent supporter of school banking, and an incorrigible deviser of gimmicks to attract the children—not always fully approved by Head Office. In 1928 he was curtly informed by Weedon that 'you clearly understand that your Pear Stunt emanates from you personally, not from the Bank'. What the Pear Stunt was remains a mystery. In the following year he was reprimanded for sending out circulars to schools without Head Office permission, though Weedon added that he had no wish to curb Westbrook's zeal. Through the 1930s he continued his merry way at the schools, with competitions and incentives involving rulers, blotters, thrift shields, and other items. And not content with catching the children young, he tried to catch them at birth, visiting the maternity hospital every week to distribute Bank money-boxes to the newly-born.

The third branch manager who stood out in the inter-war years was Albert Biggs. The originator of school banking in Tasmania, he was manager at Scottsdale for some eighteen years. He could have claimed to have worked for the Bank over a greater span of years than any other officer: in the 1880s he had from time to time performed clerical work for his father Alfred Biggs, until the official appointment of junior clerks. After that he had been accountant for the Launceston *Daily Telegraph*, then after his father's death moved to Scottsdale in 1902 to open a general store. In contrast to his father, he was a successful businessman, with a chain of stores around the north-east by 1920. In that year, however, at the age of fifty-four, he chose to take life a little more easily, relinquishing his active role in the business to become Scottsdale manager of the Launceston Bank for Savings in part of his own business premises. He performed the job with great success until retiring in 1938 when the Bank required premises of its own.

Biggs was the branch manager perhaps most complimented by Head Office. In particular, he had a special talent for half-yearly reports, and

N

earned the rare honour of being congratulated on their quality by that severe, self-appointed critic of such reports, Colonel Harrap. Biggs' reports reveal all the optimism and happy exuberance which made him one of the most popular and well-known figures in the north-east. Commenting, for example, on a rise in the price of tin in his August 1932 branch report, he recorded that 'the tin miners' earlier depressed countenances are changed to broad smiles and high hopes for the future'. A year later he was advocating extending savings facilities to Winnaleah, 'a magnificent and growing district of young, virile and up-to-date men who are adopting latest methods'. At one time timber was 'a wonderful buttress to our stability', at another time high wool prices the 'silver lining' of an otherwise clouded year. When in one particularly depressed half-year there was a record number of withdrawals, rather than hang his head in shame and make excuses as others might have done, Biggs regarded it as a wonderful thing that 'the beneficence of this Institution,—enabling persons to keep the household going, little by little, who in many cases, would *not* have saved at all without easy acccssibility for storing their surplus cash—is being appreciated in this time of stress'. Always there was a silver lining. Deservedly, Biggs lived happily on after his retirement to the age of ninety-two.

CHAPTER THIRTEEN

The Constraints of War 1939–1945

Tasmania and World War II

At the outbreak of World War II in September 1939 Tasmania was experiencing a degree of prosperity, stability and expansion unknown for any length of time since before World War I. For a while these boom conditions continued, largely unchecked and unchanged by the war. Schemes for further expansion were carried to completion, most notably the large factory near New Norfolk, planned in 1938 by Australian Newsprint Mills Limited and eventually opened in 1941, and various municipal projects. Only as Australia became more and more involved in the war and the federal government progressively extended its controls over economic and social life was the course of Tasmanian development affected, and then it was a matter of redirection rather than curtailment of the boom. Some activities were sharply cut back, others greatly expanded to further the war effort.

At a fairly early stage in the war greater exploitation of local resources was actively encouraged. Local collieries received a considerable boost as coal supplies from the mainland became more scarce. The production of flax, a strategic raw material, received particular encouragement, and already by 1941 some eight flax mills were in operation. Heavy demands for army clothing led to a large expansion of the local woollen textile industry, particularly in Launceston, while heavy demands for non-perishable foods brought into existence a large food-processing industry, including several dehydration plants in the north-west and north-east that treated a range of vegetables, especially potatoes. On a more modest scale Tasmania's engineering industries, including the Launceston railway workshops, produced some munitions for the allied forces. Overall, manufacturing employment during the course of the war rose by nearly fifty per cent.

One of the obvious economic benefits of the war to Tasmania, as to Australia generally, was the elimination of unemployment, a major problem for almost all the inter-war years. In the depths of the 1930s depression unemployment in Tasmania had briefly exceeded twenty-five per cent, and even in the more prosperous times on the eve of the war was still not much below ten per cent. The problem quickly disappeared after the outbreak of war as war production increased, and as Tasmanians joined the armed forces in their thousands; over the whole war period nearly 30,000 Tasmanians, out of a total population of less than 250,000, served in the armed forces. Indeed, from 1942, as the war effort gathered pace, Tasmania experienced a general shortage of labour.

The individual Tasmanian, of course, saw the war in a very different light. Assured employment was little compensation for the overriding tragedy of world conflict, for uncertainty, fear and family losses. In any event, if incomes were higher, the actual standard of living was probably lower, with harder conditions of work, heavier taxation and inflation offsetting rising salaries and wages. Further, with more severe rationing and increasing shortages as time passed, there was less opportunity to spend any new-found wealth.

During the war period as a whole, Tasmania apparently fared considerably worse economically than the mainland of Australia. Despite its dehydration plants and busy woollen mills, Tasmania had fewer strategic war industries than the mainland states, and because it was an island dependent for its existence on shipping, its development became more and more cramped by the increasing scarcity and cost of coastal and ocean-going vessels. From the time a German merchant-raider laid mines in Bass Strait in 1940, availability of shipping freight was a major and growing problem. The surest sign that Tasmania was faring worse than the rest of Australia was that, despite shortages of labour, there reappeared during the war a marked drift of population to the mainland, though in the absence of official figures for the later war years, its overall extent is difficult to gauge.

The immediate post-war years saw a definite, if brief deterioration in Tasmania's economic fortunes. As happened after World War I, Tasmania faced great difficulties in resettling ex-servicemen and reorganizing the economy on a peace-time basis. Unlike the years immediately following World War I, there was no world-wide re-stocking boom to facilitate an easy period of transition. Instead, the end of the war brought a sudden drop in demand for the products of war. Now without a market, the many large dehydration plants virtually suspended operations; some closed permanently, others in time converted to the production of canned foodstuffs. Similarly, the large drop in demand for army clothing resulted in a sharp decline in the production of woollen goods. As a whole, manufacturing employment was lower in 1945 and 1946 than it had been in 1944 and did not recover significantly before 1947. Tasmania's exports reflected a similar pattern, with a distinct recession from 1944–5 to 1946–7.

In the conversion to peacetime production Tasmania was further handicapped by shortages of vital materials. To some degree every state suffered from this problem, but none so much as Tasmania. The island depended heavily on mainland suppliers who naturally tended to give priority to local demands, and who furthermore were impeded in supplying Tasmania by still serious shipping difficulties. Shortages of materials were felt, particularly in the building industry. A Tasmanian parliamentary committee investigating the problem of house-building could report as late as September 1947 that the industry was still severely retarded by the lack of materials for which in all but the most basic items, such as bricks, cement and timber, it relied on mainland suppliers.

The Bank and the war effort

The immediate impact of war on the Launceston Bank for Savings was considerably greater than it had been in 1914. In its half-yearly report for February 1940, the first since the start of the war, the Executive Committee reported the loss of four of its staff to the armed forces; one had already died in action. Six months later it was recorded that thirty-eight per cent of the Bank's staff of 1939 had joined up; two years later the proportion had increased to fifty-eight per cent. In their place the Bank appointed inexperienced temporary clerks, which made for great difficulties in administration. The problem of administration further increased when in March 1942, with Japanese forces dangerously close to Australia, elaborate precautions were taken against the possibility of air raids. From then until June 1943, when the danger had receded, branch managers were required to duplicate all records of deposits and withdrawals, posting the duplicates regularly to Head Office for safe keeping.

The financing of war posed a greater and more immediate threat to savings-bank deposits than it had in World War I. The federal government was very quick to introduce the system of war-savings certificates, in contrast to World War I, when it had only been instituted in 1917. War-savings certificates, issued in small denominations at above savings-bank interest, and having considerable patriotic appeal, competed directly and strongly with savings-bank deposits. For the wealthier members of the community the federal government made almost continuous issues of war loans under various names, such as Austerity Loans, Liberty Loans, Victory Loans, and immediately after the war, Security Loans. Both war-savings certificates and loans the Bank handled and encouraged as a matter of national duty, though to its own direct cost. It even provided safe-deposit facilities free of charge for those who wished to leave their certificates or bonds at the Bank.

Perhaps the most serious problem encountered by the Bank in the war years was the pegging of its interest rate on deposits. Paying three per cent to depositors at the outbreak of the war, the Bank for Savings, along with the Hobart Savings Bank, had early reduced the rate to two and three-quarter per cent, but this failed to satisfy the federal government. Under emergency regulations the rate was fixed at two and a quarter per cent from 1 April 1942, and was to remain at that figure for more than ten years. The Bank was now squeezed on two sides: by the war-savings certificates, which although having a duration of seven years, paid a comparatively handsome return of three and a half per cent; and by the Commonwealth Savings Bank, which paid a rate normally one per cent below the trustee banks but now only a quarter of one per cent below. The Launceston Bank for Savings and the Hobart Savings Bank sent a delegation to Canberra to protest against what seemed unfair discrimination, but the Treasurer, J. B. Chifley, was, according to the Minutes of the Executive Committee of 9 April 1943, 'not at all sympathetic'.

The trend in the Bank for Savings' deposit business in the war and immediate post-war years was erratic. At first deposits rose very slowly, which is not surprising given the competition from the federal government. Between August 1939 and February 1943 the total increase registered was less than £300,000, or about ten per cent for the whole three and a half years. However, in the next three and a half years to August 1946 deposits increased very rapidly, by about ninety per cent overall. The contrast is rather startling and not clearly explicable. Perhaps as the war swung more strongly in favour of the allies, patriotic fervour diminished and government bonds and war-savings certificates lost some of their appeal, particularly as such investments would not be instantly recoverable when the war ended. Anticipating happier times ahead, many people perhaps began to plan and save in earnest, preferring to keep their money readily accessible in savings accounts. As well, almost certainly as time passed the gap between earnings and scope for spending increased, so that people were forced to save. This inability to spend seems to have applied even to school children; Westbrook, back at the Burnie branch in 1943, attributed a boom in school-banking business to the shortage of sweets. Also at the end of the war the receipt of deferred war pay gave a considerable boost to savings-bank deposits. However, the boost was only temporary, for as the Scottsdale manager observed, 'this has been offset in some measure by . . . evident anxiety in many cases to spend in a rather reckless manner'. More generally, freer spending after the war, so far as it was possible while rationing and shortages continued, clearly accounts for the slow rise in deposits for some time after August 1946. Not until 1949 did deposits again begin to rise at a fairly rapid rate.

Investment outlets for the Bank in the war and immediate post-war years were understandably very restricted. With the virtual cessation of house-building, mortgage lending was at a standstill. Fixed deposits with commercial banks were relatively unrewarding and rose only modestly. Loans made to municipal authorities, although their capital projects were highly restricted for most of the war period, overall rose substantially, with a particularly sharp rise immediately after the war. However, much the greater part of the Bank's increased funds was, as one would expect, invested in federal government bonds. Between August 1939 and February 1947 holdings of federal government stock rose from around forty-five per cent to sixty per cent of total paying assets—or back to the level immediately prior to the 1930s depression.

The Bank and its competitors

Of Tasmania's three savings institutions, the Commonwealth Savings Bank was the most successful between 1939 and 1947. In two important respects the war greatly strengthened its competitive position. Firstly, and most obvious, was the change in interest rates on deposits, imposed in 1942. Paying only a quarter of one per cent less than the trustee savings banks, the Commonwealth Savings Bank could win a much greater share of the rise in savings-bank deposits than it had been able to do when the margin was one per cent. Secondly, and less obvious, was the effect of inflation, in conjunction with the maximum size of individual deposit accounts allowed to the various institutions. Officially, the trustee savings banks had a maximum deposit size of £300, the Commonwealth Savings Bank a maximum of £500, plus another £1,000 per depositor at a somewhat lower rate of interest. While this had long been to the advantage of the Commonwealth Savings Bank, it became much more so during and after the war, as with rapid inflation depositors at the trustee savings banks increasingly came up against the £300 limit, now more carefully observed than previously, and turned to the Commonwealth Savings Bank with its more liberal provisions. Thus greatly strengthened, the Commonwealth Savings Bank, smallest of the three banks in 1939, became the largest by 1947, having increased its share of savings-bank deposits in Tasmania back to nearly forty per cent, the share it held before the trustee savings banks established branches.

While the Launceston Bank for Savings lost ground to the Commonwealth Savings Bank, it gained relative to the Hobart Savings Bank, as it had done in the immediate pre-war years, so that its overall share of total savings-bank business declined only slightly during the period. Although

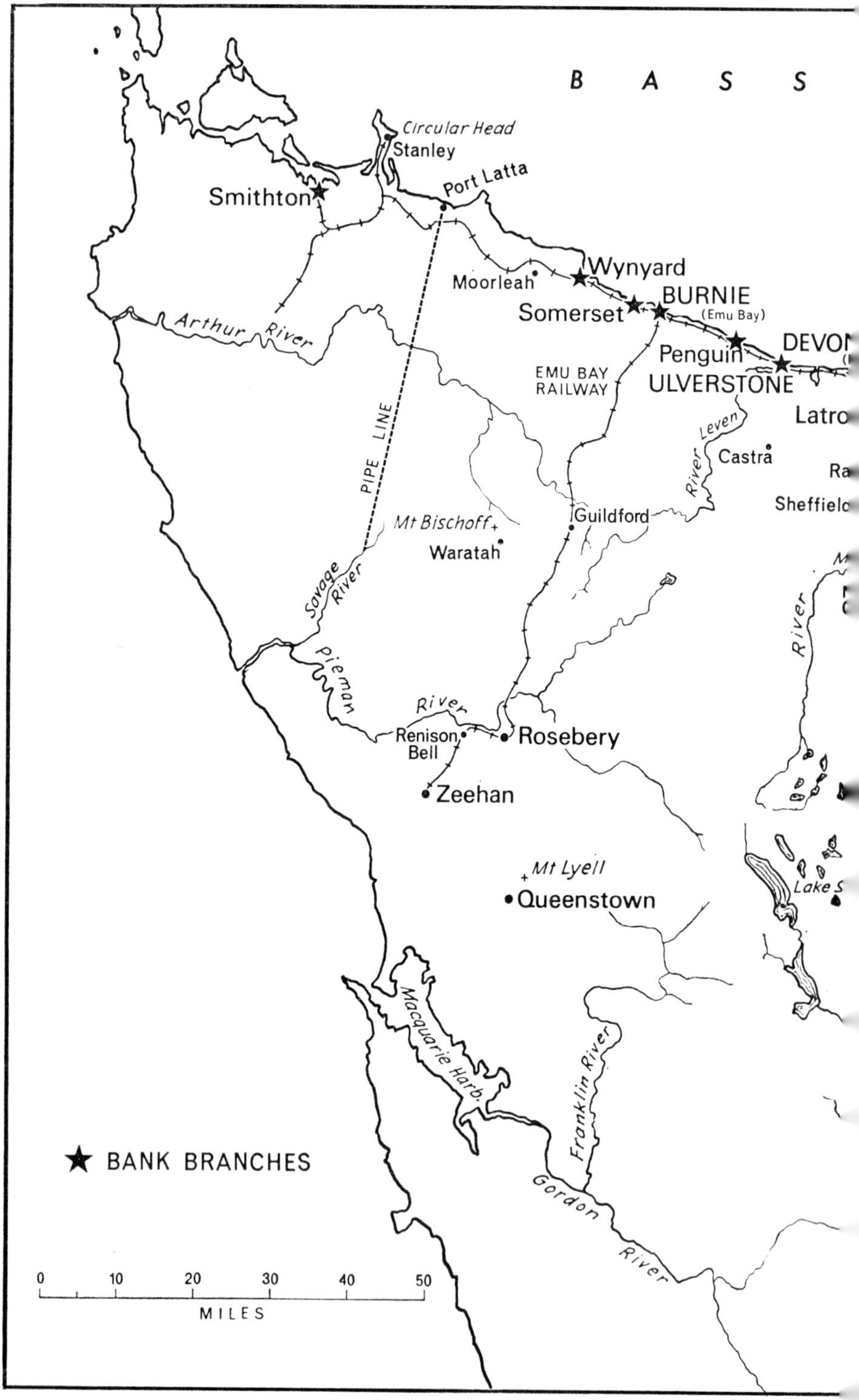

Northern Tasmania

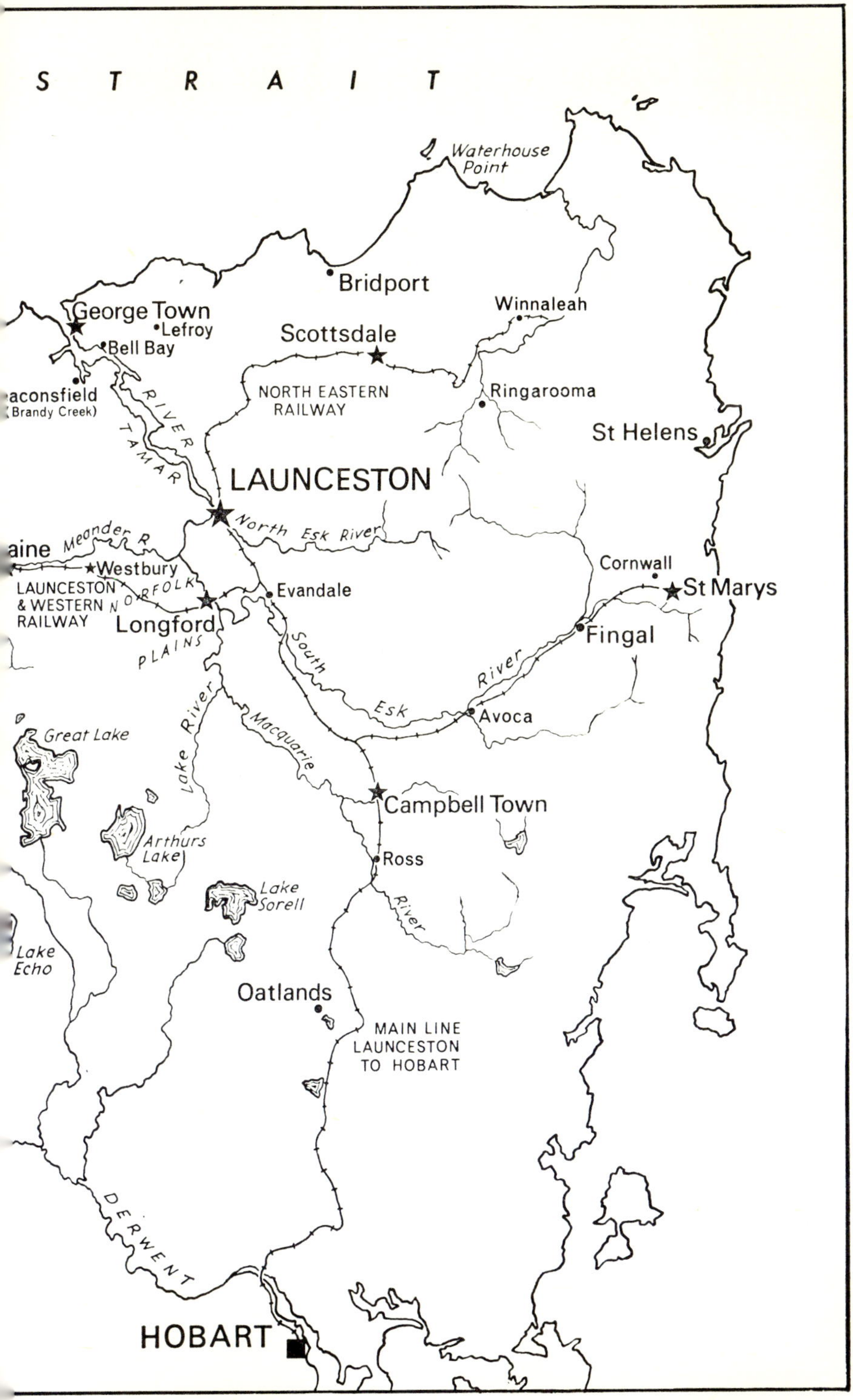

S T R A I T
Waterhouse Point
Bridport
Winnaleah
George Town
Lefroy
Bell Bay
Scottsdale
aconsfield
Brandy Creek)
NORTH EASTERN RAILWAY
Ringarooma
RIVER TAMAR
St Helens
LAUNCESTON
North Esk River
aine
Meander R
Westbury
LAUNCESTON & WESTERN RAILWAY
NORFOLK
Evandale
Cornwall
St Marys
Longford
PLAINS
Fingal
South
River
Esk
Avoca
Great Lake
Lake River
Macquarie
Campbell Town
Arthurs Lake
Ross
Lake Sorell
River
Lake Echo
Oatlands
MAIN LINE LAUNCESTON TO HOBART
DERWENT
HOBART

there is no obvious single reason for this, the Bank's active branch-building programme of the late 1930s was probably an important contributing factor. Bank officers generally had great and probably justified faith in the power of a pleasant, well-located building to attract customers, and at the outbreak of the war all but two of the Bank's nine branches, including Latrobe, operated in their own specially built premises. In November 1941 one of the remaining two, at Smithton, also acquired its own premises. The Smithton manager reported with enthusiasm that 'The building is the subject of much favourable comment, and I feel it has done much to overcome, if it has not entirely dispersed, prejudice against the Bank for its action in closing down the Branch for a period.' The success of its branches, however, can only provide part of the explanation for the Bank's success, since over the whole period from 1939 to 1947 the Bank's Head Office, probably feeling the benefit of the city's booming war industries, gained a slightly increased share of the Bank's total deposits. Whatever the complete explanation, deposits at the Launceston Bank for Savings increased substantially, relative to those of the Hobart Savings Bank, between 1939 and 1947.

For the duration of the war there was no competition between the Launceston Bank for Savings and the Hobart Savings Bank beyond routine efforts to expand business at the various branches. However, not long after the war ended, the informal truce between the two banks was broken. In May 1946 the Hobart Savings Bank planned to open a new branch at the old port of Stanley, north of Smithton, without informing the Launceston Bank for Savings of its intentions. The Bank for Savings reacted quickly, opening its own branch in Stanley just one day after the Hobart Savings Bank, even though conditions barely justified one savings bank, let alone two. The renewed competition prompted a conference between the two banks in the following month, at which it was agreed that in future each bank would notify the other of its intentions well in advance. The agreement meant little in practice, for only two weeks later the Launceston Bank for Savings learned that the Hobart Savings Bank had plans to open an agency at Longford, only fourteen miles from the Bank for Savings' headquarters. This piece of 'affrontery' the Bank for Savings countered with plans to open an agency at Deloraine, where the Hobart Savings Bank had conducted a branch undisturbed since 1920.

Whether the Hobart Savings Bank was frightened off by the vigorous reactions of the Launceston Bank for Savings is uncertain. One only knows that the Hobart Savings Bank made no further encroachment on northern territory for the time being and, in fact, in the immediate post-war years opened only one other new branch, in the comparatively 'safe' town of Oatlands, though some northerners might dispute whether this was really southern territory. In contrast, during July and August 1946 the Launceston Bank for Savings opened five new branches, on the northern plains at Longford and Westbury, south of Latrobe at Sheffield, where the Bank had opened one of its first agencies, at Penguin on the north-west coast, and at Campbell Town in the Midlands. Part of the reason for this spate of new branches was the return of pre-war employees; new branches made it easier to reabsorb them. In part also it would seem to reflect a generally more dynamic outlook by the Bank. To some extent the driving force may have come from Ronald Tyson, the manager, but it may also be significant that during 1945 and 1946 there was a considerable shake-up within the Executive Committee, with two new members, a new chairman and a new vice-chairman, renamed from 1946 president and vice-president. All five new branches, in contrast to the competition-prompted Stanley branch, which later reverted to an agency, proved in the long run to be justified economically.

In fact, there is evidence that the Launceston Bank for Savings would have been still more active, had it not been cramped by severe restrictions on building activity. From 1943 the Executive Committee had ambitious plans for remodelling Head Office and in 1945 had purchased a site for a new branch in South Launceston, as well as agreeing on plans for major alterations at Burnie. By 1948 and 1949 it had schemes for more branches, and purchased blocks of land and obtained detailed architectural plans. However, with the building industry only slowly overcoming its material shortages, and priority being given to house-building, such plans remained in abeyance until the 1950s.

CHAPTER FOURTEEN

Prosperity, Competition and Success

Tasmania since the war

Since the recession and slow reorganization immediately following World War II, Tasmania has experienced more than two decades of unprecedented expansion and prosperity. Although the smallest and least wealthy of Australian states, Tasmania has, in all essential respects, matched the outstanding growth record of the mainland. Except briefly in the late 1940s and early 1950s, the island has attracted few overseas migrants, but with little of the drift to the mainland that characterized so much of the island's history, and with a very high natural rate of increase, Tasmania's population growth has not been far behind that of Australia as a whole. Between the census of 1947 and the end of 1969 Tasmania's population increased by fifty-two per cent compared with sixty-three per cent for all Australia. Meanwhile the standard of living on balance rose rather more rapidly in Tasmania than on the mainland. In the late 1940s average personal income in Tasmania was about eighty per cent of that of Australia as a whole; by the late 1960s it approached ninety per cent of the national average.

Some of Tasmania's growth, it might be argued, has depended on the assistance of the federal government. Both through the normal system of tax reimbursement, and through special grants, Tasmania's public finances have been considerably subsidized. Yet such subsidies have only been peripheral to the island's fortunes. For example, at the peak of its importance late in the 1960s, the special grant contributed only about three per cent to Tasmania's national income. Furthermore, it could be argued with as much strength now as it was argued in the 1920s that federal economic policy has discriminated, if unintentionally, against Tasmania: in its policies towards shipping, upon which Tasmania depends more than any other state; and its protection policies towards both agriculture and manufacturing, which have greatly bolstered the mainland economy, but much less that of the island.

Essentially Tasmania's success has stemmed from its ability to sell its goods and services, particularly to the rest of Australia. One of the most publicized of its successes, and one perhaps bringing the greatest prestige, has been the post-war tourist boom. Tasmania's natural and historical attractions have for decades brought many visitors to the island, but with the greater affluence of the 1950s and 1960s, and much easier access by air or car-ferry services, the industry of recent years has dwarfed earlier performances. In the late 1960s Tasmania recorded over 250,000 arrivals and departures annually, compared with an average of around 50,000 annually in the late 1930s. A large proportion of these, it is believed, are genuine tourists, spending millions of dollars a year in the island, though the figure could not even be estimated approximately.

What is known, and in this Tasmania is unique among Australian states, is the value of Tasmania's exports of commodities; because it is an island, all shipments, whether for overseas or interstate destinations, continue to be recorded. The figures show an exceptionally high degree of dependence on external markets. Although subject to obvious fluctuations, since the late 1930s generally more than half of Tasmania's income has been earned by selling goods to overseas countries or other parts of Australia, mostly the latter; this compares with a proportion of only around twenty-five per cent at the turn of the century, a time when exports were already booming, and indicates how important the federal customs union has become to at least this one state over the years. And despite Tasmania's rapidly growing internal market there has been no tendency since the war for external markets to decline in importance. With about a six-fold increase in value since 1947, exports have maintained their dominant position and have provided the key to Tasmania's post-war success.

Tasmanian exports since the war have been outstanding for their diversity as well as their overall importance. Although not all individual figures are known* it is unlikely that any single item accounts for much more than ten per cent of the total. Exports have increased on a remarkably broad front. Within the primary sector, for example, exports of timber, a small but growing trade since the turn of the century, have continued to grow vigorously. The livestock industries have similarly contributed greatly to the overall expansion. Through the large-scale eradication of rabbits, widespread pasture improvement and other advances, sheep numbers and the volume of wool exports have been more than doubled since the war. The cattle industry, particularly dairying, has grown at a similar rate, with a rapid expansion as a result in exports of butter. From both sections of the livestock industry large export trades in meat have also developed in recent years. Meanwhile crop farming, if less dynamic, has to its credit a

* See p. 186.

major growth in exports of fresh fruit, and large new export trades in frozen and canned vegetables to the mainland.

Overall, however, manufacturing has dominated the growth of Tasmania's exports, and within this sector a small number of large firms are outstanding. Mostly these were established by World War II, and have expanded and diversified greatly since: among them Launceston's large textile factories, Hobart's zinc refinery, carbide works and chocolate factory; and the paper-making enterprises of A.P.P.M. in the north and Australian Newsprint Mills in the south. To these, since the war, have been added several major new enterprises, the two largest perhaps the paper mill of Australian Paper Manufacturers at Port Huon and the aluminium works at Bell Bay, near the mouth of the Tamar. It is some indication how important the comparatively few large establishments have been to Tasmania's progress that a major portion of Tasmania's exports is not itemized separately, since this would reveal information about individual establishments and companies. The 'other' category of exports, which includes confectionery, most paper products and aluminium, has increased more than tenfold since World War II to account now for about a third of all Tasmanian exports. Along with manufactured goods which are itemized, particularly woollen textiles and zinc products, these now account for most of Tasmanian exports.

In recent times, too recent for statistics to be available or meaningful, Tasmania has begun to participate in the great Australian mining boom. Once the mainstay of the Tasmanian economy, mining is again becoming a dynamic sector of a diverse economy. To the great copper mining and smelting complex of the Mount Lyell Company, the one major survivor of the earlier mining boom, have been added since the war large scheelite mining operations on King Island, and in very recent years two large mining enterprises in the west: the Renison Bell tin-mining company, which may yet revive some of the glories of the Mount Bischoff days and has already breathed new life into the neighbouring near ghost town of Zeehan; and the Savage River iron mine, from which pulverized ore is pumped by pipeline to the new Port Latta, west of Wynyard, and there converted into pellets for shipment to Japan.

Given the diversity of Tasmania's export growth since the war, it is not surprising that geographically population growth has been widely spread over the island. Between the two census years of 1947 and 1966 no major changes occurred in the relative importance of different regions or major urban centres. At both dates, what could be clearly regarded as 'northern' territory accounted for almost exactly half of Tasmania's population, while that in the south rose slightly to rather more than forty-five per cent. The remaining few per cent were located in the Midlands and at the various west coast mining centres. Again at each date the two 'capitals' were of approximately the same relative importance, both in relation to each other and the whole state: Hobart and suburbs were and have continued to be about twice as large as Launceston and suburbs; and since the war the two city complexes together have accounted for a little under half of the population of the whole state.

The Bank and its competitors 1947–1959

Until the late 1950s, when the entry of the trading banks into savings-bank business brought major changes, the pattern of Tasmanian savings banking continued much as it had evolved by the immediate post-war years. For the three institutions they were relatively peaceful and very prosperous years. In 1947 there were some fears about the bank nationalization plan, but these were quickly quelled when it became clear that the savings banks were not included in the proposals. From the late 1940s as the backlog of spending petered out and the boom gathered pace, deposits increased at a more rapid rate. In the late 1950s the rate of growth slowed as savings institutions met increased competition for funds from short-term debentures of public companies, and also from the share market. However, with higher rates of return to depositors and more liberal terms for depositing, deposits continued to grow and there was little cause for real concern. Overall, in the twelve years from February 1947 to February 1959 total savings-bank deposits in Tasmania rather more than doubled.

There was no major change during this period in the relative strength of the three institutions, as there had been during and immediately following the war. The Commonwealth Savings Bank continued the largest of the three banks, slightly increasing its share of all deposits from thirty-eight to forty per cent. The Hobart Savings Bank was the second largest, with a slight decline in its share of deposits from thirty-five to thirty-three per cent. The Launceston Bank for Savings remained the smallest, with a stable share of some twenty-seven per cent. The lack of relative change is striking, but in one respect deceptive. It does not reflect, as one might imagine, a lack of competition. On the contrary, the three institutions competed perhaps more strongly than before, but as it happened, over time their various efforts and advantages tended to counterbalance each other, leaving them overall in much the same position as before.

The Commonwealth Savings Bank maintained the stronger role it had acquired during and immediately after the war, and in fact slightly improved on it, for two basic reasons. Firstly, it had the advantage over the trustee savings banks of a greater maximum size for individual deposits, which more than offset the slight disadvantage in that its rate of interest was a quarter of one per cent below that of its competitors. It was an advantage which grew as time passed, because of continuing inflation and as more accounts neared or reached the maximum size allowable, now strictly enforced under Commonwealth legislation. Its importance was clearly demonstrated when the differential was altered substantially on two occasions within the period and was followed by marked changes in respective growth rates. Up to 1951 the Commonwealth Savings Bank had a maximum deposit size of £500, compared with £300 for the trustee savings banks; depositors could also place another £1,000 in the Commonwealth Savings Bank, but at a much lower rate of interest on the extra amount, so that this additional provision was probably fairly unimportant. Until that year the government bank was pulling away from the private institutions. However, in 1951 the maximum deposit size of the trustee banks was increased by law to £450, only slightly below that of the Commonwealth Savings Bank, and from then the trend was clearly reversed: the trustee banks then began to gain relative to the Commonwealth Bank. In 1956 the process was reversed when the maximum deposit at the top rate of interest paid by the Commonwealth Savings Bank was doubled to £1,000. This big new differential was only slightly offset in the following year when the trustee banks' limit was raised to £500, with provision for another £1,000 at a lower rate of interest. Equality was not finally achieved until 1959, by which time the Commonwealth Savings Bank had more than made up the ground it had lost earlier in the decade.

The other factor in the Commonwealth Savings Bank's sustained performance was the expansion of full branch facilities, part of the Commonwealth Bank of Australia's more active search for business after World War II. Early in the 1950s the Commonwealth Bank established three new branches in Tasmania, the first for some thirty years, a move which may have been influenced in some degree by the greater success currently enjoyed by the trustee savings banks. All three new branches were in the south, at Cygnet, near Port Huon, and in two of the capital's suburbs, North Hobart and Moonah. Later in the decade the Commonwealth Bank established more branches in the south at New Norfolk and at Glenorchy, another Hobart suburb. Meanwhile, in the mid-1950s, branches were established in the north at George Town, about the time the aluminium works opened, a little later at Ulverstone, then in the outer Launceston suburb of Mowbray. No figures are available for deposits at these new branches but, as they provided far more attractive and convenient facilities than the post offices, there can be no doubt that they gave a considerable boost to the business of the Commonwealth Savings Bank.

Of the two trustee savings banks, the Hobart Savings Bank was the harder hit by the Commonwealth Savings Bank's active branch policy, and this probably accounts for the further slight decline in the share of deposit business held by the southern bank. The decline might have been considerably greater if, over the same period, the Hobart Savings Bank had not largely compensated for increased competition from the Commonwealth Savings Bank by extending its activities considerably in the north, a move which caused considerable concern to the Launceston Bank for Savings. In 1950 the Hobart Savings Bank opened in Devonport, the largest and most profitable branch centre for the Launceston Bank. Not long afterwards it established a branch in another of the Bank for Savings' largest branch centres, Ulverstone; with the Commonwealth Savings Bank also at Ulverstone, the Launceston Bank for Savings now had two competitors where previously it had a virtual monopoly of savings-bank business. By the mid-1950s the Hobart Savings Bank had also established a branch in the north-western mining town of Rosebery.

Despite the more aggressive policies of its competitors, the Launceston Bank for Savings was relatively inactive in establishing new branches, and certainly there is no evidence that it ever contemplated retaliation by extending its operations to southern or even western Tasmania. In the period the Launceston Bank for Savings opened only three new branches, two of which could hardly be regarded as major extensions into new areas. The South Launceston branch, opened in 1949, was primarily for the convenience of depositors living in southern suburbs who would otherwise have banked at Head Office; and the Railton branch, opened in the following year, simply replaced an agency in an area already well served by the Bank, with branches at Sheffield, a little to the west, and at Latrobe to the north. The one important new branch was at George Town, established in 1955 following the opening of the Bell Bay aluminium plant and shortly after the Commonwealth Savings Bank had established a branch there. Apart from these new branches, the Bank also established a number of new agencies in the north.

Given that the Launceston Bank for Savings had no intention of extending beyond northern territory, its relatively inactive branch extension policy is quite explicable. It already had a well-developed branch network in the region it served, especially with the crop of new branches established in 1946. Rather than extend to new centres which might prove uneconomic, in the face of increased competition the Bank concentrated on making existing facilities as attractive and convenient as possible. From the early 1950s the Bank for Savings poured large sums of money into buying, building, altering and extending its premises, with apparently considerable success. In 1952, for example, following the amalgamation of the Australasia and the Union Banks to become the Australia and New Zealand Bank, the Launceston Bank for Savings bought the large and well-located Union Bank building at Burnie; this was to be a major factor in making the Burnie branch its largest for a number of years. During 1953 the Bank commenced the long-planned internal remodelling of and extensions to its Head Office at Launceston. In the same year it completed a new building for its branch at Westbury and also extensive alterations to its Devonport branch. In the following year the St Marys branch opened in new premises, and during the next three years new branch buildings were opened at George Town, Penguin, Longford and Latrobe; in addition, major alterations were made at Ulverstone and Burnie.

Apart from striving to provide the best possible facilities for depositors, the Launceston Bank for Savings attracted deposit business indirectly, through its lending policies. Investment in municipalities, marine boards and other local public authorities had long been recognized not only as profitable but also of considerable assistance in attracting deposits. The mutually beneficial alliance of local authorities and the Bank for Savings, with all the good will and publicity it created, no doubt gained the Bank many new customers, and in the period the Bank for Savings was particularly active in lending to authorities in northern Tasmania. Overall, between February 1947 and February 1959 its holdings of local government stock rose from less than £1 million to £3.6 million.

Perhaps even more important in attracting depositors was the Bank's role in house lending. Directly, in that borrowers were also depositors at the Bank, and indirectly, through the general good will and reputation it developed, house mortgage business meant a definite boost to deposit business, as well as a profitable investment for the Bank. When generally in Australia savings banks had long waiting-lists, the Launceston Bank for Savings lent with little delay to almost every eligible borrower. Over the same twelve years mortgage loans rose even more rapidly than investments in local government stock, from around £0.6 million to £3.7 million. By 1959 these two key outlets accounted for over sixty per cent of the Bank's investments, compared with only about twenty-five per cent in 1947.

The entry of the trading banks

In 1955 a new era in savings-bank history began when the Federal Treasurer issued the first permits to allow trading banks to operate savings-bank facilities. With these permits the Bank of New South Wales and the A.N.Z. Bank commenced savings-bank business on 19 January 1956. A few months later they were followed by the Commercial Banking Company of Sydney. Other trading banks were more cautious, taking over five years to make up their minds. Eventually, however, they followed suit, the English, Scottish and Australian Bank in September 1961, and the National Bank and the Commercial Bank of Australia in May and July of 1962 respectively. At first their savings-bank facilities were available only in the mainland states. Not until September 1959, more than three years after commencing operations on the mainland, did the A.N.Z. Bank become the first trading bank to develop savings banking in Tasmania. Two more years elapsed before the Bank of New South Wales established similar facilities in September 1961. The other four trading banks entered the field during the next eighteen months.

From the start the trading banks were subject to extensive regulations which had a direct bearing on the position of the Launceston Bank for Savings. Perhaps least welcome of these regulations was the requirement that a minimum of seventy per cent of private savings-bank assets must be held in government or government-guaranteed investments, including local government loans; mortgage loans, fixed deposits and cash holdings were not to exceed thirty per cent. This regulation also applied to the two trustee savings banks, and although they were given time to adjust their investments, the requirements had a definitely cramping effect on at least the Launceston Bank for Savings' vigorous house-lending policy. Regulations also fixed the interest rates of the private savings banks at the same rate as the Commonwealth Savings Bank, or a quarter of one per cent below that paid by the trustee savings banks. Most important of all, and most welcome to the Launceston Bank for Savings and the Hobart Savings Bank, regulations fixed a new maximum size for individual deposits, again in line with the Commonwealth Savings Bank. Initially not applicable to the trustee savings banks, possibly because private savings banking had not yet started in Tasmania, from 1 September 1958 the trustee savings banks came into line with other institutions, with a maximum deposit size of £1,500, three times the previous limit. Shortly afterwards this was increased to £2,000.

The entry of the trading banks into savings-bank business posed a major challenge to the Launceston Bank for Savings, as it did to the established institutions all over Australia, directly through the competition from six new savings banks, and indirectly through the new investment regulations to which the Bank for Savings was also subject. Yet at the same time the entry of the trading banks provided major new opportunities, and on balance might even have proved beneficial. Unlike the mainland states, Tasmania had plenty of advance warning; not until 1961, when the Bank of New South Wales followed the example of the A.N.Z. Bank, did competition really become serious, and in the meantime the Bank for Savings, along with other established institutions, had ample opportunity to prepare for battle. The considerable publicity surrounding the entry of the trading banks into savings-bank business, it is believed, provided a general stimulus to deposit business, reminiscent perhaps, as far as the Bank for Savings is concerned, of the considerable stimulus it had received from publicity many decades before in the 1840s. Above all, the now much greater maximum-deposit size eliminated the large and increasing advantage the Commonwealth Savings Bank had had, and provided the Launceston Bank for Savings, and the Hobart Savings Bank, with a range of potential depositors hitherto out of reach.

To meet the challenge of new conditions, the Launceston Bank for Savings had a particularly strong Executive Committee. Since 1951 the Committee's professional standing and responsibility had been recognized and reinforced by the introduction, under amended legislation, of fee payments for its members; in the changed conditions of the twentieth century, honorary membership had long been an anachronism inhibiting maximum efficiency. More importantly, between 1953 and 1956 there had been a complete change of personnel on the Committee as existing members, appointed before or immediately after the war, had either died or retired because of advancing years. In the long-established tradition they were replaced by leading Launceston businessmen, headed by a new president, Sinclair J. Thyne, a textile manufacturer and mayor of Launceston in 1951 and 1952. If from the same background as their predecessors, the new members of the Committee were much younger, more able to adapt to new circumstances and meet new challenges. Among them, too, were men with professional expertise of direct value to the institution, in addition to their general business experience and ability; they included an accountant, a former bank officer, and a financial agent with specialist knowledge of the credit-worthiness of potential borrowers. Furthermore, being all so recently promoted from the ranks of the General Committee they had a particular understanding of that body and worked with it in close co-operation. It was probably no coincidence that in its report for February 1956 the Executive Committee, in announcing the appointment of new General Committee members to fill the places vacated by a spate of deaths and retirements, included for the first time representatives from five different country towns—a wise and logical move given the critical importance of the Bank's country branches.

Shortly before the trading banks began to provide savings-bank facilities in Tasmania, the Launceston Bank for Savings also acquired a new general manager. In 1958 Ronald Tyson retired, after more than fifty-one years' outstanding service with the Bank. During the previous twenty-two years he had been general manager, a powerful and dynamic figure who had guided the Bank through the difficult war and immediate post-war years, and who played a large part in maintaining its successful record in the face of increasing competition. In 1954 Tyson was awarded the O.B.E. in recognition of his long service to the community. Still as alert and active as ever, he was, however, approaching the age of retirement, and on 31 August 1958 finally left the Bank with fitting tributes from all quarters. In his place the Executive Committee appointed the present general manager, B. Leslie Hooper, then assistant general manager, who had already nearly thirty-two years of service with the Bank.

Meeting new competition

While the 1960s saw a new and vigorous battle for savings-bank business in Tasmania, the law clearly imposed restrictions on the methods of competition. Rates of interest were fixed by the Reserve Bank, and the trustee savings banks' quarter of one per cent edge over other savings banks was at best of marginal importance. Now also the scope for indirect competition through investment policies was severely limited, although the Launceston Bank for Savings made the most of the opportunities allowed by law. Mortgage lending was rarely much below the maximum permitted, and when the maximum increased to thirty-five per cent in 1963, the Bank was quick to take advantage of the more favourable ratio. And at all times the overwhelming bulk of mortgage loans has taken the form of housing loans; at the time of writing these constituted about four-fifths of all mortgage loans. Again, within the minimum percentage of assets required to be held in government stock the Bank for Savings has concentrated whenever and wherever possible on investment in its most favoured outlet: the local authorities of northern Tasmania. Since February 1959 such investments have increased by almost twice the amount its holdings in Commonwealth government stock have increased, and now constitute the Bank's largest single asset. They include debentures of every municipality of northern Tasmania, five marine boards, and the Hydro-Electric Commission; there are also holdings of stock in several fire brigades and the Rivers and Water Supply Commission.

As in its battle with the Commonwealth Savings Bank and the Hobart Savings Bank of earlier years, in the 1960s the Launceston Bank for Savings concentrated primarily on the provision of the best possible physical facilities for depositors. Because the trading banks had such extensive branch networks, the Bank gave more attention to new branches, establishing four in the crucial period between the entry of the A.N.Z. Bank and that of the Bank of New South Wales. Two of these new branches were in key country centres, Deloraine and the rapidly expanding north-west-coast town of Somerset, and one was in the developing Launceston suburb of Newstead. The fourth, in Charles Street, Launceston, was established primarily to relieve pressure on the Head Office branch. Later, in 1965, the Bank established branches in the expanding suburbs of Mowbray and Kings Meadow, and in 1966 a branch in the new urban centre of East Devonport. Meanwhile, during the 1960s, the Bank's agencies were largely reorganized, because many were previously operated by trading banks, and then greatly extended. At the end of 1970 the Launceston Bank for Savings operated some twenty-four full branches, including six in the suburbs of Launceston, and fifty-three agencies, all but one in northern or at least 'border' territory.

Along with the increase in number of branches and agencies, in the 1960s the Launceston Bank for Savings continued to invest heavily in new buildings, alterations and extensions. In doing so it became, early in the decade, a leader in modern architecture in northern Tasmania. The first of its new creations was, perhaps appropriately, a thoroughly remodelled Head Office. In 1963 the old building was functionally revolutionized, with all strictly Head Office operations now conducted on a greatly enlarged first floor, leaving the ground floor for essentially normal depositor business. At the same time the Bank took the daring step of discarding the old Bank of Van Diemen's Land facade for one of modern design. The decision was made, after long deliberation, at a special meeting of the General Committee. There were many regrets, inside and outside the Bank, but the end result, a flat marble front, with a centre-piece of horizontal metal bands surmounting double glass doors, won the triennial award for the best piece of commercial or industrial architecture in Tasmania.

Only months after the remodelled Head Office was completed, the Bank opened a new eye-catching building for its South Launceston branch. Predominantly glass-walled, with a 'refreshingly airy' and efficient interior featuring Tasmanian hardwoods, the banking chamber opens on to a spacious forecourt. This and the building itself are surrounded on three sides by colonnades of tapering, sharp-edged concrete pillars. At the opening ceremony on 26 September 1963 the Mayor of Launceston had plenty of compliments to pay the Bank on its new building, while the president light-heartedly alluded to the country home of a Spanish grandee.

Perhaps encouraged by its successes of 1963, in the following year the Executive Committee accepted for its planned Kings Meadow branch a design for a much more expensive and unconventional building. When completed, it formed externally a six-sided structure composed of bold rounded arches encasing glass walls and projecting outwards from the centre of the building. Architectural opinion may have been doubtful about its merits, but there is no doubt that this flamboyant new building, opened in 1965, attracted customers, and in its short life it has proved an outstandingly successful branch.

During the 1960s the Launceston Bank for Savings made not only architectural innovations, but many others. Possibly the most important of these was the establishment of a public-relations department in 1961, when competition from the trading banks was intensifying. The State Savings Bank of Victoria had taken similar action in 1957. The public-relations office gave particular attention to the school-banking side of the institution's business. Always regarded as one of its most basic activities, both for its own sake and as a long-term investment, school banking had developed rapidly in the post-war years, along with the rapidly rising population of school children. By the end of the 1950s the Bank catered for around 150 schools and nearly 40,000 young depositors. Now the encouragement of school banking became one of the major objects of the public-relations office. From 1963 the Launceston Bank for Savings sponsored what was to be a highly successful children's quiz show on one of the local television stations, and in the following year instituted a system of annual scholarships open to children over the whole of northern Tasmania. The interest and publicity created by these and other efforts on behalf of school children have contributed largely to the continued rise in school banking, as well as to Bank business generally.

Among other new developments of the 1960s the Bank for Savings re-established facilities for fixed deposits in 1961, and in 1967, along with the Hobart Savings Bank, it made provisions for full cheque accounts, thus matching in every way facilities available at the competing trading banks. In 1967 it also instituted one of its most successful innovations, Christmas Club Accounts. Under this scheme, originally devised in the United States, people could prepare for Christmas expenditure early in the year by simply acquiring a book of fifty coupons for one dollar, two dollars, or five dollars. Gradually, in the course of the year, these coupons would be returned to the Bank with the appropriate money, and the whole amount withdrawn, with interest, at Christmas. The number of depositors taking advantage of this scheme had risen by 1970 into five figures.

A successful institution

In the highly prosperous but highly competitive 1960s the Launceston Bank for Savings was very successful. Between February 1959 and August 1970 total deposits in the Bank more than doubled. In part this reflected a substantial rise in the number of depositors, from 148,000 to 185,000, a particularly significant achievement in view of the much greater number of savings banks in operation. In part it reflected a large increase in the average size of accounts. Increases in maximum-deposit size, $20,000 at the end of December 1970, have attracted many comparatively large accounts which, in the 1950s, the Bank could not have accepted.

In the greatly changed conditions of recent years it is hardly surprising that depositors are now more diverse in occupation and background than at any time in the Bank's history. With the increasing complexity of society and blurring of occupational distinctions, it would be meaningless, if not misleading, to attempt a classification of depositors as one can for the nineteenth century. Certain limited points, however, can be made. From samples of new accounts in recent years it is clear that while depositors come from the widest range of lower- and middle-income earners, as one would expect, the unskilled manual workers, for whom the Launceston Bank for Savings and other savings banks were originally created, are now very few. They are much less important as depositors than they are in the community in general, which is perhaps some indication how state welfare has undermined the traditional nineteenth-century objectives of savings banks. A further point of interest, perhaps, is the very considerable number of strictly non-individual accounts: the multiplicity of accounts from non-profit-making organizations, the growing popularity of joint accounts, and the large number of trust accounts. Although most of the latter are held simply on behalf of children, they include many solicitors' trust accounts for large sums, which overall contribute a substantial portion of the Bank's funds; these provide one of the clearest examples of the boost given to deposits from the greatly increased legal maximum-account size.

As one would expect, the purposes for which savings accounts are held are now more diverse than at any time previously. The traditionally dominant types, the relatively idle accounts of surplus funds held for indefinite periods for indefinite purposes, still compose a large percentage of the Bank's deposits. However, the post-war years have seen a rapid rise in savings accounts operated for more specific, relatively short-term or medium-term purposes: for holidays, payments of rates or taxes, refurnishing or other major household outlays, and deposits on land or houses.

In other respects the purpose or pattern of savings accounts has changed less. Savings accounts used effectively as current accounts are still fairly rare. They are not encouraged by the Bank, and with the much greater facilities provided by trading banks, perhaps are not so sought after by depositors as in earlier years. Also, despite the affluence and full employment of post-war years, the ideal savers, the depositors who add weekly or monthly to their accounts in equal instalments, remain as few as ever. A scheme recently introduced by the Bank to pay a higher rate of interest to those who contract to save by equal instalments over three years has been very little used by the Bank's customers. Depositors dislike regular and long-term commitments as much as they ever have done. This point is further illustrated by the still comparative unimportance of higher-yielding fixed deposits.

In general terms, the Launceston Bank for Savings, in its overall record as well as the pattern, purpose and type of its accounts, has been basically similar to other savings banks in recent years. Despite strong and growing competition from other forms of investment, particularly building societies and the share market, savings banking has continued to grow and diversify in nature. The advantages of complete liquidity, safety and ease of access have attracted a large growth of funds, even though higher interest rates are available elsewhere. Savings-bank deposits have increased rapidly in every Australian state, in Tasmania as in the others. However, within Tasmania it would seem that the Launceston Bank for Savings has been distinctly, though not spectacularly more successful than its competitors.

In the past decade the Launceston Bank for Savings has suffered much less than one might expect from the entry of trading banks into savings-bank business. Certainly it has had the advantages of well-established branches, a considerable degree of local loyalty, and a slight edge in interest rates. Nevertheless, it is still a considerable achievement that, after about a decade of competition, this one savings bank, operating in only half a state, holds considerably more deposits than the total of all six private savings banks operating throughout Tasmania. Up to August 1970 private savings banks acquired a smaller share of savings-bank business in Tasmania than in any other state, and the success of the Launceston Bank for Savings is no small part of the explanation.

Perhaps more significant is the fact that of the three established savings institutions in Tasmania, the Launceston Bank for Savings has experienced the smallest reduction in its share of savings-bank deposits since the entry of the trading banks. Between February 1959 and August 1970 the Launceston Bank for Savings' share of total deposits in Tasmania declined from about twenty-seven per cent to something over twenty-four per cent. Over the same period the Hobart Savings Bank's share fell from about thirty-three to twenty-seven per cent and in 1970 its total deposits exceeded those of the Launceston Bank for Savings by little more than ten per cent. The Commonwealth Savings Bank experienced the greatest reduction from forty to thirty per cent, despite a more aggressive branch-expansion policy than the Launceston Bank for Savings and a far more aggressive one than the Hobart Savings Bank which made virtually no additions in the period. Clearly the Commonwealth Savings Bank felt the effects not only of competition from new savings banks, but the loss of its advantage in maximum-deposit size.

Perhaps one of the underlying reasons for the relative success of the Launceston Bank for Savings is that it has restricted its activities to northern Tasmania, in contrast to all its competitors which have operated throughout the state. The Bank for Savings has never seriously contemplated extending beyond the north. Such geographic concentration has meant considerable competitive advantages within the area of operations. Within this area the Bank has been able to provide an almost exhaustive network of branches and agencies; the Launceston Bank for Savings has, for example, twenty-four branches in northern Tasmania, while the Hobart Savings

Bank has nineteen throughout the state. Through its close network of branches and agencies in this restricted area, the Bank for Savings has been able to develop depositing facilities, including school banking, and borrowing facilities to a very high degree, and has all the advantages of local knowledge and not a small degree of local loyalty.

Since they were first established more than fifty years ago the Bank's branches have been perhaps the key to its development, but never more so than in recent years. Although still named after the city where its headquarters are located, and although its Executive Committee is still composed exclusively of Launceston businessmen, at least since the war the Launceston Bank for Savings has in reality been northern Tasmania's Bank for Savings. And in this it may be significant that at the time of writing five of the six senior administrators of the Bank were born outside Launceston, and that four of the six began their careers at country branches of the Bank. Certainly, since the war the country branches have accounted for most of the increase in deposits, despite the fact that Launceston itself has retained a roughly stable share of northern Tasmania's population. Just after the war Launceston accounted for about seventy per cent of the Bank's deposits. By the end of the 1950s this had declined to around sixty per cent, and at the time of writing the city accounts for less than half of all the deposits, of which about a third are at the various suburban branches. Of the country branches, which now altogether account for most of the Bank for Savings' deposits, those of the north-west coast have grown most in importance, with an increase in their share of all deposits from around twenty-five per cent just after the war to around forty per cent at the present time. Since the north-west coast is the area of northern Tasmania with the most established identity and the least allegiance in general to Launceston, this would suggest perhaps that local loyalty as such has not been the crucial factor in the Bank's success.

The success of the Launceston Bank for Savings has certainly not been achieved without cost. Successful competition has meant heavy outlays on buildings and a substantial allocation of income to maintenance and depreciation. It has also meant more staff than might otherwise have been employed; at present the Bank has over 150 staff, of whom twenty-one work solely on Head Office business. The result has been a considerable increase in costs of management relative to income, though to some extent this also reflects better conditions and higher salaries for its staff, as compared with, for example, the austere 1930s. Overall, despite a much-reduced proportionate allocation to reserves, now ample for all forseeable contingencies, the proportion of income distributed to depositors has fallen from about three-quarters in the 1930s to generally rather less than two-thirds in the 1960s.

Yet the cost has been worthwhile. A somewhat smaller proportion of income distributed as interest has been a small price to pay for the benefits which have accrued. Highly developed facilities have helped to attract some 185,000 depositors, a remarkable figure compared with the total population of the area served by the Bank, which probably does not greatly exceed 200,000. And with greater funds at its disposal the Bank has been able to invest correspondingly more in the basic social needs of the area in which it operates; mortgage loans and loans to local authorities in northern Tasmania account for well over two-thirds of the Bank's investments. The success of the Launceston Bank for Savings has meant a happy and rewarding alliance between an institution and the community it serves.

And serving the community is not a meaningless phrase. As a private but non-shareholder institution this simply is the Bank's function, and perhaps the one major respect in which it has remained unaltered during its 135 years of existence. In many respects the Bank has changed fundamentally; from a rather amateur institution to one more business-like and now highly professional; from a virtual monopoly to one facing increasing and now intense competition; and from one which originally catered for the modest needs of a handful of working-men in a town, to one serving the many and diverse needs of a large community in half a state. Throughout its history, however, the Launceston Bank for Savings has retained its basic form and object: a non-profit-making institution with allegiance neither to the government nor to shareholders but to the general public. If in this role the Bank is now by force of circumstances not so indispensable as in earlier decades, it is certainly more active and successful than at any other time in its history.

GENERAL COMMITTEE 1971

Cecil McR. Archer
Robert J. Bain, M.B.E.
Maxwell G. Cleaver, O.B.E.
John A. Ferrall
Raymond A. Ferrall, C.B.E.
G. Maurice Force
Graeme R. Ford
John Gunn
Stanley A. Guy
Sir Denham Henty, K.B.E.
Keith C. Holyman
James R. Hughes
Roy L. Hyland
William O. Layh
Gilbert C. McKinlay
Alexander P. Mitchell
Alec A. Newton
J. A. Gavin O'Dea, M.B.E.
T. Max Payne
George T. Rule
Geoffrey G. Salier
R. John Simmons
Lyall G. A. Stuart
Percy C. Thompson, V.D.
Peter J. Thyne
Sinclair J. Thyne, C.B.E.
Donald D. von Bibra, O.B.E.

CHAIRMEN AND PRESIDENTS

1891–1892	Richard Green jun.
1892–1893	Alex Webster
1893–1900	Hardwicke Weedon
1900–1903	Henry Edgell
1903–1905	George E. Harrap
1905–1908	Stuart Eardley-Wilmot
1908–1910	P. Oakley Fysh
1910–1912	William Fordyce
1912–1914	Frederick K. Fairthorne
1914–1930	Walter H. Ferrall
1930–1932	John Duncan
1932–1933	George E. Harrap
1933–1945	Albert W. Monds
1945–1952	Arthur E. Pepper
1952–1955	Alfred C. Ferrall
1955	J. Gordon Duncan
1955–1956	Algernon P. Findlay
1956–	Sinclair J. Thyne

Note: Until 1891 there were no formally-appointed Chairmen of the Executive Committee. In 1946 the title of Chairman was changed to President.

ACTUARIES AND MANAGERS

1843–1844	Isaac Sherwin
1844–1868	Henry Dowling jun.
1868–1887	George Pullen
1887–1900	John C. Cathcart
1900–1932	Hardwicke Weedon
1932–1936	John Duncan
1936–1958	Ronald S. Tyson
1958–	B. Leslie Hooper

Note: In 1918 the title of Actuary was changed to Manager.

DEPOSITORS AND DEPOSITS

Year	*Number of Accounts (Ordinary department)*	*Total Value of Deposits (All departments)* £	
1840	?	4926	
1845	455	7785	
1850	953	18,706	
1855	2125	91,429	
1860	2839	96,297	
1865	2831	64,138	
1870	3374	67,666	
1875	4367	79,988	
1880	5867	97,362	
1885	7736	122,271	
1890	9723	157,992	
1895	11,377	207,531	
1900	13,968	287,189	
1905	17,205	372,165	
1910	20,232	467,331	
1915	22,728	612,589	
1920	26,554	971,255	
1925	34,575	1,169,096	
1930	42,798	1,509,530	
1935	48,196	1,848,957	
1940	58,662	2,680,855	
1945	70,605	4,841,740	
1950	91,165	7,115,022	
1955	107,732	10,504,447	
1960	114,406	12,980,494	
1965	119,406	17,068,473	($34,136,946)
1970	138,779		$49,914,972
1971	141,154		$57,250,119

Note: As at 31 August of each year, except for 1840 (5 August) and 1845 (30 June). From 1930 onwards the number of accounts excludes school bank accounts.

Source Notes

Source notes are of two types: general references for each section to give an overall indication of the major sources used; and specific reference to quotations and to important or controversial points for which documentation is considered desirable. Complete details for each reference are given in the accompanying bibliography.

In general, no source references are given for biographical details, since these are rarely open to question and are normally derived from a wide variety of sources, including newspaper obituaries—the most important single source of information, especially for the briefer biographical sketches—advertisements, almanacs, directories, the *Australian Dictionary of Biography*, and other books and pamphlets.

Much valuable information has been supplied by the present general manager of the Launceston Bank for Savings, Mr B. Leslie Hooper, other officers at the Bank, and also the following former officers: K. Conroy, A. S. H. Emmett, C. Henri, R. H. Lewis, W. C. Shaw, R. S. Tyson, K. R. Westbrook.

CHAPTER ONE

Tasmania and Launceston in 1835

Main Sources: *Statistics of Tasmania*; *Hobart Town Almanacks*; Bethell, *The Story of Port Dalrymple*; Button, *Flotsam and Jetsam*; Fenton, *A History of Tasmania*; Hartwell, *The Economic Development of Van Diemen's Land 1820-1850*; Parker, *The Rise, Progress and Present State of Van Diemen's Land.*

References:

Page 1 Quotations from *The Times* (London), 11 August 1829.
2 'tortuous . . .' Dixon, *The Condition and Capabilities of Van Diemen's Land as a Place of Emigration*, p. 17.
3 'a harbour . . .' Dilke, *Greater Britain*, p. 95.
3 'really elegant . . .' Eyre, Autobiography, p. 96.
4 'The good . . .' quoted Whitfield, *The River Tamar*, p. 17.
4 'well fed . . .' *The Times*, 11 August 1829.
4 'allowed . . .' *Hobart Town Almanack*, 1834, p. 45.

P

Source Notes (Chapters 1–2)

A meeting of philanthropists

Main Sources: Launceston Bank for Savings, Minute-books; various bibliographical references (see general note).

References:

Page 5 Browne and the robbery: Button, op. cit., p. 168.
6 Remark by biographer of Browne: Isabella J. Mead, in *Australian Dictionary of Biography*, vol. I, p. 169.
6 Sherwin's overland ride: Bethell, op. cit., p. 120.
7 'a gentleman . . .' Plomley, *Friendly Mission*, p. 1022.
7 'a pious man' Brown, *Clyde Company Papers*, vol. II, p. 43.

The origins and philosophy of savings banking

Main Sources: This is a composite picture drawn from a variety of sources listed in the bibliography, and also from several nineteenth-century treatises not included there.

References:

Page 9 'Any class . . .' Smiles, *Self-Help*, p. 344.
9 'Of all . . .' Malthus, *An Essay on the Principle of Population*, 6th ed., pp. 407-8.

Early Australian savings banks

Main Sources: *Launceston Advertiser*; S. J. Butlin, *Foundations of the Australian Monetary System 1788-1851*.

References:

Page 11 'not arrived . . .' Evidence of Barron Field from the Bonwick Transcripts of the Bigge Commission, BT.7, p. 2850.
13 'generally work . . .' *The Times*, 7 August 1828.
13 'After the Meeting . . .' *Launceston Advertiser*, 2 October 1834.

The establishment of the Launceston Bank for Savings

Main Source: Launceston Bank for Savings, Minute-books.

References:

Page 15 'club their . . .' *Launceston Advertiser*, 12 March 1835.
15 'the crude . . .' *Launceston Advertiser*, 30 April 1835.
15 First accounts at the Launceston Bank for Savings: Ledgers (Individual).

CHAPTER TWO

The boom of the late 1830s

Main Sources: *Statistics of Tasmania*; S. J. Butlin, *Foundations of the Australian Monetary System 1788-1851*; Hartwell, *The Economic Development of Van Diemen's Land 1820-1850*; Kiddle, *Men of Yesterday*.

References:

Page 17 Tasmanian population figure for 1840 estimated from the 1842 census.
17 'it was then . . .' Glover correspondence, John Glover to Mary Bowles, 13 December 1840.

Source Notes (Chapter 2)

The Bank in an 'obscure and lethargic state'

Main Sources: Launceston Bank for Savings, Ledgers; Minute-books; *Launceston Advertiser*; *Launceston Examiner*; S. J. Butlin, op. cit.

References:

Page 18 Davies' 'beautiful' sermons: Brown, *Clyde Company Papers*, vol. II, p. 33.
18 'the tillage . . .' *Launceston Advertiser*, 23 January 1840.
18 Longford Savings Bank advertisement: *Launceston Advertiser*, 10 November 1836.
18 'obscure . . .' *Launceston Examiner*, 6 August 1842.
18 Gilles' career at the Union Bank: S. J. Butlin, *Australia and New Zealand Bank*, pp. 83-4.
19 'in the smallest . . .' William Browne to the Colonial Secretary, Colonial Secretary's Papers.

The need for legislation

Main Sources: Launceston Bank for Savings, Minute-books; Colonial Secretary's Papers; *Launceston Examiner.*

The depression of the early 1840s

Main Sources: Launceston Bank for Savings, Minute-books; Colonial Secretary's Papers; *Statistics of Tasmania*; *Launceston Examiner*; S. J. Butlin, op. cit.; Hartwell, op. cit.

References:

Page 22 'a most . . .' Bassett, *The Hentys*, p. 509.
22 'a general . . .' Brown, *Clyde Company Papers*, vol. III, p. 365.
22 Launceston's water supply: *Launceston Examiner*, 18 November 1843.
23 'a mere . . .' *Launceston Examiner*, 4 February 1843.
23 'a person . . .' *Launceston Examiner*, 6 September 1843.
24 Savings-bank legislation considered 'indispensable': *Launceston Examiner*, 25 October 1843.
24 'to make . . .' *Launceston Examiner*, 12 March 1842.

Reconstruction as an independent establishment

Main Sources: Launceston Bank for Savings, Balance-sheets; Minute-books; Colonial Secretary's Papers; *Launceston Examiner.*

References:

Page 24 Weedon's sale announcement: *Launceston Examiner*, 3 February 1844.
25 'take such . . .' Minute-book, 13 December 1843.
27 'The whole . . .' Minute-book, 29 July 1844.
28 Sherwin's family's losses: *Australian Dictionary of Biography*, vol. 2, p. 441, and *Launceston Examiner*, 29 June 1869.

The bank under fire

Main Sources: Launceston Bank for Savings, Minute-books; *Cornwall Chronicle*; *Launceston Examiner.*

References:
Page 28 'scurillous . . .' quoted in *Australian Dictionary of Biography*, entry for Goodwin, vol. 1, p. 458.
28 'a FLASH newspaper' *Launceston Examiner*, 16 April 1842.
28 'a vile press' *Launceston Examiner*, 22 November 1845.
29 'combination . . .' *Cornwall Chronicle*, 26 October 1844.
29 Goodwin's attack on the Bank: *Cornwall Chronicle*, 1 February and 20 September 1845.
29 Browne's threatened resignation: Browne Papers.
29 'notorious liar' *Launceston Examiner*, 12 November 1845.
29 'moral bandit' *Launceston Examiner*, 22 November 1845.

CHAPTER THREE

Political and economic affairs 1845-1850

Main Sources: *Statistics of Tasmania*; *Launceston Examiner*; Fenton, *A History of Tasmania*; Hartwell, *The Economic Development of Van Diemen's Land 1820-1850*; West, *History of Tasmania.*

References:
Page 30 'perfectly . . .' Scott Papers, James Scott to Thomas Scott, 8 June 1847.
31 'exceedingly precarious' and 'critical state' Brown, *Clyde Company Papers*, vol. III, p. 433.

The Hobart Savings Bank and the 1848 Act

Main Sources: Launceston Bank for Savings, Balance-sheets; Minute-books; Colonial Secretary's Papers; Tasmania, Acts of Parliament; S. J. Butlin, *Foundations of the Australian Monetary System 1788-1851*; Hobart Savings Bank, *The Centenary of the Hobart Savings Bank 1845-1945*.

References:
Page 32 'now that . . .' Walker to George Benington, 31 January 1845, quoted Backhouse and Tylor, *The Life and Labours of George Washington Walker . . .*, p. 520.
32 'I have . . .' Walker to J. B. Walker, 19 September 1855, ibid., p. 544.
32 'to all . . .' Hobart Savings Bank, op. cit., Objectives stated within.
33 Draft of Bill published in *Hobart Gazette Town* 10 January 1845: An Act to encourage the Establishment of Banks for Savings in Van Diemen's Land.
33 Interpretation of motive behind 1845 Bill: S. J. Butlin, op. cit., p. 453.

The Bank's depositors

Main Source: Launceston Bank for Savings, New-account Books.

Reference:
Page 35 Class of depositors; comparison with British savings banks: Horne, *A History of Savings Banks*, pp. 93-7.

The pattern of saving

Main Source: Launceston Bank for Savings, Ledgers.

CHAPTER FOUR

The gold discoveries and their effect

Main Sources: Scott Papers; *Statistics of Tasmania*; *Tasmanian Parliamentary Papers* (1852 Select Committee, and Immigration Reports); *Launceston Examiner*; Bethell, *The Story of Port Dalrymple*; Coghlan, *Labour and Industry in Australia*; Fenton, *A History of Tasmania.*

References:

Page 39 'fertile . . .' *Launceston Examiner*, 28 June 1851.
39 Denison's estimate of population loss: Coghlan, op. cit., vol. II, p. 629.
40 'a *most* . . .' *Information regarding the Colony of Van Diemen's Land*, p. 11.
40 'upon . . .' *Launceston Examiner*, 24 December 1851.
40 Claims about gold in Tasmania: *Launceston Examiner*, 28 February and 6 March 1852.
41 Sir Henry Young's observations: Fenton, op. cit., p. 269.
41 'this gold . . .' Melville, *Australasia and Prison Discipline*, p. 235.
42 'people . . .' Scott Papers, James Scott to Thomas Scott, 18 March 1853.
42 'the first . . .' *Launceston Examiner*, 28 March 1854.
42 'a large . . .' Stoney, *A Year in Tasmania*, p. 258.
42 'a very . . .' ibid., p. 262.
42 Roe's judgement of Launceston's water-supply: 'The Establishment of Local Self-Government in Hobart and Launceston 1845-1858', p. 37.

Booming business for the Bank

Main Sources: Launceston Bank for Savings, Balance-sheets; Ledgers; Minute-books; New-account Books; Scott Papers.

References:

Page 43 'in Launceston . . .' Scott Papers, James Scott to Thomas Scott, 26 September 1852.
44 Savings-bank figures for Victoria and New South Wales from the *Government Gazettes* of those colonies.
44 Hobart Savings Bank figures: *Hobart Town Gazettes.*
46 'The Managers . . .' Henry Dowling to William Paton, 18 March 1853, Letter-book 1849-54.
46 Draper's advertisement: *Wood's Van Diemen's Land Almanack*, 1852, p. 126.

The problem of investments

Main Sources: Launceston Bank for Savings, Balance-sheets; Loans-books; Minute-books; Scott Papers; *Launceston Examiner*; Hobart Savings Bank, *The Centenary of the Hobart Savings Bank 1845-1945.*

References:

Page 46 Hobart Savings Bank surplus of funds: Hobart Savings Bank, op. cit., p. 32.
46 Launceston Bank for Savings' refusal to open accounts: Scott Papers, James Scott to Thomas Scott, 1 September 1852.
47 'it is now . . .' ibid.

47 Bank's advertisement of mortgage loans: *Launceston Examiner*, 24 July 1852.
47 '*land is* . . .' Scott Papers, op. cit.
47 Land boom a 'mania' Scott Papers, James Scott to Thomas Scott, 14 February 1853.
48 Scott's optimism about the future: Scott Papers, James Scott to Thomas Scott, 18 March 1853.
48 '18 varieties . . .' Brown, *Clyde Company Papers*, vol. IV, p. 9.

The Bank's leaders

Sources: See general note.

References:

Page 49 Dowling's dominance: Roe, op. cit., p. 38.
51 'Well, that . . .' Smiles, *Thrift*, p. 160.

CHAPTER FIVE

The establishment of agencies

Main Sources: Launceston Bank for Savings, Minute-books; New-account Books; Colonial Secretary's Papers.

References:

Page 52 Tasmanian population figures from censuses of 1842, 1851 and 1861.
52 The north-west's development: Ramsay's *With the Pioneers* provides a wealth of information.
53 Hobart Bank's early discussions about branches: Hobart Savings Bank, *Centenary* . . . , pp. 25, 31, 33.
54 'Let each . . .' Wilmot's pamphlet, *Recommendation to the Police Magistrates of the Island to establish Branch Savings Banks*, published by James Barnard, Government Printer, Hobart Town, 1855, in Colonial Secretary's Papers (CSD 1/46/937).
54 Opening of Bank's agencies: *Launceston Examiner*, 2 January 1856.

Deteriorating fortunes

Main Sources: Launceston Bank for Savings, Balance-sheets; Minute-books; *Statistics of Tasmania.*

The post-office savings bank controversy

Main Sources: Launceston Bank for Savings, Minute-books; *Cornwall Chronicle*; *Launceston Examiner.*

References:

Page 57 Information about British post-office savings banks: Horne, *A History of Savings Banks*, pp. 168-81.
57 *Punch* verses: quoted in *Launceston Examiner*, 5 July 1862.
58 'came forward . . .' ibid.
59 *Examiner*'s claims regarding post-office savings banking: *Launceston Examiner*, 8 July and 5 August 1862.
59 Public denial by Browne: *Launceston Examiner*, 7 August 1862.

A run on the bank

Main Sources: Launceston Bank for Savings, Balance-sheets; Half-yearly Reports; Ledgers; Minute-books; Weekly Financial Statements.

References:

Page 62 Browne's claim regarding damage done to the Bank's reputation: *Cornwall Chronicle*, 1 November 1862.

62 Gleadow's comment: ibid.

CHAPTER SIX

Tasmania in the 1860s

Main Sources: Tasmanian *Parliamentary Papers* (Immigration Reports); *Statistics of Tasmania*; *Launceston Examiner*; Coghlan, *Labour and Industry in Australia*; Dilke, *Greater Britain*; Fenton, *A History of Tasmania*; Townsley, 'The Launceston and Western Railway Company' and 'Tasmania and the Great Economic Depression'.

References:

Page 65 'backwaters . . .' Coghlan, op. cit., vol. II, p. 871.

65 Reduction in wage levels: Townsley, 'Tasmania and the Great Economic Depression, 1858-1872', p. 37.

65fn. Castra failure: Cornish, *Under the Southern Cross*, p. 328.

66 'It is . . .' Dilke, op. cit., p. 94.

66 'In the south . . .' quoted by Coghlan, op. cit., vol. II, p. 1130.

66 'most painful . . .' *Launceston Examiner*, 9 August 1862.

67 'big and . . .' Trollope, *Australia and New Zealand*, p. 370.

67 Advocation of political union with Victoria: *Cornwall Chronicle* 18 March, 25 March and 19 April 1872.

67 Tasmania as a commercial adjunct to Melbourne: Coghlan, op. cit.

67 Abundance of minerals in Tasmania: e.g. Baird, *The Emigrants' Guide to Australasia*, p. 18.

67 'The curse . . .' Dilke, op. cit., p. 97.

68 'a fearful drawback' An Englishman, *The Rise and Progress of Australia, Tasmania and New Zealand*, p. 197.

68 Politicians dismissed as 'Lilliputian' Dilke, op. cit., p. 103.

68 'Launceston . . .' *Launceston Examiner*, 10 April 1862.

69 *Launceston Examiner* suggests secession: 24 June 1862.

The Bank's financial troubles

Main Sources: Launceston Bank for Savings, Balance-sheets; Ledgers; Loans-books; Half-yearly Reports; Minute-books; New-account Books.

Reference:

Page 74 Hobart Savings Bank figures: *Hobart Town Gazettes*.

Administrative reorganization

Main Source: Launceston Bank for Savings, Minute-books.

References:

Page 75 Dowling and the Launceston and Western Railway Company: see especially Launceston and Western Railway Company Minute-book 1865-7.

77 Changing character of savings banks: e.g. Payne and Davis, *The Savings Bank of Baltimore 1818-1866*, p. 29.

CHAPTER SEVEN

The first railways

Main Sources: *Cornwall Chronicle*; *Launceston Examiner*; Fenton, *A History of Tasmania*; Townsley, 'The Launceston and Western Railway Company' and 'The Tasmanian Main Line Railway Company'.

References:

Page 79 Trollope on the northern railway tangle: *Australia and New Zealand*, p. 361.

79 'mad crusade . . .' *Cornwall Chronicle*, 20 February 1874.

The development of mining

Main Sources: *Cornwall Chronicle*; Blainey, *The Rush that Never Ended*; Fenton, op. cit.; Hughes, *The Australian Iron and Steel Industry 1848-1962*.

References:

Page 81 Reputed ninety gold-mining companies: Fenton, op. cit., p. 358.

83 'you can . . .' *Cornwall Chronicle*, 12 November 1873.

83 History of the Emu Bay Railway: James, 'The Emu Bay and Mount Bischoff Railway'.

The boom of the 1880s

Main Sources: *Statistics of Tasmania*; Tasmanian *Parliamentary Papers* (on railway developments); *Cornwall Chronicle*; *Launceston Examiner*; Blainey, op. cit.; Fenton, op. cit.

References:

Page 84 'the tide . . .' Braddon's comment quoted by Denholm, 'Edward Braddon's Impressions of Launceston and the North West, 1878', p. 47.

84 'a poor . . .' Cornish, *Under the Southern Cross*, p. 289.

Launceston, centre of the boom

Main Sources: *Launceston Examiner*; Blainey, op. cit.; Reynolds, *Launceston. History of an Australian City*.

References:

Page 87 New manufacturing activities in Launceston: Leavitt, *Jubilee History of Tasmania*, vol. II, *passim*.

89 Details of the 1886-7 Launceston Industrial Exhibition: *Launceston Examiner* 15 and 16 December 1886.

89 Details of the 1891-2 Tasmanian International Exhibition: *Official Catalogue* and *Official Record*.

CHAPTER EIGHT

Revival and expansion

Main Sources: Launceston Bank for Savings, Balance-sheets; Half-yearly Reports; Minute-books; *Statistics of Tasmania*; *Launceston Examiner*.

References:

Page 90 Data on bank interest rates: Hall, *The Stock Exchange of Melbourne . . .*, pp. 246-7; *Statistics of Tasmania*.

91 Rate of interest paid by post-office savings banks: *Walch's Tasmanian Almanacs*.

91 Post-office savings-bank funds in 1890: Tasmanian Post Office, Annual Report and Returns (Tasmanian *Parliamentary Papers*).

92 George Pullen to the Tasmanian Colonial Secretary, 8 January 1880, Letter-book 1873-88. The circular itself is not in the Bank's records.

Leaders and officers

Main Sources: Launceston Bank for Savings, Balance-sheets; Half-yearly Reports; Minute-books.

References:

Page 93 'those early . . .' Chairman's Centenary speech, Minute-book, 21 March 1935.

95 'his gratification . . .' Report of half-yearly general meeting, 8 September 1888.

Investment policy

Main Sources: Launceston Bank for Savings, Balance-sheets; Half-yearly Reports; Letter-book 1873-88; Loans-books; Minute-books.

References:

Page 97 'I am . . .' George Pullen to the Colonial Treasurer, 31 December 1874, Letter-book 1873-88.

100 'taking into . . .' George Pullen to Mrs Edward Archer, 15 April 1874, Letter-book 1873-88.

100 'In your . . .' George Pullen to Basil Archer, 4 May 1887, Letter-book 1873-88.

101 The debates on the 1886 Act are reported only briefly in the *Launceston Examiner* for 27 October 1886 and 8 November 1886.

The depositors

Main Sources: Launceston Bank for Savings, Balance-sheets; Ledgers; Letter-books; Minute-books; New-account Books.

CHAPTER NINE

Tasmania and Launceston in the 1890s

Main Sources: *Statistics of Tasmania*; Tasmanian *Parliamentary Papers* (on the Bank of Van Diemen's Land, and unemployment); *Launceston Examiner*; *Walch's Tasmanian Almanacs*; Blainey, *The Rush that Never Ended*; Button, *Flotsam and Jetsam*.

References:

Page 105 Fall in Australian living standards calculated from data in N. G. Butlin, *Australian Domestic Product . . .*, p. 33.

108 Advertisement for Corporation Baths: *Walch's Tasmanian Almanac*, 1900, p. 311.

108 'a spot . . .' Button, op. cit., p. 344.

108 'rustic . . .' Just, *Official Handbook of Tasmania*, 5th ed., p. 92.

The Bank in the 1890s

Main Sources: Launceston Bank for Savings, Balance-sheets; Half-yearly Reports; Letter-books; Minute-books; New-account Books; *Statistics of Tasmania*; *Launceston Examiner.*

References:

Page 109 Figures for Hobart Savings Bank: *Hobart Gazettes.*

109 'In these days . . .' *Launceston Examiner*, 4 September 1891.

111 Figures for Hobart Savings Bank: *Hobart Gazettes.*

112 Rate of interest paid by Post Office Savings Bank: *Walch's Tasmanian Almanacs.*

Tasmania and the Bank after 1900

Main Sources: Launceston Bank for Savings, Balance-sheets; Half-yearly Reports; Ledgers; Minute-books; New-account Books; *Statistics of Tasmania*; *Launceston Examiner*; *Walch's Tasmanian Almanacs.*

References:

Page 114 'Launceston is . . .' *Handbook of Tasmania*, 1914, p. 160.

115 'one of . . .' *Daily Telegraph* (Launceston), 25 June 1900.

Signs of complacency

Main Sources: Launceston Bank for Savings, Depositors' Letter-books; Half-yearly Reports; Minute-books; *Statistics of Tasmania*; Tasmanian *Parliamentary Papers* (on State Savings Bank); *Launceston Examiner.*

Reference:

Page 120 Drain to the mainland: cf. Blainey, 'Population Movements in Tasmania 1870-1901', p. 69.

CHAPTER TEN

Tasmania and the Bank around 1910

Main Sources: Launceston Bank for Savings, Balance-sheets; Minute-books; *Statistics of Tasmania*; *Launceston Examiner.*

The Commonwealth Savings Bank

Main Sources: Launceston Bank for Savings, Depositors' Letter-books; Minute-books; Premier's Department Papers; *Launceston Examiner*; Gollan, *The Commonwealth Bank of Australia.*

References:

Page 123 'a matter . . .' James McGowen to Andrew Fisher, 29 November 1911 (telegram), Premier's Department Papers.

123 'little better . . .' quoted by Gollan, op. cit., p. 106.

124 'there is . . .' *Launceston Examiner*, 13 December 1912.

124 Reactions of State Savings Bank of Victoria: Craddock and Cavanough, *125 Years . . .*, pp. 34-6.

124 Suggestion that the Tasmanian government wanted to be rid of the State Savings Bank: Gollan, op. cit., p. 116.

125 'if the Bank . . .' Minute-book, 14 November 1912.

126 'We pride . . .' Hardwicke Weedon to W. E. Bovill, 1 September 1914, Depositors' Letter-book.

World War I

Main Sources: Launceston Bank for Savings, Balance-sheets; Half-yearly Reports; Minute-books; Tasmania, Acts of Parliament.

Reference:

Page 127 Long-run beneficial effect of war on the saving habit: Horne, *A History of Savings Banks*, p. 323.

To serve a city or a region?

Main Sources: Launceston Bank for Savings, Balance-sheets; Minute-books; New-account Books; *Censuses of Tasmania*; Hobart Savings Bank, *The Centenary of the Hobart Savings Bank 1845-1945*.

Reference:

Page 129 'Twenty . . .' *Launceston Examiner*, 31 October 1923.

Branch banking

Main Sources: Launceston Bank for Savings, Balance-sheets; Half-yearly Reports; Minute-books.

References:

Page 131 'the Board . . .' Minute-book, 24 November 1919.

132 'Cannot understand . . .' Minute-book, 28 February 1920.

132 'Telegram received . . .' ibid.

133fn. Information from half-yearly reports of the Hobart Savings Bank, held by Launceston Bank for Savings.

CHAPTER ELEVEN

Tasmania's economic troubles of the 1920s

Main Sources: *Statistics of Tasmania*; Tasmanian *Parliamentary Papers* (especially for Lyons government measures); *Launceston Examiner*; Forster, *Industrial Development in Australia 1920-1930*; Reynolds, *Launceston. History of an Australian City*.

References:

Page 136 Mining tributing parties: Blainey, 'The Rise and Decline of the West Coast', pp. 70-1.

136 Thirty per cent decline in tourism: Ogilvie and Shields, *The Case for Tasmania*, p. 24.

136 Unemployment figures for Tasmania: Commonwealth *Labour Reports.*

136 Committee Report: *Report of the Committee Appointed to Inquire into Tasmanian Disabilities under Federation*, 1925.

137 Information on pulp and paper, and shale oil, is taken from research essays by Mr S. Turton and Mr R. Bond respectively, held by the Department of Economic History, University of Melbourne.

137 'the finest . . .' *Launceston Examiner*, 28 November 1923.

137 Launceston, the official railway-engineering centre: Reynolds, op. cit., p. 158.

The Bank's performance 1919-1929

Main Sources: Launceston Bank for Savings, Balance-sheets; Branch Correspondence; Depositors' Letter-books; Half-yearly Reports; Minute-books.

The 1930s depression

Main Sources: Launceston Bank for Savings, Branch Half-yearly Reports; State Finance Committee, *Studies in the Tasmanian Economy*; *Statistics of Tasmania*; *Launceston Examiner.*

References:

Page 142 Launceston floods: *Launceston Examiner*, April 1929 *passim*; Reynolds, op. cit., pp. 165-6.

142 First evicted tenant: *Launceston Examiner*, 15 January 1932.

143 Lowest birth rate in Tasmania: Commonwealth *Demography Bulletins.*

143 Highest unemployment rate in Tasmania: Commonwealth *Labour Reports.*

143 'half-starved . . .' *Launceston Examiner*, 11 July 1935.

143 'Unfortunately . . .' John Duncan to Keith Westbrook, 28 April 1933, Burnie Branch Correspondence.

The Bank in depression and recovery

Main Sources: Launceston Bank for Savings, Balance-sheets; Branch Correspondence; Branch Half-yearly Reports; Half-yearly Reports; Minute-books.

References:

Page 144 General savings-bank statistics: Tasmanian *Government Gazette*; *Official Year Books of the Commonwealth.*

145 'I hear . . .' Letter to Wynyard manager dated simply August 1933, Wynyard Branch Correspondence.

145 'I am . . .' Letter to Smithton manager dated 17 August 1933, Smithton Branch Correspondence.

146 'this so-called . . .' Hardwicke Weedon to Keith Westbrook, February 1932, Burnie Branch Correspondence.

147 Chairman's prepared speech included in Report for half-year ending February 1932.

147 'However . . .' Minute-book, 24 September 1931.

The Bank's achievement 1919-1939

Main Sources: Launceston Bank for Savings, Minute-books; Tasmanian *Government Gazettes*; *Official Year Books of the Commonwealth.*

CHAPTER TWELVE

Note: Many points of detail in this chapter have been supplied by former officers of the Bank.

The leaders

Main Sources: Launceston Bank for Savings, Branch Correspondence; Half-yearly Reports; Minute-books.

References:

Page 153 'Mr Weedon's . . .' Minute-book, 17 December 1931.
154 Opening of the new Gorge road: *Launceston Examiner*, 3 November 1930.
154 'It is safe . . .' *Launceston Examiner*, 6 July 1932.
157 'so belittled . . .' Sub-Committee Report, 3 April 1935.

Attracting depositors

Main Sources: Launceston Bank for Savings, Branch Correspondence; Depositors' Letter-books; Half-yearly Reports; Minute-books; New-account Books.

References:

Page 158 'Officers are . . .' Head Office Circular No. 59, 30 July 1936.
158 'you will . . .' Hardwicke Weedon to Keith Westbrook, 17 September 1928, Burnie Branch Correspondence.
159 'a notable . . .' Report of half-yearly general meeting, March 1929.
159 'We do not . . .' Letter dated 29 March 1924, Depositors' Letter-book, 1921-4.
160 'The doors . . .' Tasmanian *Post Office Directory*, 1931, p. 125.

Innovations

Main Sources: Launceston Bank for Savings, Branch Correspondence; Branch Half-yearly Reports; Half-yearly Reports; Minute-books.

References:

Page 162 'Mr W. C. Morris . . .' Albert Biggs to Keith Westbrook, 8 November 1933, Burnie Branch Correspondence.
163 Hobart Savings Bank opens school banks: information supplied by Hobart Savings Bank.
163 'absolutely inert' Scottsdale Branch Report for half-year ending February 1935.
163 'teachers . . .' Scottsdale Branch Report for half-year ending August 1935.
163 Transfer of accounts to Commonwealth Savings Bank: Keith Westbrook to John Duncan, 24 July 1933, Burnie Branch Correspondence.

Efficiency and economy

Main Sources: Launceston Bank for Savings, Balance-sheets; Branch Correspondence; Branch Half-yearly Reports; Half-yearly Reports; Head Office Circulars; Minute-books.

References:

Page 166 Smithton 'very lively' at times: Letter dated 12 May 1921, Smithton Branch Correspondence.

166 Smithton manager has no wish to remain permanently: letter dated 11 June 1921, Smithton Branch Correspondence.

167 'regarding ...' Minute-book, 10 September 1929.

167 'The impression ...' Hardwicke Weedon to Ulverstone branch manager, 6 December 1927, Ulverstone Branch Correspondence.

168 Sub-Committee Report: Minute-book, 11 May 1933.

The branch managers

Main Sources: Launceston Bank for Savings, Branch Correspondence; Branch Half-yearly Reports; Minute-books.

References:

Page 171 'As you are ...' Ulverstone manager to Hardwicke Weedon, 25 October 1921, Ulverstone Branch Correspondence.

171 'only ordinary ...' Ulverstone manager to Hardwicke Weedon, undated letter, end of 1922, Ulverstone Branch Correspondence.

171 'scheming scoundrel' Hardwicke Weedon to Ronald Tyson, 27 November 1930, Ulverstone Branch Correspondence.

172 'Since ...' William Shaw to Hardwicke Weedon, 20 November 1931, Ulverstone Branch Correspondence.

173 'you clearly ...' Hardwicke Weedon to Keith Westbrook, 22 February 1928, Burnie Branch Correspondence.

174 'a magnificent ...' Scottsdale Branch Report for half-year ending August 1933.

174 'a wonderful ...' Scottsdale Branch Report for half-year ending August 1934.

174 'silver lining' Scottsdale Branch Report for half-year ending February 1934.

174 'the beneficence ...' ibid.

CHAPTER THIRTEEN

Tasmania and World War II

Main Sources: Launceston Bank for Savings, Branch Half-yearly Reports; State Finance Committee, *Studies in the Tasmanian Economy*; *Statistics of Tasmania.*

References:

Page 176 Nearly 30,000 Tasmanians in armed forces: Reynolds, *Launceston. History of an Australian City*, p. 174.

177 Tasmanian parliamentary committee investigation: *Report of the Joint Committee on Home Building*, 1947.

The Bank and the war effort

Main Sources: Launceston Bank for Savings, Balance-sheets; Branch Half-yearly Reports; Half-yearly Reports; Minute-books; *Official Year Books of the Commonwealth.*

References:

Page 177 Air-raid precautions: Head Office Circular No. 192, 27 February 1942.

178 'this has . . .' Scottsdale Branch Report for half-year ending February 1946.

The Bank and its competitors

Main Sources: Launceston Bank for Savings, Branch Half-yearly Reports; Half-yearly Reports; Minute-books; *Official Year Books of the Commonwealth.*

References:

Page 182 'The building . . .' Smithton Branch Report for half-year ending February 1941.

182 Information on Hobart Savings Bank branches: *Walch's Tasmanian Almanacs.*

CHAPTER FOURTEEN

Note: Many points of detail in this chapter have been supplied by the general manager of the Launceston Bank for Savings, and other Bank officers.

Tasmania since the war

Main Sources: *Statistics of Tasmania*; *Tasmanian Year Books*; annual reports on the Tasmanian economy (Tasmanian *Parliamentary Papers*).

Reference:

Page 184 Special grant contributed three per cent to Tasmania's national income: estimated from data in *Official Year Books of the Commonwealth* and *Australian National Accounts.*

The Bank and its competitors 1947-1959

Main Sources: Launceston Bank for Savings, Balance-sheets; Half-yearly Reports; Minute-books; Tasmanian *Government Gazettes*; *Official Year Books of the Commonwealth.*

References:

Page 188 New branches of the Commonwealth and the Hobart Savings Banks: *Walch's Tasmanian Almanacs.*

190 Waiting-lists of borrowers: R. H. Wallace, 'The Australian Savings Banks', in Hirst and Wallace, *Studies in the Australian Capital Market*, p. 287.

Entry of the trading banks

Main Sources: Launceston Bank for Savings, Half-yearly Reports; *Official Year Books of the Commonwealth*; Wallace, op. cit.; Harris, 'Private Savings Banks in Australia 1956-1960'.

Source Notes (Chapter 14)

Meeting new competition

Main Sources: Launceston Bank for Savings, Balance-sheets; Half-yearly Reports.

Reference:

Page 194 Opening of the South Launceston branch building: *Launceston Examiner*, 27 September 1963.

A successful institution

Main Sources: Launceston Bank for Savings, Balance-sheets; Half-yearly Reports; New-account Books; Tasmanian *Government Gazettes*; Commonwealth *Government Gazettes*; *Official Year Books of the Commonwealth.*

Reference:

Page 197 Comparison of Bank's deposits with Australia generally: Wallace, op. cit.; Harris, op. cit.

Bibliography

RECORDS OF THE LAUNCESTON BANK FOR SAVINGS

Balance-sheets, 1844–
  Held by the Bank for 1844-62 and 1874–, for 1862-74 reported in the *Government Gazette* and local newspapers.
Branch Half-yearly Reports, 1932-60, for Burnie, Devonport, St Marys, Scottsdale, Smithton, Ulverstone, Wynyard.
Correspondence
  (i) Head Office
  Depositors' Letter-books, 1888-1909, 1913-16, 1918-25
  General Letter-books, 1849-54, 1873-88
  Loans Letter-books, 1888-94, 1922-5
  Other Banks' Letter-book, 1921-5
  (ii) Branches
  Burnie, 1928-9, 1932-9
  Devonport, 1932-9
  St Marys, 1924-39
  Scottsdale, 1924-39
  Smithton, 1921, 1933-9
  Ulverstone, 1920-39
  Wynyard, 1933-9
Half-yearly Reports, 1862–
  Until 1888 incorporated in the Minute-books or summarized in newspapers; from 1888 separate copies held by the Bank.
Head Office Circulars, 1932-45
Ledgers (Individual), 1835-1912
Loans-books (Individual), 1864-88
Minute-books of the Managing (later Executive) Committee and Trustees (later Managers, then General Committee) 1835–
New-account Books, 1849–
Weekly Financial Statements, 1855-73

OTHER MANUSCRIPT MATERIAL

Browne Papers: diaries 1834-45; miscellaneous correspondence 1845-69 (Northern Regional Library)
Colonial Secretary's Papers, 1841-55 (Tasmanian State Archives)
Eyre, E. J., Autobiography (Mitchell Library, A.1806)
Field, Barron, Evidence before the Bigge Commission, Bonwick Transcripts (Mitchell Library, BT.7)
Glover, John, Miscellaneous Correspondence 1831-40 (Mitchell Library, Ag.35/9)
Launceston and Western Railway Company, Minute-book 1865-7 (Mitchell Library, B.47)
Launceston Harbour League, Minute-book 1910-12 (Mitchell Library, B.1095)
Oakden Letter-books, 1833-42 (in the possession of the Gillett family, Ross, Tasmania)
Premier's Department Papers, 1911-13 (Tasmanian State Archives)
Scott Papers: correspondence 1846-55 (Queen Victoria Museum and Art Gallery)
Supreme Court Papers: miscellaneous returns from the Launceston Bank for Savings (Tasmanian State Archives)

PRINTED SOURCES, OFFICIAL

Tasmania

Acts of Parliament, 1848–
Censuses of Tasmania, 1842–
Commonwealth Bureau of Census and Statistics, Tasmanian Office, *Tasmanian Year Book*, No. 1, 1967–
Government Gazette, 1844–
From 1844-81 known as the *Hobart Town Gazette*, from 1881-1906 as the *Hobart Gazette.*
Parliamentary Papers, 1840–
State Finance Committee, *Studies in the Tasmanian Economy*, No. 2, 1931/2-1935/6–
Statistics of Tasmania, 1824-39–

Commonwealth

Bureau of Census and Statistics, *Australian National Accounts*, 1948/9–
———, *Demography Bulletin*, No. 35, 1917
———, *Labour Report*, No. 1, 1912–
———, *Official Year Book of the Commonwealth*, No. 1, 1901-7–
———, *Production Bulletin*, No. 1, 1901-6–
Government Gazette, 1964–
Parliamentary Debates
Parliamentary Papers

Bibliography

NEWSPAPERS

Cornwall Chronicle, Launceston, 1835-80
Daily Telegraph, Launceston, 1881-1928
Launceston Advertiser, 1834-46
Launceston Examiner, 1842–
The Times, London, 1828-9

ALMANACS AND DIRECTORIES

Hobart Town Almanack, 1834-8
Wood's Van Diemen's Land Almanack, 1839, 1846-52, 1854-7
Walch's Tasmanian Almanac[k], 1863–
Post Office Directory, 1890/1–

BOOKS AND PAMPHLETS

An Englishman, *The Rise and Progress of Australia, Tasmania and New Zealand*. London, 1857.
Australian Dictionary of Biography (gen. ed. D. Pike). Vols 1-3. Melbourne, 1966-9.
Backhouse, J., and Tylor, C., *The Life and Labours of George Washington Walker, of Hobart Town, Tasmania*. London, 1862.
Baird, J., *The Emigrants' Guide to Australasia*. London, 1868.
Bassett, M., *The Hentys. An Australian Colonial Tapestry*. London, 1954.
Bethell, L. S., *The Story of Port Dalrymple*. Launceston, [1961].
Blainey, G. N., *The Peaks of Lyell*. 2nd ed. Melbourne, 1959.
———, *The Rush that Never Ended*. 2nd ed. Melbourne, 1969.
Brown, P. L. (ed.), *Clyde Company Papers*. 7 vols. London, 1941-71.
Butlin, N. G., *Australian Domestic Product, Investment and Foreign Borrowing 1861-1938/9*. Cambridge, 1962.
Butlin, S. J., *Australia and New Zealand Bank*. London, 1961.
———, *Foundations of the Australian Monetary System 1788-1851*. Melbourne, 1953.
Button, H., *Flotsam and Jetsam*. Launceston, [1909].
Coghlan, T. A., *Labour and Industry in Australia*. 4 vols. London, 1918.
Cooch, A., *The State Savings Bank of Victoria*. Melbourne, 1934.
Cooley, T. C. T., *Railroading in Tasmania 1868-1961*. Hobart, 1963.
Cornish, H., *Under the Southern Cross*. Madras, 1880.
Craddock, T., and Cavanough, M., *125 Years; the Story of the State Savings Bank of Victoria, 1842-1966*. Melbourne, 1967.
Cyclopedia of Tasmania. 2 vols. [Hobart, 1900].
Dilke, C. W., *Greater Britain*. London, 1868.
Dixon, J., *The Condition and Capabilities of Van Diemen's Land as a Place of Emigration*. London, 1839.
Duncan, J., *A Century of Thrift. A Brief History of the Launceston Bank for Savings*. Launceston, 1935.

Dunsdorfs, E., *The Australian Wheat-growing Industry 1788-1948.* Melbourne, 1956.

Fenton, J., *A History of Tasmania.* Hobart, 1884.

Forster, C., *Industrial Development in Australia 1920-1930.* Canberra, 1964.

Giblin, L. F., *The Growth of a Central Bank.* Melbourne, 1951.

Gill, J. S., *Launceston. The Northern Capital of Tasmania and Why.* Launceston, [1928].

Gollan, R., *The Commonwealth Bank of Australia. Origins and Early History.* Canberra, 1968.

Green, F. C. (ed.), *Tasmania: A Century of Responsible Government.* Hobart, 1956.

Griffiths, N., *A History of the Government Savings Bank of New South Wales.* Sydney, 1930.

Hall, A. R., *The London Capital Market and Australia 1870-1914.* Canberra, 1963.

———, *The Stock Exchange of Melbourne and the Victorian Economy 1852-1900.* Canberra, 1968.

Handbook of Tasmania. 2nd ed. Government Printer, Hobart, 1914.

Hartwell, R. M., *The Economic Development of Van Diemen's Land 1820-1850.* Melbourne, 1954.

Hirst, R. R., and Wallace, R. H. (eds.), *Studies in the Australian Capital Market.* Melbourne, 1964.

Hobart Savings Bank, *The Centenary of the Hobart Savings Bank 1845-1945.* Hobart, 1945.

Horne, H. O., *A History of Savings Banks.* London, 1947.

Hughes, H., *The Australian Iron and Steel Industry 1848-1962.* Melbourne, 1964.

Information regarding the Colony of Van Diemen's Land. 3rd ed. Government Printer, Hobart, 1854.

Jauncey, L. C., *Australia's Government Bank.* London, 1933.

Just, T. C., *Official Handbook of Tasmania.* 2nd ed. Launceston, 1883, and later editions.

Kiddle, M., *Men of Yesterday.* Melbourne, 1961.

Launceston Chamber of Commerce, *Annual Reports.* 1904/5, 1906/7-1913/14.

Leavitt, T. W. H., *Jubilee History of Tasmania.* 2 vols. Melbourne, 1888.

Malthus, T., *An Essay on the Principle of Population.* 1st ed. London, 1798; 6th ed. London, 1826.

Melbourne Savings Bank, *Seven Useful Pamphlets on 'Thrift'.* Melbourne, 1880.

Melville, H., *Australasia and Prison Discipline.* London, 1851.

Mercer, P. G., *Gateway to Progress. Centenary History of the Marine Board of Burnie.* Burnie, 1969.

Official Catalogue of the Tasmanian International Exhibition 1891-2. Launceston, 1891.

Official Record of the Tasmanian International Exhibition 1891-2. Launceston, 1893.

Ogilvie, A. G., and Shields, T., *The Case for Tasmania.* Hobart, 1926.
Parker, H. W., *The Rise, Progress and Present State of Van Diemen's Land.* London, 1833.
Payne, P. L., and Davis, L. E., *The Savings Bank of Baltimore 1818-1866.* Baltimore, 1956.
Plomley, N. J. B. (ed.), *Friendly Mission.* Hobart, 1966.
Poynter, J. R., *Society and Pauperism.* Melbourne, 1969.
Ramsay, C., *With the Pioneers.* Hobart, 1958.
Report of the Committee Appointed to Inquire into Tasmanian Disabilities under Federation. Hobart, 1925.
Reynolds, J., *Launceston. History of an Australian City.* Melbourne, 1969.
Roberts, S. H., *History of Australian Land Settlement 1788-1920.* Melbourne, 1924.
Robertson, E. G., and Craig, E. N., *Early Houses of Northern Tasmania.* 2 vols. Melbourne, 1964.
Savings Bank of South Australia, *Our Centenary; a history of the first hundred years of the Savings Bank of South Australia.* Adelaide, 1948.
Smiles, S., *Self-Help.* London, 1866.
———, *Thrift: a book of domestic counsel.* London, 1875.
[Stoney, H. B.], *A Year in Tasmania.* Hobart, 1854.
Thomas, H., *Guide for Excursionists from the Mainland to Tasmania.* Melbourne, 1869.
Trollope, A., *Australia and New Zealand.* Australian ed. Melbourne, 1873.
West, J., *The History of Tasmania.* 2 vols. Launceston, 1852; facsimile ed. Libraries Board of South Australia, 1966.
Whitfield, E., *History of the Launceston Mechanics Institute and Public Library.* Launceston, [1910].
———, *The River Tamar.* Launceston, [1912].

ARTICLES

Barrett, W. R., 'The Venerable William Henry Browne, LL.D'. *Tasmanian Historical Research Association Papers and Proceedings* (*T.H.R.A.*), vol. 13, no. 4, August 1966.
Blainey, G. N., 'Population Movements in Tasmania 1870-1901'. *T.H.R.A.*, vol. 3, no. 4, June 1954.
———, 'The Rise and Decline of the West Coast'. *T.H.R.A.*, vol. 4, no. 4, February 1956.
———, 'A Theory of Mineral Discovery: Australia in the Nineteenth Century'. *Economic History Review*, August 1970.
Crawford, G. H., 'The Scotts: Thomas, George and James'. *T.H.R.A.*, vol. 14, no. 1, December 1966.
Denholm, D., 'Edward Braddon's Impressions of Launceston and the North West, 1878'. *T.H.R.A.*, vol. 15, no. 2, November 1967.
Ginswick, J., 'The Tasmanian Trade Cycle: The Turning Point of the Forties'. *T.H.R.A.*, vol. 5, no. 3, August 1956.

Green, F. C., 'Hydro-Electric Development in Tasmania'. *T.H.R.A.*, vol. 8, no. 1, August 1959.

Harris, C. P., 'Private Savings Banks in Australia 1956-1960'. *Economic Record*, vol. 38, no. 182, June 1962.

James, P. C., 'The Emu Bay and Mount Bischoff Railway'. *T.H.R.A.*, vol. 10, no. 4, July 1963.

Reynolds, J., 'The Establishment of the Electrolytic Zinc Industry in Tasmania'. *T.H.R.A.*, vol. 6, no. 2, September 1957.

Roe, M., 'The Establishment of Local Self-Government in Hobart and Launceston, 1845-1858'. *T.H.R.A.*, vol. 14, no. 1, December 1966.

Taylor, H., 'The Direction of Thrift. A Savings Bank Comparison'. *Victorian Review*, October 1881.

Townsley, W. A., 'The Launceston and Western Railway Company'. *T.H.R.A.*, vol. 3, no. 1, March 1954.

———, 'Tasmania and the Great Economic Depression, 1858-1872'. *T.H.R.A.*, vol. 4, no. 2, July 1955.

———, 'The Tasmanian Main Line Railway Company'. *T.H.R.A.*, vol. 5, no. 3, August 1956.

Index

* L.B.S. Launceston Bank for Savings.

B A S S
Circular Head
Stanley
Port Latta
Smithton
Wynyard
Moorleah
BURNIE
(Emu Bay)
Somerset
DEVON
Penguin
ULVERSTONE
Latrob
EMU BAY
RAILWAY
Arthur River
River Leven
Castra
Rai
PIPE LINE
Guildford
Sheffield
Mt Bischoff
Waratah
Savage River
River
Pieman River
Renison Bell
Rosebery
Zeehan
Mt Lyell
Queenstown
Lake St
Macquarie Harb.
Franklin River
Gordon River
BANK BRANCHES
0
10
20
30
40
50
MILES